VERMONT

Picture Research by
Faith Learned Pepe

American Historical Press
Sun Valley, California

VERMONT

An Illustrated History

By John Duffy & Vincent Feeney

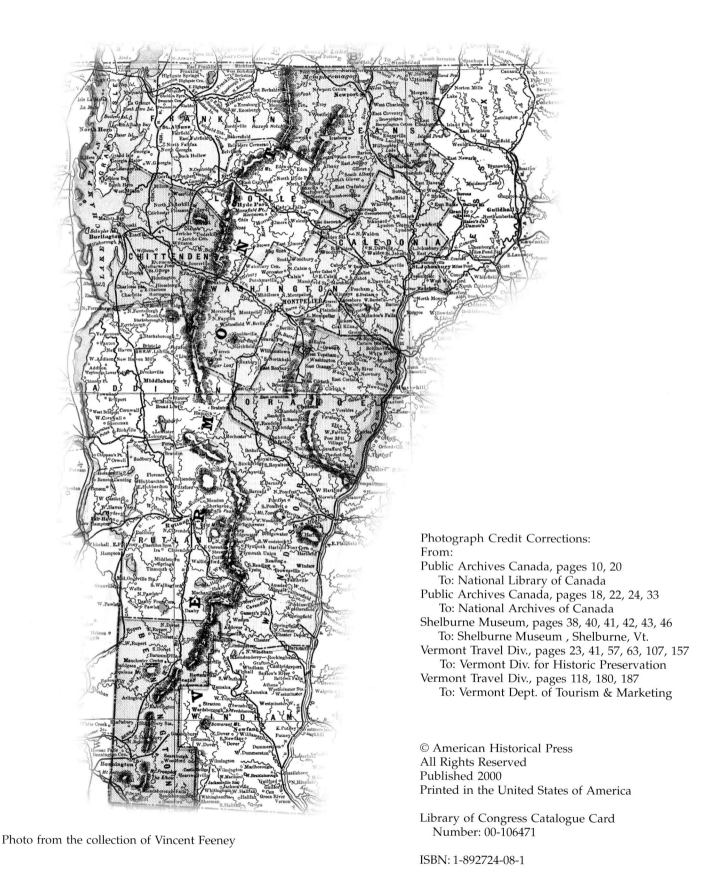

Photo from the collection of Vincent Feeney

Photograph Credit Corrections:
From:
Public Archives Canada, pages 10, 20
    To: National Library of Canada
Public Archives Canada, pages 18, 22, 24, 33
    To: National Archives of Canada
Shelburne Museum, pages 38, 40, 41, 42, 43, 46
    To: Shelburne Museum , Shelburne, Vt.
Vermont Travel Div., pages 23, 41, 57, 63, 107, 157
    To: Vermont Div. for Historic Preservation
Vermont Travel Div., pages 118, 180, 187
    To: Vermont Dept. of Tourism & Marketing

Library of Congress Catalogue Card
    Number: 00-106471

ISBN: 1-892724-08-1

Bibliography: p. 290
Includes Index

Contents

Acknowledgements

This book is greatly indebted to H. Nicholas Muller and Samuel Hand for their collection of essays from the pages of *Vermont History* titled "In A State of Nature." Marjory W. Power and William A. Haviland provided especially useful information on the Abenaki and their encounters with the founders of New France and New England in their book *The Original Vermonters: Native Inhabitants Past and Present.* William Doyle's concise and informative *The Vermont Political Tradition* was also helpful.

I am grateful to the Vermont Historical Society for nominating me to write this book.

John Duffy
Isle La Motte, Vermont

The cooperation and assistance of the Vermont Department of Tourism and the Special Collections Department of the Bailey-Howe Library at the University of Vermont in permitting the use of some of their photographs was especially appreciated.

Vincent Feeney
Burlington, Vermont

Collecting the pictures that appear in *Vermont: An Illustrated History* would not have been possible without the assistance of numerous individuals and organizations. Fifty-one Vermont institutions, collectors, and photographers contributed photographs from their collections. The remaining pictures were gathered from museums, galleries, and photo archives outside the state. Contributors are acknowledged in the photo courtesy lines. Appreciation is due all of them, as well as to anywhose names may have in advertently been omitted.

Mary Pat Johnson and the entire Vermont Historical Society library staff showed infinite patience in hauling out photos on busy days, deciphering photo orders, and coping with last-minute research problems. Connell Gallagher, Nadia Smith, and the rest of the Special Collections staff at the University of Vermont's Bailey-Howe Library were equally helpful. The Local History Room at the Brooks Memorial Library in Brattleboro often served as both reference room and caption-writing office. My search for various odd bits of information was facilitated by the expertise of Brooks Library staff members the late George Lindsey and Jerry Carbone. Others who gave generous assistance were Jeff Barry, Ruth Levin, Cristin Merck, David Proper, Bob Shaw, and Russell Smith. The late Roy Lewando provided three illustrations and a sense of humor. I am especially grateful to him, and to my three sons, for putting up with my long involvement with this project.

Faith Learned Pepe
Putney, Vermont

Introduction

Vermont: An Illustrated History tells the story of people settling, developing, and organizing the communities that have contributed in special ways to shaping the Vermont that exists today.

The story begins with a portrait of Native American life, with Vermont as the land of the People of the Dawn, the Abenaki, and recounts how these original Vermonters utilized the land and its resources to support their communities and their way of life.

With the first ventures of Europeans, such as the men of New France who followed Samuel de Champlain and settled on the shores of the lake that was eventually named after him in the seventeenth century or Major Robert Rogers, who, along with his New England Rangers, explored the intervales of the Connecticut, the years of conflict and struggle over control of the land "twixt lake and river" provide views of men and issues that continue to enthrall readers.

Yet the accounts of these early years in the seventeenth and eighteenth centuries, years of settlement and of bloody war and revolution, also show in detail how strong-willed men and women founded an independent-minded community—for fourteen years an independent Republic of Vermont.

With statehood in 1791 came Vermont's first land boom. Settlers arrived from southern New England to claim and clear the northern forests in numbers that easily made Vermont the fastest growing state in the Union by 1810. The times saw quick and handsome profits on speculative ventures in land, timber, and potash; and the first commercial connections with the northern market outlets through Canada and thus to Europe sparked after 1808 the fiery national debate over trade with Britain. The resultant Embargo Act introduced an episode that showed how Vermont's fortunes have from the earliest days been tied to large national trends and issues. Subsequently the War of 1812 is also seen as a resolution of Vermont's internal political disputes and an event that clearly marks a people in the first stages of organizing a stable community.

A young society and a dynamic people, the

The Peninsular campaign of 1862 brought the Union army within five miles of Richmond. Larkin Mead's drawing portrays "General Davison's Brigade taking possession of Mechanicsville near Richmond." A month later General Robert E. Lee's offensive closed the campaign with victory for the Confederates. From the Houghton Collection. Courtesy, Vermont Historical Society

Left
Swedish-American artist Bror Thulstrup drew this lively scene of skaters, titled Winter Carnival on Lake Champlain, *sometime around 1880. Numerous other winter carnivals have been held in Vermont over the past hundred years. Most, however, have emphasized skiing rather than skating. Courtesy, Robert Hull Fleming Museum, University of Vermont*

Facing page, bottom
At the height of the flood of 1927 water levels rose to twelve feet above street level on Main and State streets in Montpelier. The night before this view of East State Street was taken, flood waters entirely covered both cars and door transoms. Courtesy, Vermont Historical Society

Vermonters of the half-century from the War of 1812 to the close of the Civil War project the profile of a vigorous community examining, testing, and sometimes adopting many of the new ideas of how to order society that appeared on the American scene during those boisterous decades. Anti-slavery efforts, Anti-Masonic political candidates, prohibition of alcohol, labor organizations, education reform, economic panic, religious revivals, adventures westward in search of gold or fulfillment of a "Manifest Destiny" by taking new lands in the West and Southwest from Mexico: all of these events and adventures of a youthful, developing Vermont led to those awful days at Cedar Creek, Fredericksburg, and Andersonville, where Vermont's young men paid the terrible price of preserving the Union.

The Civil War cast a long shadow over the next fifty years of life in Vermont. The ubiquitous war memorial—a blue-coated Federal trooper leaning on his rifle—stands in many of Vermont's town and village greens or city centers, erected by veterans or their children throughout the 1870s and 1880s and even into the first years after the turn of the century. Memories of Vermont's service to the Union are not the only legacy of the Civil War. Technology developed in the war brought Vermont and the rest of the nation into a modern age.

Vermont changed steadily during the fifty years between the Civil War and the 1920s. A completed railway system linked almost every town with the rest of the nation by 1905. The small hill farm began to disappear as larger acreage intervale farms entered the urban markets of the Northeast and beyond to sell butter and, after refrigerated trains came into service in the late 1870s, whole milk. The products of Vermont's forests, first bulk harvested in the early years of the century for the potash market in Canada and Europe, had nearly disappeared by 1880 as forest products were sent to build the tenements and bungalows of eastern cities; to produce paper and newsprint for the increasing number of book, magazine, and newspaper readers; and to fuel the trains carrying milk and butter to market.

The make-up of Vermont's population underwent a major transformation by 1920. The biggest reason for the change was a shift in migration. From Canada and Europe came Quebecoise, Irish, Italians, Swedes, and Finns to work on farms, in mills, in the forest and lumber industries, and on railway construction; Poles and Scots came to work in the quarries. All contributed to shaping a people whose Yankee homogeneity began to fade. Rural populations shifted in urban directions to Burlington, Rutland, St. Johnsbury, and Springfield. By the 1880s electrification systems took root in larger urban centers like Burlington and Rutland. Telephones appeared in the 1890s. Social reforms were initiated, including public school reform, teacher education improvement, and establishment of public health programs.

Suffragists and temperance marchers in the late nineteenth and early twentieth century urged fellow Vermonters to institutionalize political justice for all by extending the franchise to women and generally to improve the quality of life by eradicating the socially disruptive abuse of alcohol. All of these efforts to improve economic and social aspects of life in Vermont were paralleled by the stabilization of political life. Vermont became identified with the Northern Republican Party during the Civil War, and the Republicans held control of state government for one hundred years-1862 until the election of Democrat Philip Hoff as governor in 1962.

Vermont's story is told with an appreciation for its people and its land. We see how man and nature have come together in Vermont. In the twentieth century the key events that Vermonters mark in their recent past are often those in which the works of nature and man join to shape

the development of a place where vigorous people work hard to keep vibrant a life they have chosen.

The greatest single natural disaster of the twentieth century—the Great Flood of 1927 stands as an important benchmark in both the history of Vermont's government and in the story of a people's ability to spring back from a powerfully damaging stroke.

In the 1930s, despite its electoral rejection of Franklin Delano Roosevelt, Vermont's acceptance of important New Deal programs showed a Vermont independent at the polls, but quick to realize that what's good for the country is good for Vermont.

Indeed, Vermonters have moved on toward their third century as a community still willing to examine, test, publicly debate at length, if necessary, and sometimes adopt new ideas about how to order their lives, often even to be among the first in the nation to do so, as with the state's early adoption of forceful environmental protection laws; many Vermonters also played a formative role in the nuclear freeze debates in the 1980s by bringing that crucial issue to their town meetings. The genes of its original founding fathers may not be dominant in Vermont today, but its people and the place are unquestionably still Yankee-independent, resourceful, and willing to speak out after all these years.

The Earliest Vermonters

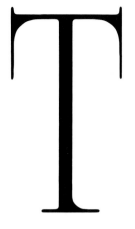

The last glacial flow covered the northern hemisphere from about 23,000 to 16,000 B.C. As the glacier began to recede the level of the world's oceans rose on the earth's surface. Marine waters flooded large sections of the northern hemisphere by 10,000 B.C. In a region that would be named Vermont nearly 12,000 years later by a physician from Philadelphia, the flooding of the ocean created what geologists call the Champlain Sea, a body of water stretching from Lake Ontario east to today's Enosburg Falls, Vermont, and south to Whitehall, New York. In valleys of the eastern side of the mountain range running north and south through Vermont, glacial melt filled the region to form a lake running from Middletown, Connecticut, to East Thetford, Vermont, known to modern geologists as Lake Hitchcock.

Archaeological remains uncovered in various locations on both the east and west sides of the mountain range, but mostly from findings in the Champlain Valley, indicate that the people archaeologists call Paleoindians were Vermont's first inhabitants. The first recognized Paleoindian archaeological site in New England was not discovered until 1920 in East Highgate on a sandy bluff looking down on the Missisquoi River south and west to Lake Champlain. The exact date of occupation at Highgate by Paleoindians is difficult to pinpoint, but archaeologists suggest that the site was inhabited after the earth sprang back from the pressure of the glacier and after the Champlain Sea receded—between 9000 and 7000 B.C.

Paleoindian tools and projectiles have also been found at Swanton, Milton, Grand Isle, Burlington, Ferrisburg, Monckton, Addison, Orwell, and other locations in the Champlain Valley. Little evidence has been found on the Vermont side of the Connecticut Valley, but a site dated around 9000 B.C. has been found in New Hampshire on a tributary of the Connecticut River.

These original Vermonters survived on food from the Champlain Sea. Even as it subsided, the sea contained many marine mammals and fish—various whales and seals, probably most of the species of fish found in the western reaches of the Atlantic Ocean, including the salmon and smelt (which remained landlocked after the sea receded), as well as crustaceans and shellfish. As the habitat changed from tundra conditions to forest, moose, caribou, elk, deer, and other large meat animals were available for the Paleoindians' diet.

The locations of archaeological remains of the Paleoindians suggest that their movements in Vermont followed the easiest routes—the waterways. In fact, travel would continue along these waterways with later native Vermonters, as well as the European settlers who came to join them, on into the modern era of steamboats, railroads, and, finally, hard-topped highways. These waterways included the Missisquoi River to Swanton and Highgate; the Lamoille to Milton and Fairfax; a protected bay of Lake Champlain in South Hero; the Winooski River at Burlington's Intervale, Colchester, and Essex Junction, and much further upstream on a tributary of the

Winooski in Moretown; and the Otter Creek near Brandon.

The populations of these early Vermonters were probably not very large. Anthropologists estimate their numbers at less than ten people per 100 square kilometers, with the densest populations probably near the Champlain Sea. Living units were probably single families or bands of a few related families averaging fifty people.

Sometime during the eighth millenium B.C., however, Vermont was apparently depopulated. As the glacier receded farther, environmental changes continued to occur. Vermont's spruce and fir forests began to be replaced by pine and oak. Smaller animals such as the fox, marten, lynx, and wolf could survive well in such a habitat, but larger animals such as the deer, bear, elk, and moose found less forage and their populations—and thus a major food supply for Paleoindians—declined. The ice-age animals, including the mastodon and the moose-elk, also became extinct in the eighth millenium B.C., with the last dated mastodon remains in the Northeast placed at 7200 B.C. The earth's surface produced the Champlain Sea's final ebb tide between 8200 and 7400 B.C., taking most of its rich marine life with it, for an evolutionary period of 800 to 1,000 years is too brief a time for most marine organisms to adapt to fresh water conditions. Only a few—salmon, smelt, and lamprey—survived landlocked, and that most curious of creatures, the eel, continues to migrate from the Atlantic Ocean to Lake Champlain's fresh headwaters to live out most of its adult life until returning to the ocean to spawn.

Today investigations of the remains of the earliest inhabitants of this region suggest that the great environmental changes after the glacial period brought about important alterations in human living patterns from approximately 7000 B.C. to 1500 B.C. As the climate warmed (for a time around 3000 B.C. to an average of three degrees warmer than today), vegetable and animal life changed, too. The environment of the Paleoindians required them to develop new skills for gathering plant and vegetable food sources and new hunting skills to catch and kill deer, bear, and the smaller animals of a forest land, which by about 2000 B.C. was roughly similar in tree species and general coverage of the Northeast to what the first European visitors found on their arrival 3,500 years later.

As archaeological investigations continue in Vermont the story of the earliest Vermonters from the post-glacial period up to the arrival of the first Europeans seemed to form two chapters, which tell of two separate ways of life developing over 3,000 to 5,000 years—first the Archaic and then the Woodland cultures.

The Archaic culture was based on hunting and collecting wild roots, nuts, and vegetables and animal food materials. As with the Paleoindians, early Vermonters living in the Archaic period depended on hunting as an important means of food, clothing, and shelter. Deer, bear, moose, beaver, other smaller fur bearers, and migrating waterfowl were their meat staples. Wild plant foods, however, were more important and available in Archaic times than they had been for Paleoindians. An interesting aspect of the Vermont Archaic people was a burial practice that involved the extensive use of red ocher. This ritual connects these early Vermonters with people of both the Ohio River Valley and the maritime regions of Canada, where similar burial practices were highly developed.

In the third millenium B.C. great cultural changes occurred in the central section of the continent. By 600 B.C. nearly 40 percent of the food supply of the inhabitants of what is today known as the American Midwest was derived from domesticated and cultivated vegetables—squash, maize, gourds, and sunflowers. Techniques and tools for cultivating, collecting, storing, and preparing these foods developed and their remains are found, for example, in frequently unearthed pieces of pottery. Hunting remained important for a meat supply, and a new tool for getting meat more efficiently than a spear, even when it was hurled with the aid of an atlatl,

came into use with the development of the bow and arrow. By 300 B.C. these and other important changes had transformed life among most of the native peoples of the continent into a pattern that archaeologists call the Woodland culture.

Vermont's version of the Woodland culture is identified by the development and appearance of such artifacts as pottery and certain food remains, especially fish and gathered vegetable or root remnants. It was a way of life still heavily dependent on hunting, but, in a region with relatively short growing seasons, less dependent on plant cultivation than the culture of the Ohio River Valley or other fertile, temperate regions of the continent. The village sites of these Woodland period inhabitants of Vermont indicate patterns of living in which hunting, fishing, and gathering wild plants were important activities. There is little indication of corn growing before about A.D. 1300.

The famous Colchester jar, similar in style to pottery made by St. Lawrence Iroquois between 1400 and 1550, was found in 1825 by a Burlington surveyor. Courtesy, Robert Hull Fleming Museum, University of Vermont

Large settlements of more or less continued occupation existed near the mouths of major river waterways in the Champlain Valley and on the Connecticut River, with smaller living sites found upriver. This pattern remained in place to greet the first European visitors to the region in the 1600s.

Students of early Vermont life generally agree that by the seventeenth century A.D. the pattern of life among Vermont's native people was distinguishable from their linguistically related neighbors to the east and north, the Micmac, Maliseets, and Passamaquoddies, (collectively known as the Wabanakis); their Mohawk adversaries to the west; and the southern New England Algonquians. The original Vermonters were named by another native people, the Montagnais from north of the St. Lawrence River. They called these people, who lived south and east from them, "People of the Dawn": Abenaki. In their own language, however, the original Vermonters called themselves Alnôbak, meaning "ordinary people."

These ordinary people of Vermont consisted of several independent groups on the eve of their encounter with the first ripple of European waves of westward migration. The main groups of western Abenaki living in Vermont consisted of the Sokoki and Cowasuck groups, who lived on the middle and upper Connecticut River; a substantial settlement living near the mouth of the Missisquoi River in northwestern Vermont; and other smaller sized settlements on the Lamoille and Winooski rivers and Otter Creek. Smaller related families seem to have lived in the larger islands of Lake Champlain.

In their areas of settlement and contingent hunting-gathering territories, the population of the Abenaki of Vermont at the time of first contact with Europeans—roughly A.D. 1600—has been estimated at one person per square mile. Evidence suggests that a settlement like the Missisquoi Village contained about 300 people. The Sokoki (the people who separated), a large band of 500 Abenaki, established a new village in 1636 at Fort Hill, New Hampshire, less than one mile across the Connecticut River from Vermont. By

Above
In 1609 Samuel de Champlain explored the lake which now bears his name. This seventeenth-century engraving The First Battle of Lake Champlain, *showed the French explorer with his Algonquin allies, fighting a group of Iroquois Indians on the New York side of the lake. Courtesy, Vermont Historical Society*

Facing page
In 1608 the French explorer Samuel de Champlain laid the foundations of the city of Quebec. During the following win- ter he heard tales from the Algonquin Indians of a large lake surrounded by mountains lying to the southwest. On July 4, 1609, Champlain, accompanied by two of his countrymen and a party of sixty Indians, entered the lake to which he gave his name. Although there is no proof that Champlain actually set foot on the soil that later became Vermont, he saw the Green Mountains to the east, and thus became known as "the discoverer of Vermont." From the Wilbur Collection. Courtesy, Bailey/Howe Library, University of Vermont*

contrast, southern New England's relatively more hospitable climate and productive soil and sea supported a native population of nearly 100,000 when Europeans began communicating the devastating diseases that reduced the native population immediately prior to the first permanent plantations at Plymouth and Massachusetts Bay in the early 1620s.

Two dates in the seventeenth and eighteenth centuries mark the entries of white Europeans

into the land of the Abenaki. Fort Ste. Anne was built by soldiers of France on Isle La Motte, the northernmost island of Lake Champlain, in 1666. This frontier outpost of New France was not maintained long, however, as the French probed deeper into the lake valley to build forts and establish settlements at Crown Point and Ticonderoga on the west shore of the lake. In 1724 Massachusetts Bay colonists built Fort Dummer in southeastern Vermont, bringing the first English-speaking permanent settlers to the region. The Dutch had earlier settled Fort Orange, today's Albany, on Henry Hudson's river in 1624 and began to move into the upper Hudson River valley and the lower Champlain Valley by 1700.

The first European account of entering the region came from the French sailor-explorer Samuel de Champlain. In July of 1609 Champlain realized that a successful settlement at Quebec required friendly relations with the various Algonquian peoples living within trading and raiding distances of the French outpost. To cement such relations, Champlain joined in an Algonquian war party against the Iroquois south and west of Quebec on the shores of the great lake that fed the Iroquois (Richelieu) River. Cham-

plain and the war party entered the lake from the Iroquois River on July 14, 1609. He noted "four beautiful islands . . . formerly . . . inhabited by savages . . . but . . . abandoned since they had been at war" with the Iroquois. After remarking on his observation of the first chestnut trees he saw in America, Champlain noted that "there is a great abundance of fish of a good many varieties."

Champlain then went on to introduce the first Vermont fish story: the tale of the marvelous *Chaousarou*. This fish, from Champlain's description, seemed to be a grotesque mixture of garpike, sturgeon, and his Indian guides' talents for pulling the legs of gullible visitors. "The longest, as these people told me, is eight or ten feet," he said. His description of the fabulous *Chaousarou* is based in part on his own sighting of a five-foot-long fish, probably a garpike, and information given to him by the Algonquian-speaking Indians, some of them probably Abenaki, he accompanied in the war party. "This fish," Champlain recorded, "fights all the others in the lakes and rivers, and is wonderfully cunning, to judge from what the people have assured me, which is, that when it wishes to catch certain birds, it goes into the rushs or weeds which border the lake in several places, and puts its snout out of the water without moving at all, so that when the birds come to light on its snout, thinking that it is the trunk of a tree, the fish is so skillful in closing its snout, which had been half open, that it draws the birds under water by the feet."

A serious mind may feel compelled to question the truth of Champlain's story from a biological basis—"Did the garpike ever grow to ten feet?" "Was it really a sturgeon?"—and the anthropologist might be attracted to the folklore features in this tale of the cunning *Chaousarou*. A Vermonter, however, will recognize an impulse behind the story that will bring a good chuckle. It was a cunning fish, indeed, and a cunning storyteller who recounted to Champlain, assuring him of its truth, this marvelous and first Vermont fish story.

From
New France
to
New England

*S*amuel de Champlain's 1609 foray up the lake he chose to name after himself and his violent encounter with the Iroquois near the later site of Fort Ticonderoga was the great French explorer's only voyage into Vermont's waters. Other Europeans did not venture into this portion of the American interior for nearly forty years afterward. Meanwhile French settlements from the Bay of Fundy to *la rapide la Chin* (the China rapids), close by the Indian village of Hochelaga on the St. Lawrence River, grew slowly under Champlain's guidance during the first quarter of the seventeenth century. Between 1608, when he founded Quebec, and his death in 1635, Champlain's work and exploration up the St. Lawrence assured an increasing flow of valuable beaver furs to Europe. He resisted colonization plans that might have competed with the fur trade. Trading posts, not colonies of farmers, were the tools of French exploitation in these early years. Other European settlements began to grow in the South and East when the Dutch and English planted colonies on the seaboard during the 1620s

Beginning with his first voyage to America in 1603, Champlain established good relations with fur-trading Hurons and Algonquins in the St. Lawrence Valley region. In 1611 he constructed a trading post on the site of Montreal. Charles W. Jeffery's idealized painting of Champlain Trading With the Indians *depicts the French explorer engaged in commerce with his Native American allies. Courtesy, Public Archives Canada (C-103059)*

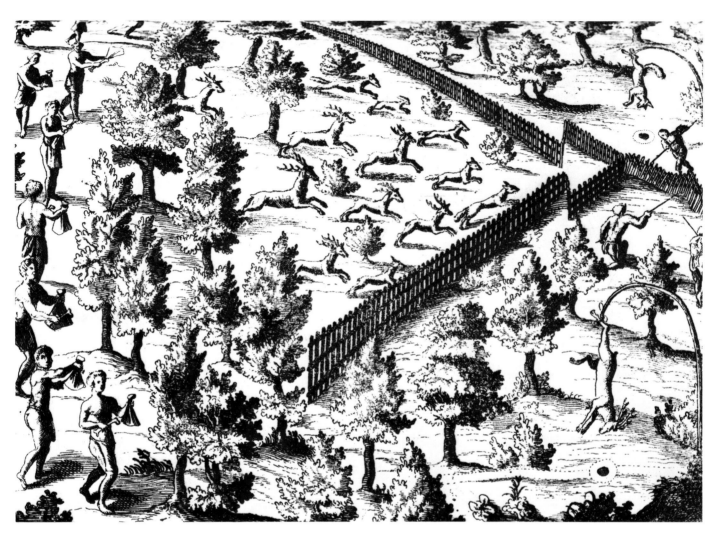

and 1630s.

In the very year that Montagnais and Abenaki Indians paddled Champlain's canoe up the beautiful lake south of the great St. Lawrence River, Henry Hudson, an English sailor employed by the Dutch, sailed a ship smaller than even the *Mayflower* up another great river south of Champlain. On the *Half Moon* Hudson sailed past the island of Manhatoes, the future site of New York City, to the rapids less than 100 miles south of Champlain's devastating musket blasts at the Mohawks in July 1609. Fort Orange, called Albany by the British, was settled fifteen years later by a company of Dutch fur traders. In 1626 the same entrepreneurs, the Dutch West India Company, bought for sixty guilders' (or sixty dollars') worth of trade goods the entire island of Manhattan from Indian inhabitants. By the 1630s small Dutch communities took root north of Fort Or-

This picture of a Huron Deer Hunt appeared in Champlain's 1632 Voyages in New France, published in Paris. At that time the North American fur trade was dominated by the French, who operated a series of trading posts in the St. Lawrence-Great Lakes area. Various Native American tribes of the North-east, including Sokoki Abenaki and their Iroquois enemies, competed fiercely with each other for control of the fur trade. The Hurons allied themselves with the French, but were dispersed by the Dutch-supported Iroquois in 1649. Courtesy, Public Archives Canada (C-113066)

ange, as the Dutch for the most part retained friendly relations with the Indians. By the 1660s Schenectady had the character of a small Dutch hamlet.

New England, the coastal region northeast of New Netherlands and southeast of New France, had already been settled by the English through the 1630s and 1640s. The line of settlement pressed west from Plymouth Plantation and the Massachusetts Bay Colony from the mid-century on, so that by 1700 settlements in New England spread up the Merrimack River into New Hampshire and west beyond the Connecticut River. In 1664 the Dutch, under command of Governor Peter Stuyvesant, surrendered New Amsterdam and all of New Netherlands—territory stretching from the Delaware to the Connecticut—to a small English fleet, thus establishing English control over what soon became the Provinces of East and West Jersey and New York. Fort Orange was renamed Albany, and New Amsterdam became New York after the Duke of York, who took possession of all these lands by a royal grant from his brother Charles II in the largest gift of land ever made by an English ruler.

By the 1630s the Dutch traders at Fort Orange were dealing in furs coming from the upper reaches of the Connecticut River watershed. Then moving westward from the coastal plantations of Massachusetts, English fur traders also began to obtain furs from the Sokoki Abenaki who lived in the Connecticut Valley. By 1635 William Pynchon controlled the Connecticut fur trade from his base in Springfield, Massachusetts. The account books of his son John, who succeeded him in 1652, reveal his most successful year to have been 1654, when he exported 3,723 pounds of beaver pelts from America to England. In addition pelts of otter, muskrat, mink, marten, lynx, fisher, fox, and sable were shipped to fur-hungry buyers back home. In the meantime French traders supported by missionaries of the Catholic Church and armed forces of the Governor of New France increased the frequency of their contacts with Vermont's Abenaki inhabitants. Even the Sokoki Abenaki, who lived for most of the century in southeastern Vermont and bordering New Hampshire (a region considered part of Massachusetts in the 1600s), traded with the French as early as 1642. Church records of Notre Dame de Montréal in the 1660s indicate that Sokoki Abenaki were traveling a long distance from the eastern section of Vermont to attend church rites with friends in French, not English, America. Yet Champlain had left a deadly legacy when he blasted Mohawks to death on the shores of his namesaked lake in 1609.

The land bounded by the Connecticut River in the East and Champlain's great lake in the West remained largely unknown to Europeans during most of the seventeenth century. Small settlements from the Hudson River Valley into southwestern Vermont by second and third generation Dutch colonists occurred late in the seventeenth and into the eighteenth centuries. English adventurers did not travel so far North and East until compelled by war with the French and their Indian allies. This also occurred in the late seventeenth and early eighteenth centuries after the raids on Deerfield and other English settlements in Massachusetts.

During this time sections of Vermont became military highways and fortified bastions for armed forces in the intensified combat, first between the natives living in an area that stretched from Western Maine through New Hampshire, southern Vermont, and on West into, first, New Netherlands and, after 1664, New York. During the last quarter of the seventeenth century and on into the 1760s the conflict was between the French and their Indian allies—often Abenaki—on one hand, and the English expanding north from their lower New England and New York settlements on the other.

From about 1630 to 1675 Native Americans—mainly Sokoki Abenaki and their Iroquois enemies from the West in New York—engaged in extended campaigns of war and terror against each other over the control of fur trade in the Connecticut River Valley and west into New York. After a disastrous defeat in 1628 at the hands of the Iroquois, the Sokoki lived as tributaries of the Iroquois for nearly thirty years. Only the westward invasion of smallpox infections from the Connecticut River Valley stanched Iroquois attacks and allowed the Sokoki and other Abenaki to trade fur with both the English at Springfield and the Dutch at Fort Orange. The Sokoki Abenaki were not left alone by the Iroquois, however. Throughout the 1650s and early 1660s, raiding armed forces of up to 400 men ranged back and forth across southern Vermont as Abenaki and Mohawk warriors attacked settlements in either tribe's homelands. One vengeful Mohawk foray ranged as far east as Maine seeking out and terrorizing native communities for nearly six months. From 1663 to the end of the decade, Mohawk and Sokoki forces battled in the Connecticut River Valley. The Sokoki fort on top of a commanding spot at Fort Hill, New Hampshire, was beseiged unsuccessfully by Mohawks in 1663, with a loss of nearly 200 men. By 1670 the largest Abenaki settlements in the southeastern portion of Vermont had been dispersed by these conflicts. Only a small settlement at today's Vernon held on into the 1670s.

In the meantime the French had not ignored the lake and land to the south of them. In 1660 there were fewer than 6,000 French settled along the St. Lawrence River. Fearing the powerful fighting forces of the Iroquois to the south and west, the French governor built forts along the Richelieu River flowing out of Lake Champlain. In 1665 Fort Ste. Therese and, closer to the lake, Fort St. Louis at the Chambly Rapids were constructed as defensive outposts.

Then in 1666 Sieur de Courcelles, governor of New France, set out with 500 men south across the ice of Champlain's lake, following the great explorer's route with the same intention of a punishing raid against the Mohawks. In unfamiliar territory south of the lake, however, the French missed the Mohawk villages and finally returned home after a few slight encounters with Mohawk war parties, having lost sixty men from the winter hardships on their journey.

Yet Governor de Courcelles did not surrender France's interest in the great lake of Champlain and the surrounding land. In the summer of 1666 he directed the construction of another fort to the south of Montreal, this time on the first large northern island in Lake Champlain. Fort Ste. Anne, on Isle La Motte, thus became the first European settlement in Vermont. With the fort on Isle La Motte as the last base, another raid south against the Mohawks was launched up the

Above
Samuel de Champlain left a deadly legacy when he assisted his Algonquin friends in overcoming a force of Iroquois in 1609. Seeking vengeance for past acts of violence, the Iroquois embarked on a vicious series of raids against the French and their Algonquin allies, beginning in 1641. This eighteenth-century French etching shows an Iroquois Warrior *equipped with various implements of war. The Iroquois were considered particularly bloodthirsty by their Abenaki enemies, who called them "maneaters." Courtesy, Public Archives Canada (C-3163)*

Facing page
A chapel—the first church of Sainte Anne in the United States—was established at Fort Sainte Anne at Isle La Motte in 1667. The chapel and fort were abandoned three years later, but a second chapel and a pavilion were erected on the original site in 1894. The chapel and pavilion, today known as Sainte Anne's Shrine, memorialize the first French settlement in Vermont. Courtesy, Vermont Travel Division

lake in the autumn by the French. The result was so devastating that the Mohawks sued for peace. While relations between most of the Native Americans and the French remained peaceful for almost another quarter of a century, the last years of the seventeenth century brewed violent outcomes for both English and French with the native inhabitants living in and around Vermont.

Between 1675 and 1700 the British population of what is now Massachusetts, Connecticut, Rhode Island, and New Hampshire rose from approximately 75,000 to 130,000 inhabitants. Not until after the British conquest of New France, however, did the French population in all of North America exceed 100,000. The pressures of an expanding British population in Massachusetts, for example, led to purchases of Indian land and British settlements that, by 1687, inched up the Connecticut River even into today's Vermont and New Hampshire.

Such population and migration pressures were bound to lead to conflict and combat as the British moved deeper into northern New England. The first notable incident of British-Indian conflict was a two-part episode in the fall of 1675 at Deerfield, Massachusetts, and the following spring at Turner's Falls on the Connecticut. In September 1675 Indians attacked and killed sixty settlers at Deerfield. When the ice left the Connecticut in the spring, returning salmon, shad, and eel brought Indians to the traditional fishing encampment at Turner's Falls. One hundred sixty British settlers from Hadley attacked the camp on May 19, 1676, while the Indians, nearly all women and children, slept. Most of the Indians were killed. These events delayed for a while British movement up the Connecticut. Northfield, for example, had been so completely destroyed in an Indian raid that the settlement was evacuated in 1675. The Indians also dispersed. Some went west to a village on the Hoosic River called Schaghticoke. Others went north to set-

tlements on Lake Champlain. One group moved to an Indian settlement already established on the lower Winooski. Still other groups traveled as far north as the Missisquoi Abenaki village, or even to Odanak and Trois Rivieres in the St. Lawrence Valley.

From about 1680 to 1763 British and French North America were the scenes of some of the cruelest and bloodiest encounters between two great European powers bent on world domination. In the forests of Pennsylvania, New York, and New England, on the frigid waves of the Atlantic, and before the walled bastions of New France bitter and violent struggles in the eighty years of worldwide conflict between France and England were fought. The waters of Vermont—principally Lake Champlain, the Winooski River, Otter Creek, the White River, and the Connecticut River—were the main highways for the grand strategies of France and England's military leaders as they conceived plans to attack and conquer each other's strongholds: the citadel at Quebec, Albany's defenses against the French from the north, and Fort St. Frederic and Carillon, the great stone forts at the narrow head of Lake Champlain.

Today as one sits in a Burlington waterfront restaurant and looks west across a calm lake to the distant lights of New York's shore, it is difficult to imagine a time when the pleasant waters of Lake Champlain and the civilized amenities along its shores were instead highways of warfare and death, where small native settlements seldom felt the comforts of safety and security. From the 1680s to the 1760s armies of 200 to 3,000 men marched and canoed the forests and great lakes of northern New England, Quebec, and New York. From the North came the French and their Algonquian allies, usually the Abenaki. From the South came the English and Dutch with their Mohawk friends.

New France controlled a vast area, with a southern boundary that ran from the Atlantic coast (near today's Castine, Maine) through Maine and New Hampshire and across southern

Count de Frontenac, Governor of New France, launched his first attack on English and Dutch settlers in Schenectady. Frontenac's forces, including Abenaki Indians from Vermont, continued their raids on the English and their Iroquois allies in the Champlain valley up until 1694. This statue of the Count is by Philippe Hébert. Courtesy, Public Archives Canada (C-7183)

Vermont to the southern reaches of Lake Champlain. Later in the eighteenth century two great stone forts were constructed on the Lake—Fort St. Frederic on the west shore, controlling a narrow constriction of the lake, and then Fort Carillon, which the British later named Ticonderoga after its capture in 1759. From Champlain across northern New York, far above the Mohawk Valley, the boundary of New France ran to Lake Ontario where the French Governor Frontenac built an important fort in the 1690s. From here westward the French, despite some English claims to the contrary, considered all to be New France, including the great run of the Mississippi south to the Gulf of Mexico. The French called the expanse of territory *pays en haut*—the far west high up the St. Lawrence River.

The English controlled everything south of the line and east from the Alleghenies. By comparison with New France, New England was only a pocket on the eastern seaboard. The expanding population of the English in North America, from Virginia to Massachusetts, pressed firmly against New France's southeastern boundary. Thus the first violent conflicts with the Abenaki in the middle Connecticut River Valley led in the 1690s to King William's War, a decade-long conflict that marked the first chapter of an eighty-year struggle between France and England for the control of North America.

The prelude to King William's War was a vicious exchange of raids between the French and the Iroquois from 1687 to 1689. In 1687 the French sent a powerful force of regular army, wild woodsmen—*courier de bois*—and uncontrollable western Hurons, over 3,000 men in all, into western New York where they attacked and destroyed several Indian villages and numerous fields of standing crops. Seneca victims of the Huron were cut up and boiled in huge kettles. In return 1,500 Iroquois avenged the French attack of 1687 in April 1689, and erased the settlement of La Chine, a village upstream from Montreal. Men, women, and children were massacred, as the French had killed the Seneca. Some

of them were tortured, burned, and roasted like spitted pigs over fires in retaliation.

In the 1690s the first phase of King William's War brought some of these horrors to the Champlain Valley. The French commander during this decade was the Count de Frontenac, Governor of New France, sent by Louis XIV in 1690 for his second tour of duty as governor, though he was seventy years old.

Frontenac quickly launched his campaign against the English and their Iroquois allies. In January 1690 he sent 200 French and Indian raiders across the ice of Lake Champlain to Schenectady, where they killed nearly seventy English and Dutch settlers. Frontenac's force, including Sokoki Abenaki from Vermont, raided into coastal Maine and southern New Hampshire into the early 1690s. In retaliation a force of 750 men from Massachusetts and Connecticut, with an equal number of Iroquois, all headed by Fitz-John Winthrop, grandson of Massachusetts Bay's first governor, John Winthrop, headed north into the Champlain Valley to punish the Abenaki at Missisquoi for their raids on Salmon Falls, Maine, and ultimately, Winthrop thought, to push on to attack Montreal.

Upon reaching the lake, however, Winthrop's force found they had insufficient boats or canoes to transport 1,500 men and supplies down the lake to their destination. Most of this large party of raiders returned home. Captain John Schuyler, however, carried on with a band of Dutchmen intending to revenge with Mohawk help the winter raid on Schenectady. A nine-day journey by boat down the valley took the Dutch and Indian party to La Prairie, south of Montreal, where they killed six French settlers, took nineteen prisoners, and destroyed 150 cattle.

The Schuylers' presence in the Upper Hudson and Champlain valleys was strongly asserted through three generations from the 1680s well into the revolutionary period of the 1770s. John's brother Peter was well-known by all of the native people of the region. They pronounced his name "Quider" and Abenaki from Missisquoi, led by

Chief Sadochquis, traded with the Schuylers at Schaghticoke in 1685. Two years later Mohawks, called "Peter Schuyler's Indians" by the Abenaki, were hospitably received at the Missisquoi village. June 1691 saw Peter Schuyler lead a force of Dutch, Indians, and English by canoe down Champlain once again to Montreal. Unlike his brother John's nine-day forced march through the wilderness a year earlier, Peter Schuyler's troop moved leisurely across the summer waters, resting long enough at the mouth of Otter Creek to build a stone breastwork fort. Finally in August, after pushing on past the Abenaki settlements on the Lower Winooski and further north at the Missisquoi and skirting the remains of the French fort at Isle La Motte, Schuyler and his

In 1612 the Dutch entered the fur trade. They cultivated good relations with the Iroquois Indians of the Northeast, from whom they obtained their pelts. Captain Johannes Schuyler, pictured with his wife Elizabeth Staats Schuyler, participated in several military engagements between 1697 and 1701 to protect Dutch and Iroquois fur-trading interests from the French and their Indian allies. Portrait attributed to John Watson. Courtesy, The New York Historical Society

men beached their canoes upstream from the fort near Chambly Rapids on the Richelieu. Pushing on toward Montreal, Schuyler got no further than La Prairie, where alarms helped increase the French defenses to outnumber their English, Dutch, and Indian attackers. Schuyler and his companions were lucky to return safely to Schenectady with few losses.

Frontenac kept up the pressure on the English and their Iroquois allies through 1691 and 1692. In 1692 a force of 300 men, some of them hard-bitten regulars of the Carignan-Salieres regiment that had first come to New France in 1665, killed and captured English-allied Iroquois on the northern forest hunting grounds, taking two of them to burn at the stake in the town square at Quebec. The following January, 600 Canadians and Indians set out south from Isle La Motte, the jump-off station for southern raids, across the ice of Champlain to Mohawk country west of Schenectady. There they destroyed three Indian towns and captured 300 Indian women and children. Peter Schuyler and a small troop of Dutch and Indians again pursued the French raiders back into the Champlain Valley. Starting out with insufficient supplies for their hastily assembled pursuit across the frozen wilderness of New York and Vermont, Schuyler's company was forced to resort to cannibalizing some Abenaki captives. Schuyler shared the grisly meals until sated by the sight of a hand floating in his soup.

From 1694 until the Peace of Ryswick concluded King William's War in 1697, the murderous ferocity of the Franco-English struggle shifted east of the Champlain Valley to Massachusetts and the Atlantic coast. In 1698 Frontenac died knowing the lands to the west and south, including Lake Champlain and Lac Sacrement (as the French called Lake George), were crucial to France's control of the New World.

The next violent episode in the eighty-year-long conflict between France and England was Queen Anne's War, lasting from 1702 to 1713. Northwestern New England and New France in the Champlain Valley continued to broil with murderous exchanges of raids by English pushing north, as French and Abenaki marched south to prevent English settlement in the Connecticut River Valley. The most famous event of Queen Anne's War originating in Vermont was the 1704 raid by French militia, Missisquoi Abenaki, and some Mohawk Catholic converts from the Caughnawaga mission on St. Lawrence's south shore against the settlement at Deerfield, Massachusetts. At dawn on February 29, 1704, Major Hertel de Rouville led an attack force of 200 French and 142 Abenaki against the English settlement. In less than an hour the French and Abenaki had killed forty-seven English and taken 120 prisoners.

The journey back to Chambly on the Richelieu took twenty-five days in March by foot up the Connecticut and the White rivers, across the mountain backbone of Vermont, down the western waterways, and over the ice of Champlain to the open water of the Richelieu River. Deerfield's Reverend John Williams survived the captivity to add his account of the experience to the many popular eighteenth-century Indian captivity narratives. Williams' *Redeemed Captive* recounted the death of nineteen prisoners as they trekked across Vermont on that gruesome and deadly journey. Williams also preached what was probably the first Protestant sermon in Vermont while on the captive march to Canada. His text for the moment was apt: "Hear, I pray you, all people, and behold my sorrow: my virgins and my young men are gone into captivity."

One of the last raiding parties from Vermont in Queen Anne's War to pierce the defenses of New England was led by a man who for nearly thirty years would frustrate, harry, and punish the northward pressing English settlements of the Connecticut River Valley. A Woronoco from Westfield in Massachusetts known as Greylock drifted north after King Philip's War in the 1670s. Greylock first settled with Mahicans, Sokoki Abenaki, and others at Schagticoke on the Hoosic River. By 1712 he had moved north to live at Missisquoi and led a raid against Northampton that year. His first notable exploit, however, was in August 1723, when he led a series of raids against Northfield and Rutland, Massachusetts, and, despite pursuit by scouts and horse troops, returned unscathed with captives to Missisquoi. He went back to Northfield again in October to raid and further harass the English.

Greylock's late summer and autumn raids in

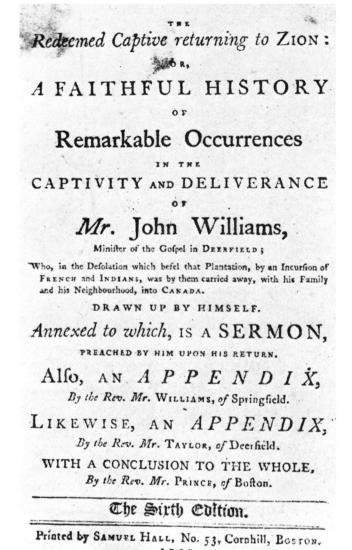

THE
Redeemed Captive returning to ZION :
OR,
A FAITHFUL HISTORY
OF
Remarkable Occurrences
IN THE
CAPTIVITY AND DELIVERANCE
OF
Mr. John Williams,
Minister of the Gospel in DEERFIELD;

Who, in the Desolation which befel that Plantation, by an Incursion of
FRENCH and INDIANS, was by them carried away, with his Family
and his Neighbourhood, into CANADA.

DRAWN UP BY HIMSELF.

Annexed to which, IS A SERMON,
PREACHED BY HIM UPON HIS RETURN.

Also, AN *APPENDIX,*
By the Rev. Mr. WILLIAMS, *of* Springfield.

LIKEWISE, AN *APPENDIX,*
By the Rev. Mr. TAYLOR, *of* Deerfield.

WITH A CONCLUSION TO THE WHOLE,
By the Rev. Mr. PRINCE, *of* Boston.

The Sixth Edition.

Printed by SAMUEL HALL, No. 53, Cornhill, BOSTON.
1795.

During the French and Indian wars, English captives were marched to Canada and held as prisoners until friends or relatives ransomed them back. In 1704 French-allied Indians attacked and burned the English settlement in Deerfield, Massachusetts. One hundred nineteen prisoners were forced to walk approximately 300 miles north through the Green Mountains to Montreal. In his narrative The Redeemed Captive *the Reverend John Williams recounted the painful details of the enforced march. Courtesy, Vermont Historical Society*

1713 led the Massachusetts government to send Lieutenant Timothy Dwight up the Connecticut to a point not far downstream from today's Brattleboro, where he built a stockade named after William Dummer (on whose land it stood). Dwight and forty-five men, including twelve Mohawks, were the entire garrison.

Even as Fort Dummer was being built in June

1724, Greylock again fell upon Deerfield, Northfield, and Westfield, returning finally to Missisquoi, after having eluded English scouts for nearly five months. One English detachment had sat fruitlessly waiting for Greylock's band at the mouth of Otter Creek for nearly a month.

Hoping to catch Greylock at Missisquoi before his spring raiding could start, Massachusetts sent a force of snowshoed militia under an indifferent command into the northern forest toward the Abenaki fortress near the foot of Lake Champlain in March of 1725. A month of wandering in the mountains without even finding Lake Champlain failed to turn up Greylock. He appeared again in Massachusetts in May, however, with raiding parties on the Connecticut. In July Massachusetts sent another force of fifty-nine men led by Captain Benjamin Wright to seek out this Indian scourge of the English, but they failed to go beyond the mouth of the Winooski River. In the meantime Greylock had raided Deerfield and Fort Dummer.

Finally in 1726, as Greylock camped at Otter Creek poised to raid the South again, the Abenaki of Missisquoi and Odanak agreed to peace with the English. What in Massachusetts the English called Dummer's War and the Abenaki today still call Greylock's War was followed by a period of peace for the Champlain and Connecticut valleys. English settlements in today's Vermont spread northward, as Westminster, known first as New Taunton, was founded in 1737 and the Sokoki Abenaki sold their land at Vernon on 1739.

The French moved south in earnest during the 1730s. Much of the Champlain Valley had been granted as *siegneuries* by King Louis XV by the 1740s, and French settlements consisting of initially a handful of people and then nearly a thousand began to take shape first in today's Alburg and then at Fort St. Frederic on Crown Point in 1731 and soon after the village at Chimney Point on the east shore of Champlain across from the fort.

Church records of the 1730s and 1740s at Fort

St. Frederic reveal another amazing aspect of the mighty Greylock. In his seventies Greylock fathered two children who were baptized at Crown Point: Marie Charlotte in 1737 and John Baptiste in 1740. Although not an Abenaki himself, for nearly thirty years Greylock's victories and fortunes were tied to the Abenaki of Missisquoi, where in his later years he lived in what European visitors called "Greylock's Castle," a stockade fort on the Missisquoi not far from the center of today's Swanton.

Since King Philip's War in the 1670s the Abenaki of northern New England had been in sporadic yet ferocious conflict with an expanding English population. Never surrendering unconditionally, as did native tribes of southern New England in the 1670s, the Abenaki of Maine, Lower Canada, and Vermont militarily resisted English encroachment until the final conquest of their French allies under the Marquis de Vaudreuil at Montreal in 1760.

The demise of French power in the Champlain Valley occurred as but a campaign that Samuel Eliot Morison has called "the real First World War." The French and Indian War in America was part of the global contest between France and England that saw naval battles in the Caribbean, the North Atlantic and the Indian Ocean, as well as large land battles on the continent of Europe, the Indian subcontinent, and the wilderness of North America. These conflicts involved Prussia and other European states, as well as France and England. Some of the first great modern military field officers of France and England—men of the caliber of Montcalm and Wolfe—died in this worldwide conflict. English control of India—which would last for 200 years—was accomplished in this Seven Years' War. England's control of French Canada was also accomplished, but England's thirteen North American colonies remained submissive for just twelve years after the Treaty of Paris concluded the war in 1763.

The events of this "first world war" occurring in and around Vermont are marked by such names as Abercrombie, Amherst, and Rogers for the English and their colonial allies, and Montcalm and Dieskau for the French. The names of Vermont Abenaki leaders allied with the French in this final conflict with the English have unfortunately not come down to us through the years. Names of important places were Fort William Henry on Lake George, which the French and English fought over twice; the two forts on Lake Champlain: Carillon, which the English renamed Ticonderoga after Lord Jeffrey Amherst captured it in 1759, and Fort St. Frederic, which the English rebuilt and renamed Crown Point also in 1759. The French settlement across from Crown Point, called *Point a la Chevalure* was abandoned in 1759, leaving only chimneys standing where a modest French village once existed.

With the final retreat of the French from the Champlain Valley in 1759, and the construction of the Crown Point Military Road from Lake Champlain east to Fort Number 4 at Charlestown, New Hampshire, on the Connecticut River, Vermont's future as a settlement of English colonials and then independent Americans was assured. Only one episode in the French and Indian War remained to be acted out across Vermont by Major Robert Rogers and his company of rangers.

Under orders from Lord Jeffrey Amherst at Crown Point, Rogers and a party of 200 men set out by boat on September 12, 1759, from Crown Point for the largest known village of Abenaki in the region, Odanak, at the mouth of the St. Francis River on the St. Lawrence. As in earlier Anglo-French conflicts the Abenaki of Missisquoi withdrew from their exposed position in Vermont and moved first to Alburg, at the outlet of Lake Champlain into the Richelieu River, where Père Etienne Lauverjat had built a chapel in 1744. After the fall of Carillon and Fort St. Frederic the French withdrew ten miles down the Richelieu to Isle aux Noix, where Abenaki with the dismantled chapel from Alburg joined them in building fortifications on the riverbank. Other Abenaki residents of the Missisquoi village and probably some from the smaller village on the

PLAN
du FORT
CARILLON

Left
Construction of Fort Carillon was begun by the French in 1755. On July 8, 1758, French Commander Montcalm and 3,600 men victoriously held the fort against a frontal assault by British General Abercromby and an army of approximately 15,000. A year later Lord Jeffrey Amherst captured the strategically located fort and renamed it Ticonderoga. Courtesy, Special Collections, University of Vermont Library

Bottom
In the late 1750s the Champlain Valley was the scene of fighting between the British and French. Lieutenant Thomas Davies painted this watercolor in 1759. The inscription read, "A View of the Lines and Fort of Ticonderoga with the Encampment of his Excellency Major General Amherst . . . ." The French had recently destroyed the fort and retreated northward. By fall of that year General Wolfe defeated the French at Quebec and the British controlled Canada. Courtesy, The New York Historical Society

lower Winooski withdrew to Odanak.

The English and their American colonials believed a punishing raid on the Abenaki at Odanak would discourage the natives from supporting the French during an English attack on Montreal in the coming spring of 1760. At the very moment Rogers' company set off down the lake, however, France's fate in North America was being sealed as the English forces led by Wolfe attacked Quebec. At this time, Wolfe is said to have recited the lines from Thomas Gray's *Elegy in a Country*

Churchyard: "The paths of glory lead but to the grave." Wolfe, victorious but dead on the Plains of Abraham, illustrated the elegy before the closing of the conquest on September 13. Rogers' adventure against the Abenaki at Odanak, while not nearly as glorious as Wolfe's, almost led to his own mortal end.

The journey down Lake Champlain for Rogers' company of 200 started uneventfully, but plans began to unravel as they entered the northern reaches of the lake. First a keg of gunpowder

exploded, disabling forty of the rangers who then returned to Crown Point. Then the fleet of boats with supplies for the return journey, left beached on the south shore of Missisquoi Bay, was discovered by the Abenaki watch guards from the deserted Missisquoi village.

The remainder of Rogers' adventure has been told in two contrasting versions. Rogers' own tale, later retold by novelist Kenneth Roberts, had Rogers and his rangers surprising the Abenaki as they lay in a drunken sleep. They were then forced to beat a hasty retreat when a French and Abenaki force was drawn to the village by the sound of the English guns. Rogers and his men struggled heroically without supplies, foraging for nuts and lilly roots, as they made their way back to the Connecticut River where, to their dismay, the supply party sent from Fort Number 4 to meet them had failed to make the rendezvous. Starving and nearly dead after three months of wandering through the northern wilderness, Rogers returned to Crown Point on December 1, 1759, over the Crown Point military road with a report of killing 200 natives at St. Francis, losing only six men there, and rescuing five captives.

The French and Abenaki tell another version of Rogers' raid. The French report of the attack records a body count of only thirty dead Abenaki. The Abenaki account, an oral tradition still sustained in Vermont's Abenaki community today, has been handed down over four generations by descendants of two families who were living in the village at Odanak in the fall of 1759. In Abenaki tradition, a Mahican accompanying Rogers warned the residents of Odanak about Rogers' raiding party the night before the rangers were to attack, thus many villagers escaped before Rogers arrived.

Whatever the true results of Rogers' raid, Wolfe's victory at Quebec was so complete that the attack on Odanak, even Rogers' version of it, had little effect on French rule in Canada. In 1760 the English drew plans to attack Montreal with a three-pronged force that included Amherst's army pushing north down the Champlain Valley from Ticonderoga and Crown Point. The conquest of French Canada was then completed in September 1760, and the Treaty of Paris in 1763 ended French occupation of Vermont.

While agreement in Europe might have relieved Anglo-French enmity, the pressures of a growing English colonial population pushing into northern New England—one of the original causes of the French and Indian War—increased the likelihood of new conflicts over the rightful ownership of what would soon officially be called Vermont. New England's militiamen, like Rogers' rangers, had been tramping through Vermont on military campaigns for nearly eighty years. Accounts of unpopulated rich intervales, good water supplies, and plenty of timber made this northwest corner of New England increasingly attractive to inhabitants of Connecticut, Massachusetts, New York, and New Hampshire.

Thousands of square miles of undeveloped land offered rich opportunities to clever men, the sort that New Hampshire, beginning with Benning Wentworth, its first governor, frequently seemed to throw up into positions of leadership. In 1741 New Hampshire's boundaries were defined and its government established, with Wentworth at its head. Ordered by the Crown to maintain Fort Dummer on the west shore of the Connecticut River, Wentworth quickly assumed the authority to grant land charters and lay out towns in the vast tract between the Connecticut and Lake Champlain, reserving choice lots for himself in every grant. In 1750, despite objections from New York, Wentworth chartered Bennington as his namesake town.

Settlers on both sides of the Green Mountains busily set about clearing lands and building homes in what by the early 1760s were being called the New Hampshire Grants. With the conclusion of the French and Indian War and the Treaty of Paris in 1763, New York disputed Wentworth's grant and demanded that the Bennington grant be withdrawn. Wentworth and New York's Governor Clinton agreed to adjudication of their differences by the King, who ruled in

Above

Benning Wentworth, Governor of the Province of New Hampshire from 1741 to 1767, began issuing charters to towns on the west side of the Connecticut River in 1749. Ignoring New York's claim to the Connecticut River as its eastern boundary, Wentworth audaciously issued a grant to the township of Bennington, located forty miles west of the river, in 1750. Within fifteen years Wentworth granted charters to 137 other townships. He had also made a fortune by selling off approximately 65,000 acres of land he had reserved for himself. Painting by Joseph Blackburn. Courtesy, New Hampshire Historical Society

Top, right

Gerardus Stuyvesant was granted a 12,000-acre tract of land by the New York authorities in 1739. The New York holders of the patent claimed it extended into Shaftsbury and Bennington, towns which were settled by families holding New Hampshire titles during the 1760s. The land dispute boiled over in 1769 when a Yorker survey team appeared on James Breakenridge's farm in Bennington and was angrily confronted by a group of Hampshire settlers, some armed, who told the surveyors to leave. Painting by Thomas McIlworth. Courtesy, The New York Historical Society

1764 that all land west of the Connecticut River came under the jurisdiction of the province of New York. Wentworth submitted to the royal judgment, having already granted 131 townships throughout the region, though few settlers had moved into them. Benning Wentworth's land grant scheme eventually collapsed in a scandal, however, and his nephew John Wentworth succeeded him as governor.

Though Benning Wentworth was no longer governor of New Hampshire, his land grant scheme planted seeds of trouble that grew and increased under his nephew's rule. The contest between holders of New Hampshire grants and the authorities of New York continued into the years of the Revolution. Once again groups of armed men marched across the land now called the New Hampshire Grants by some and New York by others. Sheriff posses of up to 700 men, bent on evicting settlers from lands granted to them by Wentworth, faced men of the Grants who were equally intent on holding their claims. Eventually these settlers organized Committees of Safety in several of their towns. The first forms of civil government had been established. In the turmoil and tumult of the Hampshire Grants controversy there could be seen the earliest signs of a Vermont community.

These Indians and Squaws Of Lower Canada *may well have been Abenaki, the original native American people of Vermont. During the eighteenth century Abenaki were forced north by English colonists. By the mid-nineteenth century, when Cornelius Krieghoff produced this lithograph, its Abenaki community frequently traveled into Canada to visit the Abenaki at Odanak. Courtesy, Public Archives Canada (C-56)*

Vermont Abenaki Indians participated in the famous attack on Deerfield, Massachusetts, in 1704. Reverend John Williams, who was one of 120 captured in this raid, later published a narrative in which he recounted details of the forced march through the Green Mountains of Vermont to Canada.

Above

In 1953 Grandma Moses painted three pictures of the Battle of Bennington. Although many of the details are historically accurate, the first two versions include the monument that was erected to mark the site of the battle. When it was pointed out to Grandma Moses that no monument existed at the time, she painted a third version without it. Courtesy, Grandma Moses, The Battle of Bennington. *Copyright 1973, Grandma Moses Properties Co., New York*

Right

This hand-painted drum, captured by American troops in 1777 during the Battle of Bennington, depicts British soldiers on horseback. "See here, men! There are the Redcoats," General John Stark was reputed to have said to his men before mustering them to battle on the afternoon of August 16, "Before night they are ours, or Molly Stark will be a widow!" By nightfall the British had surrendered and the enemy dead, wounded, and captured totaled over 900. Courtesy, The Bennington Museum

A Landscape View of Bennington, *painted by Ralph Earl in 1798, is one of the few known eighteenth-century American landscape paintings. Earl's view of Bennington depicts Governor Isaac Tichenor's homestead in the center foreground, the Parson Dewey house at the far right, the General David Robinson house, and the gambrel-roofed Elijah Dewey house, now the Walloomsic Inn. All are still standing. The artist portrayed himself sketching the scene in the lower left-hand corner. Courtesy, The Bennington Museum*

This watercolor depicts a military encampment during the War of 1812 at Tyler's farm on Lake Champlain's Missisquoi Bay near Highgate. Between battles, two Indians paddle peacefully across the lake. Nothing is known about the artist, "Benson," but the Tyler family still owns the camp site. Courtesy, Shelburne Museum, Shelburne, Vermont

Above
Not long after Thomas Water-man Wood was elected to the National Academy of Design, he paid tribute to his hometown of Montpelier by painting The Village Post Office. *Although the interior may have been taken from a store in Williamstown, Vermont, the figures in this scene were mostly Montpelier residents. The postmaster was Wood's Uncle Zenas, and the storekeeper was a local church organist. Courtesy, New York State Historical Association, Cooperstown*

Right
In 1861 the Vermont Historical Society commissioned Burling-ton artist Charles Heyde to cre-ate this coat of arms for official state purposes. The mountains depicted by the artist are Cam-el's Hump and Mount Mans-field as they might have been viewed by Samuel de Cham-plain in 1609. The motto "Ver-mont, Freedom and Unity," re-fers to the fact that Vermont was independent before joining the Union and continued the tra-dition of independent thinking thereafter. Courtesy, Shelburne Museum

When Alvan Fisher painted this bucolic view of Brattleboro in 1830 the town already had gained a reputation as being "the richest village of its size in New England." Its manufactures included paper, wool, cotton, hats, stoves, and lead pipes. Flatboats carried local products downstream to commercial centers, and steamboats made regular stops in Brattleboro. The horse pictured in the left foreground was the son of "Figure," pro-genitor of Vermont's famous Morgan horses. Courtesy, The Stephen Greene Press from Before Our Time: A Pictorial Memoir of Brattleboro, Vermont from 1830 to 1930. Copyright 1974 by Harold A. Barry, Richard E. Michelman, Richard M. Michelman, Richard M. Mitchell, and Richard H. Wellman. Published by The Stephen Greene Press, Brattleboro, Vermont. All rights reserved.

When Mrs. Samuel Haskins of Glover, Vermont, appliqued this "Crazy Quilt" during the Civil War era she used scraps of cloth to make a patchwork depicting many aspects of farm and family life in Vermont. She included domestic and wild animals and even added a few exotic ones such as a giraffe and a lion. Courtesy, Shelburne Museum

Left
The Dutton House is one of many historic houses that were moved from their original sites, reconstructed, and restored by the Shelburne Museum. Built in 1782 by Salmon Dutton, the massive kitchen fireplace and bake oven served as a center of family activities for generations. Courtesy, Shelburne Museum

Below
J. and E. Norton, manufacturers of the famous Vermont stoneware with cobalt blue decorations, made this water cooler for use in the lobby of the Hotel Putnam in Bennington sometime between 1850 and 1859. The landscape with deer and bird is supposed to be a view of Bennington. Courtesy, The Bennington Museum

Left
Seth Warner was leader of the Bennington division of the Green Mountain Boys. Following the surrender of Fort Ticonderoga in 1775, Warner's division attacked and captured Crown Point. Courtesy, Vermont Travel Division

Above
The Mount Mansfield Hotel, which opened in 1864, boasted accommodations for 500 guests, all "on a magnificent scale." The extravagance of the hotel's wealthy clientele elicited mixed reactions from a local historian of the period, who worried about the effect on the young of the idle rich "whose main business . . . seems to be to 'fare sumptuously!'" Courtesy, Robert Hull Fleming Museum, University of Vermont

Left
In 1864 the Howe Scale Company was obviously as proud of its modern factory shops as of its manufacture of "Howe's Army Scale," pictured in the paint shop at the bottom of this advertising poster. To emphasize the Howe Scale Company's contribution to the war effort, the poster depicts a brigade of Union soldiers marching past the office. Courtesy, The Shelburne Museum

Facing page
In the late nineteenth century the Dr. B.J. Kendall Company of Enosburg Falls poured as much as $75,000 a year into advertising "Kendall's Spavin Cure." This versatile liniment was reputed to cure most aches and pains of horses and other animals, as well as those pertaining to "human flesh." The large mansard-roofed building in the background of this handsome lithographed poster is the B.J. Kendall Company, which once employed twenty men and thirty women. Courtesy, The Shelburne Museum

Above
When James Hope painted this View of Clarendon Springs, Vermont, *in 1853, the curative properties of the town's mineral springs had already been famous for fifty years. According to Abby Hemenway's* Vermont Gazetteer, *both the Clarendon and Green Mountain Hotels were "the annual resort of great numbers of pleasure-seekers and invalids from all parts of the country." Courtesy, The Currier Gallery of Art*

Left
Waiting For the Mail *on a cold winter morning provided an opportunity for combining gossip with shopping. In 1941, when Harry Shokler made this print of the scene in front of the South Londonderry Store, many Vermont post offices were still located within the local general store. Courtesy, Vermont Historical Society*

Above
According to Crockett's History of Vermont, *the village of*
Newbury contained a "most el-
egant church" in the 1790s that
housed the only church bell in
the state. For centuries before
the colonists arrived, the area
along the oxbow at Newbury was
inhabited by a community of
Abenaki Indians. Courtesy, So-
ciety for the Preservation of New
England Antiquities

Right
When the Fairbanks scale busi-
ness grew and prospered during
the latter half of the nineteenth
century, its founders and man-
agers built themselves dignified
and spacious houses on the hills
around St. Johnsbury. The
landscaped grounds of Gover-
nor Fairbanks' mansion Pine-
hurst, built in 1852, were much
admired in their time. From the
Wilbur Collection. Courtesy,
Bailey/Howe Library, Univer-
sity of Vermont

St. Johnsbury, Vt. Pinehurst.

Felix Kelly's 1975 painting of The Sidewheeler Ticonderoga *at Fort Ticonderoga on Lake Champlain depicts the fort and sidewheeler steamship as they might have looked after the ship was launched in 1906. The building on the left of the Ticonderoga is the Pavilion, built in 1820 by William F. Pell. When the Ticonderoga was retired from service in 1953, Electra Havermeyer Webb bought it and had it moved overland to its present site at The Shelburne Museum. Courtesy, Shelburne Museum*

Luigi Lucioni's 1931 painting of The Village of Stowe, Vermont, *depicts a peaceful community dominated by the spire of its white church. Construction of ski trails on Mount Mansfield was started in 1933 by Civilian Conservation Corps workers, and a year later the first United States Olympic women's ski team trained there. Today the village of Stowe is a thriving ski resort. Courtesy, The Minneapolis Institute of Arts, Estate of Mrs. George P. Douglas*

A Revolution, a Republic, and Statehood

For the men and women of southern New England who contemplated migration north during the late 1760s and 1770s, "going into the Grants" offered the dubious opportunity of settling land that for the next twenty years would be racked with legal contentiousness, armed conflict, and protracted uncertainty about the safety and future of their community. The concrete terms of this life assured the new people of the Grants dramatic, sometimes violent, even deadly, conflict in the continuing land grant controversy. Legal and political contests carried on first under English rule before the Board of Trade in London and then King George III, himself. Later disputes took place in the forum of the newly independent Continental Congress. Settlement in the Grants promised residents a life of continual fear that either a New York court officer and posse or later a troop of British infantrymen or Canadian Indians would drive them from their new homes and land, if not simply shoot them.

Yet these first settlements of second and third or more generation New England men and women on lands claimed for over 100 years by the French and inhabited for thousands by the aboriginal people, the Abenaki and their predecessors, formed communities that survived the American Revolution, established themselves as a republic, and eventually joined the United States as Vermont, the fourteenth state. The twenty-odd years between New Hampshire's Governor Benning Wentworth's resignation and Vermont's joining the Union were exciting times.

By the mid-1760s Benning Wentworth had granted well over 100 townships on the west side of the Connecticut River, some of them within twenty miles of the Hudson River and others north to the eastern shore of Lake Champlain. The Province of New York, recognizing the loss

Left
Stephen Fay's tavern in Old Bennington became headquarters for Ethan Allen's Green Mountain Boys beginning in 1770. There Allen and his cohorts organized guerilla operations to protect their land titles against conflicting New York claims. Outside the tavern a snarling stuffed catamount facing westward toward New York became a symbol of the Green Mountain Boys' determination to defy their Yorker enemies. Courtesy, Vermont Historical Society

Above
During the 1770s Ann Story and her five children lived in the wilderness area that later became Salisbury, Vermont. When the Revolution broke out she volunteered her services as a spy for the Green Mountain Boys. "Give me a place among you, and see if I am the first to desert my post," are the words attributed to her in Daniel P. Thompson's nineteenth-century novel The Green Mountain Boys. *According to her contemporaries, "she feared neither Tory, Indian, nor wild beast." Illustration by Roy Lewando, Jr.*

of grant fees and taxes it would suffer if Wentworth's grants were sustained, petitioned the Crown for jurisdiction in all of the region east to the west bank of the Connecticut River. The royal response came back declaring "the Western bank of the Connecticut, from where it enters the province of Massachusetts Bay as far north as the forty-fifth degree of northern latitude, to be the boundary line between the said two provinces of New Hampshire and New York." Wentworth was furious over losing jurisdiction in the New Hampshire Grants, but recommended to the proprietors and settlers due obedience to the authorities and laws of the colony of New York.

By 1767 Benning Wentworth's handiwork in his New Hampshire Grants had planted a population of less than 10,000 settlers from lower New England. Some one to two thousand Abenaki lived in the Champlain Valley and other river intervales. A few tiny French settlements remained in the northern lake valley and as far up the Winooski as present-day Montpelier. Yet 1767 was the end of Wentworth's land ventures in the Grants. He resigned to avoid disgrace over his shady land transactions and for disobeying the Royal order to cease activities in the territory disputed by New York.

The final years of the 1760s saw an aggressive New York asserting its authority in the Grants. First in 1768 New York divided the Grants into Cumberland County, consisting of all the land lying east of the central mountain range (roughly today's Windsor and Windham counties). Then in 1770 Gloucester County was created, running from the Canadian line south to Cumberland County, east to the Connecticut River, and west to the Green Mountains. All areas west of the mountains south from Canada, New York declared Albany County. When a New York court sat in the Cumberland County shire town of Chester in 1770, Hampshire Grant landowners with Wentworth titles denied New York jurisdiction over them and threatened violent action against the court's officers. A convention of towns met at Bennington and declared they would re-

sist forcefully any New York claims on their land. During an attempt by New Hampshire grantees in 1770 to persuade a court at Albany to sustain the legitimacy of Wentworth land grants, Ethan Allen struck an early combative note in a controversy that developed quickly into violence. "The gods of the valley," Allen warned New Yorkers in ominous scriptural echoes, "are not the gods of the hills." When New York's attorney general failed to comprehend Allen's cautionary metaphors, Allen assured the Yorker lawyer that if he "accompanied him to Bennington Hill, it would be plain to him."

These contentious days spawned the irregular troop of Green Mountain Boys, who would six years later enter the Continental Army as a regular regiment in the fight for independence from England, complete with the battle experience of resisting and evicting Yorkers to strengthen them.

Probably the most colorful figure in Vermont's early history, Ethan Allen is remembered as a hero of the Revolution and leader of the Green Mountain Boys. When in 1770 the Attorney General of New York Province suggested that Allen should desert the cause of the Green Mountain farmers, he responded, "the gods of the hills are not the gods of the valley." Following the Revolution Ethan and Ira Allen were instrumental in launching Vermont as a separate state. Courtesy, Vermont Historical Society

Above
Aristocratic James Duane was an influential New York lawyer who held title to disputed lands north of Bennington. After Duane and John Kempe instituted suits in 1771 to eject settlers holding New Hampshire titles, Ethan Allen and his Hampshire friends responded by openly resisting New York authority. When Governor Tryon of New York offered twenty pounds for the arrest of the "rioters," Allen and his friends countered by offering twenty-five pounds for the apprehension of Duane and Kempe. Courtesy, Vermont Historical Society

Facing page
Vigilante justice was sometimes administered by the Green Mountain Boys against "Yorker" trespassers during the pre-Revolutionary War era. This early engraving depicts a Yorker from Arlington being hoisted to the sign of the catamount at Fay's tavern in Bennington to serve out his sentence of hanging "in an armed chair . . . for two hours, in sight of the people." On the right another Yorker receives the application of the "beech seal" to his bare back. Despite such violent resistance to New York authority, no lives were lost in these border disputes. Courtesy, Brooks Memorial Library

In the early 1770s Green Mountain Boys controlled the lands west of the mountains as roving rangers, despite the efforts of New Yorkers to combat them.

The principal targets of the Green Mountain Boys were New York sheriffs, surveyors, and landjobbers (real estate agents). The conflict became so intense that New York's Governor William Tryon requested the support of British regular troops from General Frederick Haldimand in 1773. The British refusal of military aid led New York to a propaganda war, including the infamous ultimatum known as the "Bloody Act." The Bloody Act was a proclamation ordering the immediate hanging of any Green Mountain Boy captured by the New York rangers. Ethan Allen and other prominent leaders of the Green Mountain Boys were indicted in absentia by a court in Albany. The governor of the province offered a twenty-pound reward for their capture after the Green Mountain Boys had evicted a Yorker from land he had claimed under a New York title, tore down his house, and burned the lumber. The New York reward for the Green Mountain Boys' capture was countered by Allen and the others, who proclaimed they would pay a reward of ten pounds for the apprehension of James Duane and John Kemp (two notorious New York officials) and their delivery to the Catamount Tavern in Bennington. The deflating "one-upmanship" of Yankee humor appeared early in the story of Vermont and its origins.

These antics of the Green Mountain Boys and earlier episodes of thwarting Albany County sheriff Ten Eyck when he attempted to arrest and evict Bennington's James Breckinridge infuriated New York authorities during the years immediately preceding the Declaration of Independence by the thirteen colonies. New York appealed to the Board of Trade in London and then to the King to adjudicate the dispute in favor of the New York claim to lands in the Hampshire Grants. The recommendations of the British Board of Trade, and then the King's Privy Council, as transmitted to America by Lord Dartmouth, was unsatisfactory to New York, however, for it forbade collecting further exorbitant fees for the New York land grants and ordered amicable settlement of disputes. When General Haldimand refused military aid to re-outfit the fort at Ticonderoga and re-establish a stronghold at the ruins of the French fort on Crown Point, there seemed to be little hope for New York to prevail unless it developed amicable relations with the people of the Grants. Yet when Governor Tryon offered public offices to settlers in Bennington and other towns in the Grants a

convention at Manchester passed a resolution forbidding any man to hold office under New York authority. New Yorkers were declared public enemies by the same convention. In 1774 the good citizens of Chester declared themselves free of the authority of New York.

Objection and resistance to British rule were simultaneously mounting along the eastern seaboard of North America. Citizens of Massachusetts, for example, prevented the King's Court from sitting in Boston and established their own Provincial Assembly. Committees of correspondence formed throughout the colonies to assure a flow of accurate information. Independence was a growing movement, which led to the first session of the Continental Congress at Philadelphia in 1774. A convention of Cumberland County residents of the New Hampshire Grants passed resolutions of their own spirit of independence, too.

Then in March of 1775 the "first blood of the American Revolution" was spilled at Westminster in the New Hampshire Grants. According to witnesses, citizens of Westminster armed only with clubs from a nearby woodpile occupied the courthouse to prevent a New York judge from holding session. After sufficient bracing with rum

a New York sheriff and his posse marched and fired upon the courthouse's occupants. Two men were killed, and the Westminster Massacre, as it came to be called, within two days drew over 500 armed men from the surrounding countryside to release the remaining courthouse occupants from arrest by the sheriff and give voice to both anti-New York and anti-British sentiments. When New York Governor Cadwallader Colden asked General Thomas Gage at Boston for help in suppressing what he called a "dangerous insurrection," Gage refused to send troops. He knew that a larger explosion was coming in eastern Massachusetts. In the meantime men of the Grants convened at Westminster on April 11 and resolved "to lay their grievances before his most gracious Majesty." Ethan Allen, John Hazeltine, and Charles Phelps were directed to compose the petition to the King, but the Battle of Lexington on April 19 forever put an end to expressions of loyalty to a foreign sovereign by any representative body in the land soon to be called Vermont.

The final years of the 1770s were formative years for Vermont in both political and military terms. Soon after the start of the American Revolution in 1775, the Green Mountain Boys launched into a series of military battles in and around Vermont, which came to an end with a final devastating raid by Indians, Tories, and a few British regulars on the village of Royalton in 1780. The capture of Ticonderoga on May 10, 1775, by the Green Mountain Boys and a force of men from New Hampshire and Connecticut, under Ethan Allen and Benedict Arnold, provided both a signal victory for the Yankees and a complement of artillery to be sent overland for the seige of Boston. The subsequent capture of the British outpost at Crown Point by Seth Warner and the Green Mountain Boys and the easy taking of a British ship at St. John in Canada on the Richelieu River downstream from Lake Champlain gave Americans complete control of the ancient and strategically important military routes of the Champlain

Valley.

Victories on the lake were not enough for leaders of the American forces, however, so an expeditionary force was sent north to conquer, or at least neutralize, British Canada in late 1775. The first rash attack on Montreal by Ethan Allen cost the Americans the most colorful of the Green Mountain Boys when Allen was captured outside

the city's walls. He was taken to England in irons and spent nearly three years of the war a prisoner in England, Ireland, Halifax and New York until his release in 1778. Despite Allen's capture the Americans under General Richard Montgomery pushed on with the attack against Montreal and Canada, eventually taking the city and marching on to link up with Benedict Arnold before Quebec-the destination of Arnold's heroic march through the northem forests from Massachusetts. This American adventure was thwarted, however, when Quebec stood firm against the American attack. A dangerous retreat to Ticonderoga was saved from disaster by the aid of Seth Warner and a force of Green Mountain Rangers, who rushed down lake to help the American force back to safety at the head of Lake Champlain.

Encouraged by the rout of the Americans from Canada, a British naval force on Lake Champlain, near Valcour Island, drove Benedict Arnold's newly built fleet from the waters in 1776. After the capture of Crown Point, however, the great chain barrier below Ticonderoga prevented the British from carrying on their attack against the American-occupied citadel and Fort Independence on the east shore of the lake directly across from Ticonderoga. By the end of 1776 more than 5,000 men filled both Ticonderoga's bastions and the earthwork star fort, batteries, and hospital across the lake on Mount Independence.

From 1776 until August 1777 political activities in the Grants pointed toward the formation of a new state. A series of conventions held at Dorset produced resolutions to form the New Hampshire Grants into a separate political entity unattached to either New York or New Hampshire. On January 15, 1777, the fifth of these conventions was held in Westminster, where the New Hampshire Grants declared themselves an independent state-New Connecticut. In March the final draft of the New Connecticut Declaration of Independence was published. It was reaffirmed by another convention on June 7 at Windsor, at which time, on the recommendation of Dr. Thomas Young of Philadelphia, "Ver-

mont" was adopted as the new name to replace New Connecticut.

News of a British force threatening Ticonderoga in the first week of July hastened the adoption of Vermont's Constitution by the convention at Windsor on July 2 in the midst of a thunderous rainstorm. The abandonment of Ticonderoga in mid-July 1777 by the remaining American force of about 2,000 brought on the only battle of the American Revolution actually fought in Vermont when the rear guard of the Yankee retreat was attacked at Hubbardton. Two regiments from Massachusetts and New Hampshire, including Seth Warner's, suffered heavy losses, and the village of Hubbardton was burned by the British who suffered heavy losses as well. In the meantime a full Yankee force under General St. Clair had marched via Rutland, Dorset, and Manches-

ter to Fort Edward in New York. Some troops were left to man forts at Rutland, Pittsford, and Castleton, but most settlers had been driven south by the threat of the British army under General John Burgoyne marching south toward Albany.

Yet Burgoyne's army of nearly 10,000 British regulars, Canadians, Indians, and German mercenaries desperately needed supplies, and in mid August Burgoyne sent Colonel Friedrich Baum and his Hessians, together with a large force of Indians and Tories, to capture the Yankee stores held at Bennington. The fighting actually took place in Hoosick, New York, as a defense of the battle stores at Bennington. Troops were sent from New Hampshire's Fort Number 4 at Charlestown under General John Stark, and some troops from Massachusetts lent support. As a result the Battle of Bennington saw Seth Warner's

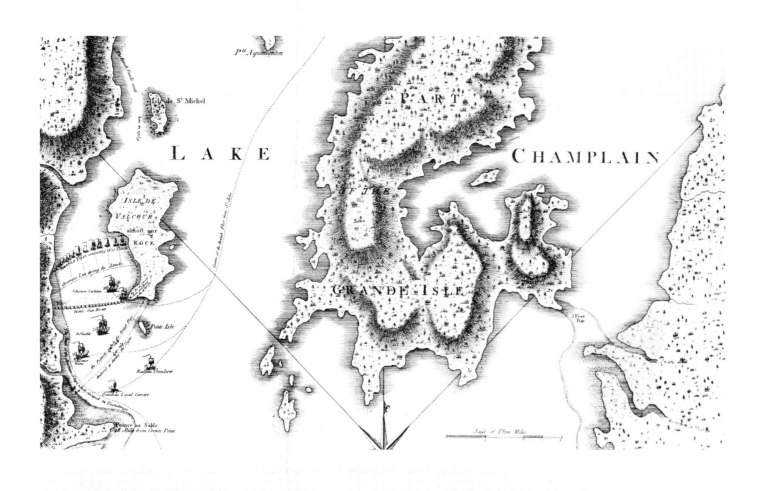

Facing page, top
William Faden's 1776 map depicts the naval maneuvers of the Battle of Valcour Island. On the morning of October 11, Benedict Arnold's sixteen American vessels were anchored between the New York shore and Valcour Island. Their position forced the British to attack from the south. By nightfall the superior British gunboats had badly battered the American fleet. Arnold slipped his remaining ships through the British lines under cover of darkness, but was eventually forced to abandon and burn them. Courtesy, Special Collections, University of Vermont Library

Right
On July 8, 1777, a group of delegates from the "separate state of New Connecticut" met at Elijah West's tavern in Windsor to adopt the Constitution of the Independent Republic of Vermont. The Windsor Constitution was the first in the country to prohibit slavery and to establish universal manhood suffrage. Today West's tavern is known as the "Old Constitution House." Courtesy, Vermont Travel Division

Facing page, bottom
This watercolor from the Royal Collection at Windsor Castle by British officer Henry Gilder, depicts the Battle of Valcour Island, October 11, 1776. Commander Benedict Arnold's fleet, drawn up in a semicircle between Valcour Island and the New York shore of Lake Champlain, is being engaged by a line of advancing British gunboats. Two days later Arnold's fleet was defeated as it sailed toward Crown Point. Rather than surrender, Arnold ran his ships ashore, burned them, and escaped to Ticonderoga. Courtesy, Vermont Historical Society

Right
On January 15, 1776, Vermont declared herself a free and independent republic. Between 1776 and 1791 the Republic of Vermont issued its own copper coinage. Reuben Harmon of Rupert was granted the exclusive right to coin copper by the Vermont House and Council. William Cooley, a goldsmith who had emigrated to Rupert from New York City, made the dies. This 1786 coin shows the sun rising from behind the Green Mountains. The ploughshare in the field beneath represents the republic's chief industry. Courtesy, The Bennington Museum

Green Mountain Rangers and other militia decisively defeat the British on August 16. This great boost to Vermont's morale in the late summer of 1777 led to the last convention at Windsor of that year. There constitutional provisions were adopted to allow the first elections and meeting of the legislature, the first constitutional prohibition of slavery in North America, and the first establishment of universal male suffrage.

Meanwhile Burgoyne's army was still aimed at Albany, though his future in the northern theater of war offered gloomy prospects after Bennington. Burgoyne wrote to his superior, Lord George Germaine, that "the Hampshire Grants

...hang like a gathering storm upon my left." The storm burst when Seth Warner's regiment of Green Mountain Rangers joined the Continental Army at Saratoga and helped to soundly defeat Burgoyne's British and German troops.

After Burgoyne's defeat Vermonters felt confident enough to take back Ticonderoga. A force of rangers led by Ebenezer Allen, Ethan and Ira's cousin, captured the vantage point of Mount Defiance, where British guns had looked down on Ticonderoga. Allen sent a few rounds from the captured guns into the fort, and the Americans quickly recovered the ancient bastion. Among the captives taken with the British were Dinah

Above
The British claimed a victory at Hubbardton when Hessian reinforcements commanded by Baron Reidesel charged and successfully routed American troops. In this bloody two-hour Revolutionary battle, the Yankees suffered losses of 96 dead and wounded, as compared to enemy casualties of 174 dead and wounded. Courtesy, Special Collections, University of Vermont Library

Facing page
Following the abandonment of Ticonderoga the retreating rear guard of the American forces was attacked by the British at Hubbardton on the morning of July 7, 1777. The Green Mountain Rangers, led by Seth Warner, and a Massachusetts regiment initially held firm against the enemy, but were defeated when British

reinforcements arrived. From F.W. Beers Atlas of Rutland County, Vermont (1869). Courtesy, Special Collections, University of Vermont

Top, right
General John Burgoyne commanded the British expedition from Canada against the colonies during the American Revolution. In addition to 7,000 regular soldiers, Burgoyne's troops included Mohawks and Hessian mercenaries. Following the defeat at Bennington, Burgoyne was forced to surrender at Saratoga on October 17, 1777. He called Vermonters "the most active and rebellious race on the continent." From the Wilbur Collection. Courtesy, Bailey/Howe Library, University of Vermont

Matthis and her son, black slaves of a British officer. Though standing in New York, Ebenezer Allen extended the new freedom of the Vermont

Constitution to Matthis and her son, allowing them to go wherever they wished.

The concluding years of the 1770s took the high revolutionary excitement of pitched combat with the British from northern New England into the mid-Atlantic and southern colonies, where it finally ended in 1781 at Yorktown, Virginia. Yet not all residents of Vermont were committed to independence from the British Crown, even as the war was ending. The troops sent earlier to defend Bennington had been paid by selling property appropriated from Vermont Tories, a method of fund-raising proposed one night by the financially imaginative Ira Allen. Those Vermonters whose property unwillingly supported the war effort secretly nursed and sometimes even openly professed continued allegiance to the King. In the meantime the Continental Congress failed to extend the union of the thirteen original states to Vermont during the late 1770s and early 1780s. New York repeatedly raised objections to admitting Vermont to the Union because, they argued, such admission denied New York's claim to jurisdiction over territory

Viewed by some as a self-seeking opportunist and a devious politician, Ira Allen was probably the most influential figure in Vermont's early history. The youngest brother of the more famous Ethan, Ira Allen was var- *iously a land speculator, a Green Mountain Boy lieutenant, a diplomat, an historian, and a founder of the University of Vermont. From the Wilbur Collection. Courtesy, Bailey/Howe Library, University of Vermont*

first disputed in the New Hampshire-New York land grant controversy of the 1760s. Ethan and Ira Allen, now owners of large tracts of land in the northern Champlain Valley through their Onion River Company, played significant political roles during the 1770s and 1780s as Vermont manipulated and negotiated back and forth with the Continental Congress, agents of the British government (especially Frederick Haldimand, who was then Governor General of Quebec), and officials of the new State of New York.

Vermont came to govern itself as a community of freemen on March 12, 1778, when the first constitutionally provided elections of state officers produced Thomas Chittenden, a native of

Guilford, Connecticut, the first governor and Joseph Marsh the lieutenant governor. Chittenden owned a large tract of land on the banks of the Winooski River, but had been forced to withdraw to the southern part of the state with the British advance into the Champlain Valley. He returned to Williston in 1787 to serve as governor of Vermont, except for one term (1789 to 1790), from 1778 to 1791.

Until the establishment of the state capitol at Montpelier in 1805 the General Assembly met annually on first the east side of the Green Mountains in 1778 and then in 1779 at Bennington. Thereafter the Assembly's seat was rotated across the mountain backbone of the state. On the initiative of the Wheelock family of Hanover, New Hampshire (sons of Eleazer Wheelock, founder of Dartmouth College), efforts were mounted to establish the capitol on the Connecticut River and expand Vermont to the east by annexing sixteen towns in New Hampshire. These blatant moves to aggrandize Vermont aroused the antagonism of both New Hampshirites and New Yorkers, who complained that their lands were illegally accruing to the growing profit of backers of a scheme to establish a Greater Vermont that would contain large portions of New York and New Hampshire. Massachusetts then laid claim to portions of southern Vermont under terms of the ancient Plimouth Plantation Royal Grant. Congress, meanwhile, considered adjudicating the claims by the three states, all of which were currently seated in Congress. Vermont had no voice, in either the Union or Congress, in settling the disputes with the three states already in Congress. The proceedings seemed to ignore Vermont's very existence. Congress, however, quickly realized that the dispute promised trouble for the small, constitutionally weak United States and attempted to resolve it.

Three momentous actions occurred in Vermont in June 1779. First, Vermont charged that the Congress of the United States tended to endanger Vermont's liberties. Then, in language reminiscent of the American Declaration of In-

dependence, Vermont declared itself independent and free of the authority of the Continental Congress. Finally, in an ominous gesture of defiance, Vermont further declared itself free to enter into a Treaty of Peace with England.

Perhaps the most aggressive actions of Vermont in these years was the scheme to annex sixteen New Hampshire towns, and the subsequent offers of protection to New York towns lying east of the Hudson River if they wished to join Greater Vermont. From the point of view of Congress the most threatening actions by Vermont were heard in rumors circulated in Philadelphia that the Allens were negotiating with General Haldimand for peace with England and alliance with Canada.

In 1779 British peace commissioners were in fact in America offering general terms of peace to the rebellious colonists. With the Allens playing central roles because of their large land holdings in the northern Champlain Valley, Vermont

Top
Thomas Chittenden spent the early years of his life as a farmer in Salisbury, Connecticut. Convinced by Ethan and Ira Allen that limitless opportunities existed in the Hampshire Grants, he purchased a large tract of land bordering Lake Champlain in 1774. His support of the Allen brothers in the movement to free the Grants from New York jurisdiction gained him support as a popular leader. From the Wilbur Collection. Courtesy, Bailey/Howe Library, University of Vermont

Left
Frontispiece from the early American play The Contrast, *by Royall Tyler. Tyler's play contrasted the simple republican virtues of the true American with the foppish attitudes of pseudo-Americans. A later work,* The Algerine Captive, *was written in Guilford, where Tyler settled in 1790. Courtesy, Vermont Historical Society*

settlements to the west who felt alienated from Albany, and potential provincial allies in Canada. Some opposition to the Allens' fast dealings and suspicious correspondence with the British began to develop in Vermont, however, by Jacob Bayley from east of the mountains and Isaac Tichenor, a New Jerseyan transplanted to Bennington, who played increasingly important roles in opposing the Allens in Vermont's public affairs.

Then while in Paris in 1781 Benjamin Franklin obtained a captured letter from Lord George Germain to Sir Henry Clinton that outlined the British efforts to bring Vermont back into alliance with the Crown. This news and Vermont's hegemonic intentions toward New Hampshire and New York caused some in Congress to call for a military invasion of Vermont. In a now famous letter of warning written in 1783 General George Washington cautioned against an invasion of Vermont: "It is not a trifling force that will subdue them," he said. "The country is very montainous . . . . The inhabitants for the most part are a hardy race, composed of that kind of people who are best calculated for soldiers . . . ."

Washington subsequently played an important part in bringing Vermont into the Union. He advised Governor Chittenden to pull back Vermont's boundaries from the recently claimed sixteen towns of New Hampshire and the eastern New York towns. Yet even after the British final defeat at Yorktown, Ira Allen kept alive the question of allying with Canada, a connection of obvious value to the Allens because of their growing land holdings near the Canadian border. The Treaty of Paris in 1783 finally established the Canadian boundary at the forty-fifth parallel, thus excluding any part of Vermont from Canadian territory and clearly defining the northern border of the Republic of Vermont.

From the closing of the war in 1783, through the adoption of the United States Constitution in 1789, until the final admission of Vermont as the fourteenth state in 1791, the independent Republic of Vermont grew and prospered on both sides of the Green Mountains. In the first federal

soon realized that playing British and Canadian threats against New York or New Hampshire claims would dampen Congress's enthusiasm to settle the long-standing land dispute in New York's favor. The Allens wove complicated alliances among New Hampshire towns, New York

Census of 1791, Vermont's population numbered 85,000. Guilford and Bennington were the largest towns, with 2,400 and 2,300 each, respectively. Coins and currency were issued. Though experiencing some economic distress in the mid-1780s, when Assemblyman Alexander Hamilton urged New York to settle the Vermont land claim disputes by accepting $30,000 from the new republic, Vermont was able to bring that twenty-five-year controversy to conclusion by payment in full of $30,000.

With this dispute finally put to rest, Vermont's admission to the Union was cleared. Ironically the first political unit of the United States to abolish slavery in its constitution, Vermont entered the Union paired with a slave-holding state, Kentucky. Northern Congressmen saw Vermont as a balance to southern interests with Kentucky's admission.

The revolution and the republic passed in seventeen lively and often dangerous years for Vermont. They were years that laid a base for nearly twenty years of boom times, until 1812 and "the second war of independence from England."

Boom Times, Factions, and War Again

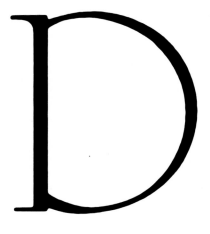

During the twenty years between its admission to the Union in 1791 and the outbreak of a second war with England in 1812, Vermont drew thousands of immigrants. Most of them were from southern New England. Census reports spell out just how attractive both Americans and Europeans found Vermont. During its first thirty years as part of the United States its population nearly tripled. Beginning in 1791, with 85,000 people, Vermont's population grew to 154,000 in 1800; 217,000 in 1810; and 235,000 in 1820.

Travelers also saw the appeal of life in the Green Mountains and their valleys. Timothy Dwight, President of Yale College, remarked after visiting Vermont in 1798: *From the richness of its soil; the variety and value of its products; the salubrity of its climate; the rapid increase of its population; the hardihood, industry, and enterprise of its inhabitants . . . [Vermont] cannot but be regarded as one important nursery of the human race and as a country where a great mass of happiness and virtue may be fairly expected in future ages.*

A "great mass of happiness," however, could not be expected without a great deal of hard work. Virtue would vary by individuals and place.

By 1800 Vermont was showing many symptoms of a developing community. Even before joining the United States in 1791, Vermont established a postal service. The University of Vermont was founded in Burlington in 1791 through a gift of 4,000 pounds from Ira Allen. Middlebury College was founded with assistance from Gamaliel Painter in 1800. Newspapers had appeared in Vermont in 1780 when Timothy Green and the Spooner brothers briefly published the *Vermont Gazette* (or *Green Mountain Postboy*) in Windsor. At Bennington, Anthony Hasewell's *Vermont Gazette* (or *Freeman's Depository*) appeared in 1783 for a longer run than its earlier namesake across the mountains in Windsor. Among the great wave of immigrants in the 1790s was Samuel Williams, a refugee from Harvard College whose personal financial difficulties sent him north to escape his creditors, co-found the *Rutland Herald* in 1794, publish the first literary journal in the state (*The Rural Magazine* from 1795 to 1796) and play an important role in the

Above
This anonymous view of Middlebury shows the town and college as they looked during the first decade of the nineteenth century. Middlebury College was the seat of three religious revivals between 1805 and 1811, a period in which missionaries from southern New England concentrated their energies on evangelizing backsliding or atheistic Vermonters. As a result of these revivals, over half of the college's student body professed renewed faith. Sarah Cleghorn bequest. Courtesy, Special Collections, University of Vermont Library

Facing page
"My neighborhood to Middlebury College made me bitterly feel the disparity in educational facilities between the sexes," wrote Emma Willard, who lived in the town of Middlebury between 1809 and 1819. To remedy this situation she opened a female seminary in her home. This school and the one she later opened in Troy, New York, offered an academically demanding curriculum which included courses in mathematics, history, natural philosophy, and physics. Courtesy, Vermont Historical Society

early years of the struggling University of Vermont.

In 1791 about half of Vermont's population lived in the counties west of the Green Mountains. The great tracts of land purchased there by Ethan and Ira Allen's Onion River Company during the early 1770s had appreciated enormously in value. In 1799 Ira himself was reputed to own over 120,00 acres in the state, which he had originally bought for prices as low as fifty cents to one dollar per

acre. By 1800 land in the Champlain Valley was selling for ten to twenty dollars per acre. Leading figures of the Revolutionary period sustained their positions of influence through control of huge tracts of land. Governor Thomas Chittenden, for example, reportedly owned over 40,000 Vermont acres, mostly in the Winooski River Valley, during the 1790s. In the meantime the General Assembly assured wide ownership by parceling out grants of land in sections of less than fifty acres.

On the east side of the mountains, migration north up the Connecticut River and its tributaries was not as rapid as in the Champlain Valley. Until about 1820 Newbury remained a frontier point east of the mountain range, and settlement north of that town in Caledonia, Orleans, and even Lamoille counties would not reach a peak until the 1820s and 1830s.

On a walking trip in 1842 historian Francis Parkman passed under a green canopy enclosing the stump-covered woods of Orleans and Essex counties. As the settlers' guest, Parkman slept in one-room log cabins that were typical of the first step in taming the still-primeval northeastern Vermont forest. In the southeastern corner of the state at Brattleboro, however, President Dwight of Yale College noted in 1798 that the village was "one of the prettiest objects of the kind and size within my recollection." Even Newbury, though a jumping-off spot for journeys into the northern wilderness, was considered by Dwight to be a "new Eden."

Signs of a developing and maturing community were seen throughout Vermont during the 1790s. In 1789 the Reverend Nathan Perkins of Connecticut had toured Vermont, but was saddened to find it a place of "no Sabbath, no ministers, no religion, no heaven, no hell, no morality." Before the century had ended, however, the great evangelical movement that was sweeping across America had made its way to Vermont and Congregationalists, Baptists, and Methodists—the Evangelical United Front, as it came to be called—found Vermont a welcoming place. Churches of these denominations were built throughout the state during the 1790s.

This was a country where travel was accomplished only over rough and rutty tracks. Reverend Perkins, going from Burlington to Williston on May 12, 1789, stated he "rode through the woods [for] fourteen miles, [with] the riding as bad as it could be." Communication and transportation systems were needed to assure Vermont's growth. By 1810 roads, turnpikes, regular stagecoach routes, reliable postal service, and even a canal to route traffic around the great obstacle of Bellows Falls on the Connecticut began to flesh out the primitive network by which Vermonters could visit, trade, and generally communicate with each other and the rest of the world.

Plans for canals connecting both ends of Lake Champlain to the important markets of Montreal

and New York began to take shape as early as 1791. Vermonters quickly recognized that their produce in the 1790s needed the market outlets of the population centers to the north and south of them. Clearing the land for farming produced two products much needed at both ends of Vermont's major water transport routes—timber and potash. Lake Champlain and the Connecticut River carried large and annually increasing amounts of these products north into Canada and south to lower New England. In addition, as the century turned, Vermont's output of sheep and cattle also grew, and the markets in Albany, Montreal, and lower New England also began to receive Vermont livestock in increasing numbers. By 1820 an observer in southern New Hampshire, on the road to Boston, counted in one winter's day "from 50 to 100 sleighs pass from Vermont . . . to Boston with dead hogs, pork, butter, cheese . . . and load back with store goods. They have generally two horses and travel forty miles a day with a ton weight."

Agricultural products were not the only results of early Vermonters' energetic efforts. Alexis de Tocqueville, an insightful French observer of American manners, noted in the 1830s that "al-

most all the farmers of America have combined some trade with agriculture." In a predominantly agricultural economy, "the shop outback" was the place in dreary winter months where farmers produced chairs, barrels, firkins, rakes, and iron tools, while the women made homespun cloth. What was not used at home or on the farm was often bartered or peddled. In a Vermont folk song of 1787 "the ingenious mechanic[s]" of Marlboro are praised for producing and trading all kinds of household tools and "braided bark mittens." Soon after 1800, however, woolen and cotton mills were spinning cloth in large amounts. By 1809 over a million yards of cloth were being produced annually in Vermont.

Furnaces in Vergennes and elsewhere provided sufficient iron for blacksmiths and other forges throughout the state by 1800. Iron ore ex-

Above
Vermont-made butter was being transported to Boston as early as 1854 in refrigerated railway cars. At that time butter and cheese production took place in farm dairies, similar to the one pictured. Although this farm couple continued to make butter at home in the early part of this century, most of the state's butter and cheese was being commercially produced in dairy plants and creameries by 1880. Courtesy, Vermont Historical Society

Facing page, top
This anonymous drawing shows the First Bridge at Bellows Falls, constructed in 1784 by Enoch Hale of Rindge, New Hampshire. The bridge spanned the Connecticut River between Bellows Falls and Walpole, New Hampshire. Four years later the first charter for building a canal in the United States was issued, enabling boats to bypass the rapids of Bellows Falls. Sarah Cleghorn bequest. Courtesy, Special Collections, University of Vermont Library

Facing page, bottom
In this engraving Weathersfield sheepbreeder William Jarvis (right) appears to be pointing out the outstanding attributes of an enormous Merino sheep. New England's burgeoning textile industry stimulated a sheep-raising boom that peaked in Vermont about 1840. Competition from New Zealand, Australia, and the West put most Vermont sheep farmers out of business by 1870. Courtesy, Vermont Historical Society

traction was not a long-lived industry in Vermont, but marble quarrying, an industry that grew and remains productive in the late twentieth century, made its first diggings in Middlebury, while copper diggings commenced east of the mountains in Strafford.

Distilleries that were often capitalized with out-of-state money, occasionally with money raised by state-chartered lotteries, appeared at strategic locations. According to one observer the distance from markets usually allowed distillers "to get grain cheap." In 1790 distilleries were expensive ventures, but the returns could be quite handsome. A distillery constructed at Middlebury in 1791 with money from Canadian backers cost $5,000. Another was built at Rutland in 1792 from the proceeds of a legislatively approved lottery that raised over $10,000. The advertisement for this venture claimed that the General Assembly's motives in this case were "well known to have arisen from their patriotic desire to encourage the beneficial manufacture of brandies, strong beere, etc."

Lotteries were, in fact, a popular method for raising both private and public funds in the first twenty years of the State of Vermont. Churches, roads, and bridges were built and the state debt paid by lottery. By Acts of the General Assembly, the State of Vermont ran twenty-five lotteries between 1783 and 1806. Private bills in the legislature authorized many more, as in the lottery for the distillery in Rutland in 1792. Martin Chittenden, son of the Governor, was a manager of the Rutland distillery. Most likely paternal favor helped speed his lottery bill into law.

Yet Yankee ingenuity played in more than political and economic arenas. For a part of New England that was still pretty much a frontier, Vermont obtained a surprisingly large number of patents during its early years. The United States Patent Office, or its predecessor in the President's Office, granted eleven patents for various kinds of mills to Vermonters previous to 1830. In addition, between 1790 and 1830 thirty-four of the one hundred twenty-two patents obtained

Above
The illegitimate son of a black father and white mother, Lemuel Haynes became known as one of the most erudite and witty ministers in New England. Born in West Hartford, Connecticut, and bound out as a servant in his childhood, Haynes served as minister of the Rutland West Parish for thirty years. In 1804 he became the fourth recipient of a master's degree from Middlebury College, although he never attended classes there. His marriage to a white schoolteacher, Elizabeth Babbitt, was a long and happy one. Portrait by Eu-gene Bischoff, 1940. Courtesy, The Bennington Museum

Facing page
According to Abby Hemenway's Vermont Gazetteer, *early Vermont women were the principal producers of textiles. They "picked their own wools, spun their own yarn, drove their own looms . . . wove their own carpets, quilts, and coverlids . . . ." A number of thrifty Vermont housewives continued to weave cloth for home use up into the twentieth century. From the Porter Thayer Collection. Courtesy, Brooks Memorial Library*

by Vermonters were for various kinds of factory machinery. With only nineteen patents granted in those forty years, agriculture was a modest third in the list of enterprises. Patents were also granted for a spring-pen ruler and a method of teaching "the art of writing by lead plummet" in 1812, according to patent office records.

Even as commercial activity increased and Vermont matured as a community, economic and political interests clashed in a series of conflicts that signaled a new and complex stage in the political life of Vermont. Until the 1790s politics in Vermont had been dominated by singular personalities in coalitions like the Arlington Junto, led by Thomas Chittenden. With the death of Ethan Allen in 1789, Thomas Chittenden in 1797, and the bankrupt exile and pauper's death of Ira Allen after the turn of the century in Philadelphia, parties rose to shape the direction of Vermont's political life and held sway late into the twentieth century. Politics in Vermont took on many features of the national scene.

No sooner had Vermont entered the Union in 1791 than the first man, of what today appears to be an endless train of presidential candidates, made his way to Bennington in pursuit of the nation's first office. While on a botanizing trip with fellow Virginian James Madison, Thomas Jefferson came to Vermont in May 1791 seeking support for his presidential candidacy. The nation's first political parties were the Federalists, backers of a strong national government, and the Democratic-Republicans, who favored constitutional protection against a powerful central government. Each party had persuasive leaders. Alexander Hamilton spoke for the Federalists, and Thomas Jefferson and James Madison led the Democratic-Republicans. In Vermont the Federalists quickly gained support on the eastern side of the Green Mountains among lawyers, ministers, and merchants. Prominent among these was Woodstock lawyer Charles Marsh, the brother of Vermont's first lieutenant governor Joseph Marsh, part of the group earlier characterized by Ethan Allen as "the pettifogging mob" from the eastern part of the state. The Democratic-Republicans held sway west of the mountains, and when Jefferson defeated Adams in 1800 for the presidency he won every county on the west side of the state. While Vermont's Federalists sympathized with England's anti-French posture after the outbreak of the French Revolu-

tion in 1789, Jefferson's support for the democratic ideals of the French Revolution prompted some Vermonters to form Jefferson Societies to promote "liberty, fraternity, and equality" in a Vermont they felt was threatened by Federalist anti-democratic policies.

With the death of Thomas Chittenden and the election of Federalist Isaac Tichenor, called "Jersey Slick" for his Newark birthplace, party conflict came to center stage in Vermont's political theater. When the Federalist-dominated General Assembly sat in 1798 at Vergennes in the heartland of Jeffersonian supporters, the Federalist majority asserted partisan strength and refused to reelect a number of Jeffersonian judges, including Israel Smith, Chief Justice of the Supreme Court.

One of the last Green Mountain Boys to play a prominent and stormy role in Vermont's politics during this era of rising party power was Matthew Lyon of Fair Haven. An Irish immigrant who first married Ethan Allen's cousin and then, after her death, a daughter of Thomas Chittenden, the fiery tempered Lyon participated in both the capture of Fort Ticonderoga in 1775 and the debacle at Hubbardton in 1777. As the founder of Fair Haven, he also established a number of businesses there, including a store, a hotel, a

there as well), though best remembered for the
physical violence of combat with his opponents,
also clearly demonstrates the increasing importance of party politics in Vermont and the new
nation. None of his opponents was a minor figure on the political scene. A dispute between
Lyon and Nathaniel Chipman over land ownership restoration claims by Tories, whose property was confiscated during the Revolution to
pay for Vermont's military expenditure, burst into
punching and gouging when Lyon accused
Chipman of dishonestly supporting Tory
interests.

Elected to Congress in 1798, Lyon heatedly opposed President John Adam's pro-British policy
and again fell to physical combat on the floor of
the House of Representatives, this time with Federalist Congressman Roger Griswold of Connecticut. Lyon's violence was mitigated some in
1798 when he published *The Scourge of Aristocracy*,
a Jeffersonian newspaper dedicated to opposing

paper mill, forges and iron furnaces, and a
newspaper.

Lyon's career, both in Vermont and as a member of Congress from Vermont (he later moved
to Kentucky and was elected to Congress from

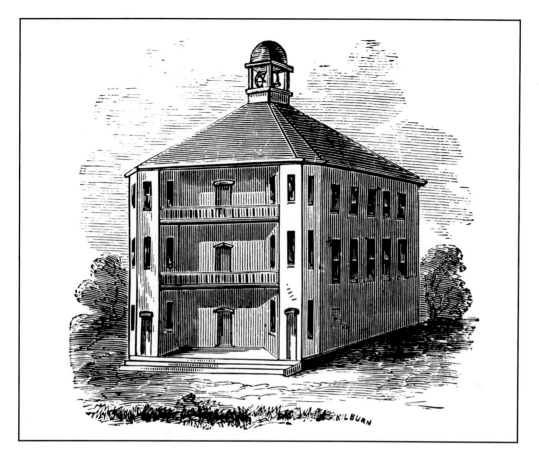

Left
Vermont's first State House, completed in 1808, was a simple three-story frame building similar in design to many other New England meeting houses. The fifteen-member Council of Censors convened on the third floor. Members of the House sat on simple pine benches on the first floor. From the Wilbur Collection. Courtesy, Bailey/Howe Library, University of Vermont

Facing page
During President Thomas Jefferson's embargo on trade with England from 1808 to 1809 Vermont sent livestock to Canadian markets over the desolate terrain of the Green Mountains on a route throught Mount Mansfield's Smugglers Notch leading, ironically, into Jeffersonville and on to the border. Photo by Peter A. Moriarity

pro-British Federalist policies. His opening editorial tone remained belligerent, however, as he proclaimed that while Federalist "aristocratic [newspapers will be] vomiting forth columns of lies, malignant abuse and deception, the *Scourge* will be devoted to politics."

The Federalist-dominated Congress had passed the Alien and Sedition acts, laws that claimed to protect national security but were really intended to suppress opposition voices like Lyon's. Within two days of the *Scourge*'s publication a Federalist grand jury was impounded, and an indictment was handed down against Lyon two days later. Lyon was brought to trial in federal court for prosecution by Charles Marsh of Woodstock. Lyon conducted, simultaneously, his own defense against the sedition charges and his campaign for reelection to Congress. After a brief trial he was convicted, fined $1,000, and sentenced to four months in the Vergennes jail. Not intimidated by his opponents' legal victory, Lyon, still in jail, won the Congressional election by nearly 600 votes in a runoff. With support from

Jeffersonians around the country, Lyon's fine was paid and he was free to return to Congress where in 1800, despite Federalists continuing to call him "a notorious and seditious person," Matthew Lyon cast the decisive House vote for Thomas Jefferson to become president in the thirty-sixth ballot after neither Adams, Jefferson, nor Aaron Burr failed to poll a majority of the general electorate.

Lyon departed Vermont in 1801 for Kentucky, where he was again elected to Congress. While Lyon's highly vocal and intensely physical part in the drama of Vermont's party politics brought national attention to Federalist efforts at suppressing civil liberties, his party needed seven years to gain control of the governor's office and a majority of both the General Assembly and the Vermont representation in Congress.

Jefferson's presidency did not always please even Democratic-Republican Vermonters, however, especially after he rammed the Embargo Act through Congress in 1807 and 1808. The act prohibited trade with England, including its Ca-

nadian territories; imposed severe restraints upon Vermont's commercial activity; generated intense political debate; and threatened serious civil disruptions. Vermont and the Province of Lower Canada (Quebec) were economically interdependent. Timber, beef, grain, and ashes for soap manufacture moved north into Canada both overland and on Lake Champlain. Canadian goods, often of British manufacture, came south for Vermont's and lower New England's markets. The first phase of the Embargo Act, passed in late 1807, applied only to seaport trade and thus promised increased trade activity for Lake Champlain and Vermont's border communities. The land embargo of March 1808, however, soon threatened to close down all trade with Canada. Vermonters were quick to respond to this threat to their commerce with northern markets.

Smuggling and a general tolerance for illegal commerce with Canada grew hand in hand. During James Madison's first term as president, before the War of 1812 broke out, some Vermont newspapers, especially longtime anti-Jeffersonian Federalist journals, condemned the embargo as an infringement on individual liberties and an unnecessary hardship for Vermonters to endure. In some instances smugglers were even acclaimed heroes as partisan feelings heated up during the years from 1809 to 1812.

The single most memorable episode in the story of anti-embargo antagonism in Vermont was the infamous *Blacksnake* affair. The *Blacksnake*, a forty-foot, single-masted cutter, was one of the most notorious and successful smugglers' ships on the lake in 1808. Regularly eluding militia and federal customs officers at strategic spots like Windmill Point in Alburg, as well as on the waters of Missisquoi Bay and Lake Champlain, the *Blacksnake* (called so for its tarred hull) carried potash into Canada and manufactured goods into Vermont, with seeming impunity.

In 1808 its crew attempted to prevent federal and militia officers from impounding the boat as it lay beached upstream from the lake on the Winooski River while waiting to load potash for Canada. The smugglers resisted and killed three of the government men, but were arrested quickly, both at the scene of the fight and later at the border while trying to escape into Canada.

The *Blacksnake* trial stirred intense partisan feelings between Embargo-supporting Republicans and anti-Jefferson Federalists. Ethan Allen, Jr., a staunch Federalist, was dismissed from jury duty in the smugglers trial for asserting the smugglers' total innocence in the case. Royall Tyler, Chief Justice of the Supreme Court, presided at the Burlington court that found most of the *Blacksnake*'s crew guilty. Among them, Cyrus Dean was found guilty of murder and hanged in Burlington on November 11, 1809, before a crowd of 10,000 spectators.

As the embargo seemed to signal certain prospects of war, Jeffersonian and Federalist partisans further heated up the internal political battle. Vermont's 200,000-plus population from 1808 to 1812 was well informed by over thirty newspapers expressing the full range of political opinions at the time. Federalist newspapers claimed Britain and the United States would soon amicably resolve their differences, and the embargo only exacerbated international tensions. According to the Jeffersonian press, England was "perfidious Albion," with whom Americans had better prepare to wage war.

The succession of Vermont governors after Thomas Chittenden up to the War of 1812, as well as the instances when their parties held majorities, is worth noting. With the death of Chittenden in 1797, Isaac Tichenor, a confirmed Federalist seeking to link Vermont with the party of Hamilton and Adams, served from 1797 to 1807 when Israel Smith, former Jeffersonian Chief Justice of Vermont's Supreme Court, served for one year. Through most of these years Democratic-Republicans controlled the General Assembly. In 1809, after being out of office one year, Tichenor, an anti-embargo man, recaptured the governor's office for one year, only to quickly lose it after urging compassion for the *Blacksnake*'s crew, including Cyrus Dean, and thereby

Royall Tyler, who was once engaged to John Adam's daughter, is best known as a playwright. He moved his law practice from Boston to Guilford in 1791. Between 1801 and 1812 he sat on the Vermont Supreme Court and served as its Chief Justice from 1807-1812. His wife, Mary Palmer Tyler, was the author of one of the first American books on childcare. From the Wilbur Collection. Courtesy, Bailey/Howe Library, University of Vermont

earning charges of treason from his Jeffersonian opponents. Tichenor was succeeded by Democratic-Republican Jonas Galusha, who held the office from 1809 to the outbreak of the war in 1812.

As the war loomed near Vermont's anti-war Federalists elected Martin Chittenden to the governor's office. Though the son of founding father Thomas Chittenden, Martin quickly declared he was "not able to see the necessity of war." So unnecessary did he find it, in fact, that in 1813 he tried to recall Vermont's Third Brigade of the Third Militia Division from New York, where it had been called to join General Wade Hampton's ill-fated expedition against Canada. This inept military venture in the northern theater against Canadian forces was thwarted at Chazy, New York and Chateauguay, Quebec in September and October. From their camp at Plattsburgh the Vermont militia's officers responded, "We shall not obey your Excellency's order for returning, but shall continue in the service of our country."

Vermont was obviously not united on the question of war with distant England and neighboring Canada. In February 1812 Jeffersonians mounted a demonstration in support of the national administration's war policy at Vermont's five-year-old State House in Montpelier, only to have anti-war Federalists disrupt the event with speeches attacking the war. At Rockingham in September, army enlistment officers were obstructed by anti-war Federalists. An anti-war group in Bennington broke up a militia muster. Federalists charged that Jeffersonian Democratic Societies were "instruments of Napoleon." Jeffersonians countered these charges by accusing Federalists of forming secret societies to plot secession of New England from the Union.

The charges that Federalists were considering secession was not totally unsupported by events of that dissention-ridden wartime era. On October 6, 1814, the Massachusetts legislature called for a New England Convention at Hartford, Connecticut, in order to present "their public grievances and concerns, . . . [including] defence against the enemy . . . and also to take measures, if they shall think proper, for procuring a convention of delegates from all the United States, in order to revise the Constitution thereof."

Federalists strength in New England was scattered, however, for they controlled the five states only by slim majorities. The Convention ruled out plans of secession as moderates came to control the meeting. Vermont, moreover, had declined to participate officially in the convention. Matthew Lyon's old Federalist foe, Nathaniel Chipman, warned Vermont's Federalists against discussing regional problems with "potential Separatists." While Boston and other southern New England seaport districts might have felt the need for the Federalist convention based on the damage to maritime activities the war with

Left
Montpelier's first Pavilion Hotel (pictured) was built as a tavern in 1807. The building was replaced by a more elaborate five-story structure in 1876. Courtesy, Vermont Historical Society

Bottom
The second Pavilion provided the best in accomodations for visitors to the state's capital. The hotel is pictured circa 1900. Courtesy, Vermont Historical Society

Facing page
The third Pavilion building is a modern steel-reinforced version of its predecessor. It houses the museum, offices, and library of the Vermont Historical Society, as well as state offices. Courtesy, Vermont Historical Society

England was causing, Vermont had only recently dealt with a very real, nearly disastrous immediate threat—the greatest military force ever to enter the Champlain Valley.

In August 1814, nearly fifty miles north of the border just outside of Montreal, General Sir George Prevost commanded over 10,000 British veterans of the Napoleonic campaigns; the Canadian militia, including the French Canadians under Lieutenant Colonel de Salaberry, who had thwarted Wade Hampton at Chateauguay; and a small force of Indians, some from the Odanak Abenaki, who probably sought an opportunity for restoration of the lands on the Missisquoi that they had lost to the Allens in legally questionable land dealings after the Revolution. This army, the last great military force to use the ancient Champlain route to conduct its campaign, was the strongest, best disciplined, and most completely equipped army ever sent to North America.

With only 1,500 regular troops and a few thousand militiamen (including Vermont troops who came back to New York when called from the homes they had returned to after the first defeat at Chateauguay), American defenses on the south bank of the Saranac River at Plattsburgh Bay were bulwarked by forts built on the riverbank and a bit north at Cumberland Head. An American squadron commanded by Thomas MacDonough was anchored in Plattsburgh Bay. On September 11, 1814, a British fleet, part of which went on to bombard Burlington, entered Plattsburgh Bay and engaged MacDonough's fleet in a murderous exchange of cannon, musket, and small arms fire. Anchored abreast, the British flagship *Confiance* and the American flagship *Saratoga* battered each other until one-fifth of the American's crew was dead and her starboard battery silenced. MacDonough turned his ship completely around at anchor, however, and fearlessly pounded the *Confiance* and three other English vessels with his port battery until the English surrendered.

A MONSTER.

FRIGHTFUL AS TEN FURIES!!

TERRIBLE AS HELL!

The following is copied from the JOURNAL kept by Mr. Jacob M. Berriman, during his tour to the Westward of Fort Recovery.

May 27, 1794. THIS morning about an hour after sunrise as we proceeded on our rout about a mile west from the place where we had lodged the preceding night, we were alarmed by a terrible barking of our dogs a-head, & all eagerly pushed forward to take possession of the game thus pionted out by our faithful dogs. About a quarter of a mile a-head we discovered the most terrible Monster which human eyes ever beheld, to which our dogs dare not approach; but only stood barking at a considerable distance. At the sight of so monstrous a creature, every hair on our heads seemed to stand on end with fear: Though we had no reason to apprehend ourselves in danger, for he was busily employed in destroying a large Panter, which seemed as incapable of resistance, as a common squirrel would have been in competition with one our dogs.

We halted, and placed ourselves to the best advantage in order to view his manner of dispatching the Panter, which he did by winding his tail around him and drawing to such a degree as to crush and break his bones, which we could frequently hear sounding like the snapping of a whip, accompanied by the most hidious howls of the agonizing animal. A consultation was next held in order to choose the most effectual method of attacking so formidable an enemy. It was finally determined, that one of the company should go back to the house and procure a horse, on which one of us, being mounted and armed with a musket, should approach within a convenient distance of the snake, and giving him a well-aimed shot, should retreat precipitately in case he was attacked.—Accordingly the person appointed, proceeded back to the house, and in less than an hour returned mounted on a horse well calculated for the purpose. It was then concluded to suspend our attack till he should have devoured his game; which he did in the following manner:—After having broken all his bones, as above, he licked him with his mouth till he appeared all over wet and slippery, and then swallowed him without much difficulty. The large animal which he had now gorged appeared to have greatly abated the agility of his motion, which we thought a circumstance much in our favor;—but on the other hand, we were not without great apprehensions of his scales being so hard that a ball could not penetrate them—However, having mounted the horse myself, I attacked him in the manner above described, and, after giving him three shots, he was so far disabled that we all approached with long gads, and dispatched him without much further difficulty. It was not till about two o'clock in the afternoon, that we accomplished a part of our business so satisfactory, both to our fears and curiosity—. We had now an opportunity to view him leisurely, and such a mixture of horror and beauty, I believe was never before seen blended in one object. After we had drawn him out straight, we proceeded to measure his dimensions, which we did exactly, and found him to be no less than 36 feet 2 inches in length and the largest part of his body to be 3 feet 1 inch in diameter—His eyes were indescribably large and piercing—His head was of a most beautiful changeable green, towards the top inclining to a yellow, but darker towards his neck and round his jaws—Upon the top of his head was a large oval black spot—His neck was incircled with three rows of spots of the most beautiful crimson—His back, from his neck nearly to the end of his tail was covered with scales of the most beautiful green I ever beheld, on each side was a row of large black scales, between two small red stripes. His belly was perfectly white along the middle, but bearing upon a yellow towards each side. The next part of our business was to determine upon the best manner to dispose of the skin, which we looked upon as a most valuable part of our game.

As the day was so far spent that we could not complete the skinning of it before dark, and as we could not possibly carry it away whole, we concluded to leave it until morning. Accordingly we went back to the abovementioned hut, and in the morning returned with knives, and in about three hours we completed the business to our satisfaction. The skin we carefully washed and stuffed it with hay until it was dry, when we opened and rolled it up for the convenience of carrying.

☞ As many persons, perhaps, will doubt the truth of the above account, they may satisfy themselves by calling at Mr. PEAL's Museum in Philadelphia, where the Skin was presented.

PRINTED AND SOLD AT WINDSOR—(VT.)
1812.

Left
This broadside was designed to inspire Vermonters to patriotic fervor during the opening days of the War of 1812. It recounted a tale of a monstrous panther-eating snake, which symbolized the monster of British imperialism threatening to devour the fiercely independent Vermont catamount. Courtesy, Vermont Historical Society

Facing page
On September 11, 1814, a British fleet entered Plattsburgh Bay and engaged the American fleet in a murderous exchange of fire. Fighting took place simultaneously on land, with British soldiers outnumbering Americans two to one. The American victory on Lake Champlain proved to be a turning point in the war. Sir George Prevost's huge land forces withdrew into Canada, thus ending the threat from the north. Courtesy, Special Collections, University of Vermont Library

Though outnumbering the land forces, Prevost was so discouraged by the naval defeat that he retreated to Canada.

The American peace commissioners in Ghent, Belgium, were highly encouraged by the news of MacDonough's victory on Champlain and good American results at Baltimore. Though the burning of the White House on August 24, 1814, by the British diminished American spirits a bit, deadlocked negotiations were broken in mid-October, at the very moment the Hartford Convention rejected secession. The London *Times* described the happenings on the Chesapeake Bay off Baltimore and on Lake Champlain as a "lamentable event to the civilized world." The Duke of Wellington, England's hero of the Napoleonic War, advised British Prime Minister Lord Castlereagh, "you have no right from the state of the war to demand any concession of territory from America." In the words of historian Samuel Eliot Morison, the "victory at Plattsburgh proved to be the decisive action."

The political conflicts that marked the era of the Embargo Act and the War of 1812 ultimately saw the Democratic-Republicans rise to control Vermont's political life for the next ten years. Modest prosperity returned to Vermont after the war, though boom times would never come again. Population growth stabilized and almost started to decrease when the western migration began to pull Vermonters away in the thirties and forties. Through the 1820s, however, Vermont and the rest of the nation entered an era of good feeling. Disruption and dissention would not occur again with truly violent outcomes until the dispute over the abolition of slavery. In the meantime Vermonters went about the business of clearing more forests and beginning to build public and private institutions such as schools, town halls, hotels, inns, and turnpikes—the hallmarks of a maturing community.

Fifty Years of Social Dynamism

FREE SOIL
UNION CONVENTION!

The Freemen of the Fourth District,

**Without regard to party, opposed to *extending* and *perpetuating*
the curse of *slavery* in any territory under the control of the Federal Government, and opposed to the election of Cass and Taylor, are
requested to meet in Mass Convention at SOUTH HARDWICK, Wednesday, Aug. 30, at 10 A. M.**

**L. P. POLAND, *Esq. of Morristown*, and *A. J. ROWELL, Esq.*
of Troy, with others, will address the Freemen.**

By order of the PEOPLE.

If a single characteristic could be said to mark Vermont in the decades between the War of 1812 and the Civil War of 1861 to 1865, it was a condition of constant agitation or "social ferment," in the words of historian David Ludlum. The social ferment of the post-War of 1812 era ran a course that led ultimately to the most powerful of all civil disruptions—the war which finally and violently resolved the great question of national union. In those nearly fifty years before the Civil War, Vermont experienced a series of social movements, which themselves contributed to the organization of Vermont as a community. Such movements as the religious revivals of the 1820s and 1830s, or the peculiarly Vermontish support of the anti-Masonic movement during the 1830s, the great temperance crusade and its promise to correct the socially destructive effects of excessive consumption of alcohol, and various other social reform movements clearly mark this era as a formative time. Improvement of public education, prison reform, organization of labor, and, finally, the rising cry for the abolition of slavery

LOWELL OFFERING

December, 1845.

"Is Saul also among the prophets ?"

A REPOSITORY
OF ORIGINAL ARTICLES, WRITTEN BY
"FACTORY GIRLS."

LOWELL: MISSES CURTIS & FARLEY.
BOSTON: JORDAN & WILEY, 121
Washington street.
1845.

Entered according to Act of Congress, in the year 1845, in the Clerk's Office of the District Court
of the District of Massachusetts.

Left

Harriot Curtis was one of over 1,000 Vermont women who went down to work in the mills of Lowell, Massachusetts, between 1820 and 1850. As coeditor of the Lowell Offering, *the first magazine in the United States to be written entirely by women, she was outspoken in her views concerning equal pay for equal work. "Time is time, labor is labor," she wrote, ". . . and we could never understand why a man's time and services were, in fact, more valuable than women's when the labor was equally as well performed by one as the other." Courtesy, Sophia Smith Collection, Smith College*

Facing page, top

"Western Fever" infected hundreds of Vermonters following the Panic of 1837 and reached epidemic proportions by the 1840s and 1850s. Farmers, fed up with trying to scratch a living from Vermont's rocky soil, needed little enticement to set forth in search of more fertile pastures to the West. Both the Gold Rush and railroad transportation speeded up the great migration from Vermont. By the 1870s Vermont had given over half its native-born population to the rest of the country. Advertisement from the Vermont Phoenix, *November 2, 1838. Courtesy, Brooks Memorial Library*

Facing page, bottom

Lorenzo Dow was one of many revivalists who sought converts in the Vermont countryside during the first two decades of the nineteenth century. "Crazy Dow," as he was called, made an annual trip north from Connecticut to visit his three sisters in Hardwick. During these annual visits he traveled a circuit through Washington and Caldonia counties, preaching hellfire and damnation to the unrepentant. A theatrical and dynamic speaker, Dow attracted large crowds all over New England, in Canada, and even in Europe. Courtesy, Brooks Memorial Library

Western Fever ! !

THE subscriber being desirous of removing to the West, offers his farm for sale, pleasantly situated in Halifax, containing about eighty acres of choice land, fairly proportioned between mowing, ploughing and pasturing.—and an excellent sugar orchard, and apparatus for sugaring—well watered—plenty of orcharding—together with a first rate house, slated roof, barn, sheds, and all necessary out-buildings in first rate order and condition. Said farm is situated in the neighborhood of Reid's Mills, and on the new stage road from Boston to Albany, called the Green River Road. Said farm will be sold, together with the hay, grain, stock, farming tools, &c. &c. all in good order and condition.

NATHAN MARSH.

Halifax, Oct. 20, 1838.   4w8

shaped a Vermont that demonstrated the ultimate value of these movements as socially organizing processes. Vermont became a community because of them.

For at least the first twenty years after the War of 1812, until the Panic of 1837 and the severe economic hardships of the late 1830s, religious revivals and the social reformation that flowed from them were feverishly pursued, sometimes with puritanical zeal. Religious revivals had been a regular feature of American life since the arrival of the first New England colonists in the seventeenth century. Intense religious emotions and feelings of conversion and salvation were common facts among the various Dissenters and Separatists who settled Massachusetts, Connecticut, and Rhode Island. In the mid-eighteenth century, prior to the Revolution, a powerful revival, enflamed by the highly charged sermons of English preacher George Whitfield as he traveled the eastern seaboard, swept the American colonies in what was called the Great Awakening. After the war, however, a generation of American leaders, including many in Vermont, found their spiritual and intellectual needs best served in the ideas of Deism, if not plain atheism. Many Americans, indeed, many Vermonters, may have

nodded agreement with Benjamin Franklin's letter of 1790 to President Ezra Stiles of Yale: "As to Jesus of Nazareth, . . . I have . . . some Doubts as to his Divinity; tho' it is a question I do not dogmatize upon." From the point of view of Reverend Stiles' clerical brothers of southern New England, Vermonters were not only nodding agreement with Dr. Franklin, they had in fact turned their backs on religion altogether. The task orthodox divines gave themselves was to restore—to revive—religion and Christian behavior in Vermont.

The earliest revivals around the turn of the century were aimed at civilizing a rambunctious frontier society. It was clear to the clergy of Connecticut and Massachusetts that Vermont was a faithless, heathenish, irreverent place prone to blasphemy, drunkenness, licentiousness, and atheism. After all, it had been the home of Ethan Allen, the tutelary spirit of Vermont's infidelity. Allen's ponderous attack on revealed religion—on the very basis of traditional New England

Calvinism—in his 1785 book *Reason, Man's Only Oracle* seemed to justify the free and easy social decorum of frontier life in Vermont by its rational exposition of natural religion. The story of Allen's death in 1789—falling on the ice from his hay-filled sled after a February night of heavy drinking with fellow veterans of the Green Mountain Boys on Lake Champlain's South Hero Island—was a tale often told with prim satisfaction by the clergy. Nineteenth century historians, however, later told a story that suggests the reformers had a valid purpose. Looking back on Manchester from some fifty years into the century, one historian of that town claimed that life in its early years justified calling Manchester "an immoral place. Drinking, gambling, and whoring were common." From a mid-century vantage point, Daniel Thompson, Montpelier's historian-novelist, described a Sodom on the upper Winooski:

Gambling was a common practice, libertinism found too many victims in the unsophisticated, unsuspecting and therefore unguarded female community. All these stained the records of the week days, while the sabbaths were desecrated by horse racing, match shooting, street games, holly day amusements, visiting and pleasure parties.

When Nathan Perkins contemplated Ethan Allen's grave during his tour of Vermont he observed that the "awful infidel . . . [was] one of the wickedest men that ever walked this guilty globe." Yet Thomas Paine and his *Age of Reason* had to share some of the guilt with Allen. Thomas Robbins, on a missionary tour of Vermont in 1796, noted that "The Age of Reason is greedily received in Vermont." Paine, with a lucid prose that made his thinking more accessible than Allen's *Oracle,* quickly became the bible of Vermont's freethinkers. There were, Robbins noted, ". . . some very obstinate deists here . . . . Infidels in religion are apt to be democrats in politics." From the Reverend Perkins' point of view Allen, Paine, democratic thinking, and frontier freedom had dreadful effects: "[Half the people] would chuse [sic] to have no Sabbath—no ministers—no religion—no heaven—no hell—no morality." Perkins summed up the view of Vermont from the genteel parlors of southern New England's parsonages: "Scarcely any politeness in the whole state."

Soon after 1800, however, religion began again to attract the attention and energies of America. A national convention of Presbyterians and allied Congregationalists in Philadelphia formed a United Front to evangelize their backsliding atheistic compatriots. Vermont was a principal target of missionaries from southern New England, especially from the Standing Order clergy of Connecticut. The first wave of revivals swept across the young republic and into Vermont in the first decade of the nineteenth century. Nearly every town of any size experienced a revival. Addison County's Congregational churches saw twelve revivals in less than ten years. Middlebury College alone was the seat of three revivals between 1805 and 1811. Of the college's one hundred fifty students, over half professed a change of life in favor of religion.

The War of 1812 slowed the advance of religion among Vermont's "heathenish hordes." Intense political disputes between Federalists (with whom the Congregationalist clergy were closely allied) and freethinking Jeffersonian Democrats over the embargo and subsequent war with England forced religion down one grade on the social agenda. "The state of religion is low and unpromising," moaned one missionary in 1812, "stupidity with regard to the concerns of a future state generally prevails." Meanwhile the spotted fever epidemic of 1813 to 1814 killed 6,000 Vermonters without regard to the future state of their souls and thinned out church rolls for a time. War, pestilence, and hints of famine during food shortages caused by twelve months of frost in frigid 1816 offered revival preachers fertile grounds for kindling religious fires once again.

From 1817 to the devastating Panic of 1837 and its depressing aftershocks, the religious life of

This mid-nineteenth-century engraving of the Vermont state seal included two peaceful cows resting beneath a pine tree. Pine sprigs were worn by Vermonters who fought at Plattsburgh during the War of 1812, and later by those who fought in the Civil War. Cows were an appropriate symbol for rural Vermont. The dairy industry grew following the Civil War, and by the early 1920s, there were more cattle than people in the state. Courtesy, Vermont Historical Society

Vermont—indeed its very social fabric—vibrated with excitement. Revivals often triggered the formation of benevolent societies in church groups. Asa Burton, a famous teacher of Congregationalist clergy, reported to the 1817 General Convention of Congregationalist Ministers that "the whole Protestant world [is] alive to the great and blessed object of relieving human suffering, of dispelling human ignorance, of redeeming the human character from its corruption and its guilt, and bringing the whole family of Adam to a participation in . . . Christianity." The benevolent impulse came as a wave in a flood tide of religious emotions that swept the American scene in the 1820s and 1830s.

Usually marked as beginning in 1815 at a giant revival in Cane Ridge, Kentucky, that was attended by over 20,000 fervent old and new believers, America's Second Great Awakening raged across the United States through the 1820s. It burned with great intensity through New York's Genessee County under the direction of Charles Grandison Finney, and swept into Vermont in the mid-1830s, where the acrobatic exhortations of a former circus rider, Jedidiah Burchard, led anxious Vermonters to profess renewed faith and join their neighbors in a revived community of saints—or at least a community of souls enflamed by fiery revival rhetoric. Burchard and other radical preachers brought into the church a great flock of new members during the 1830s and increased the rolls of Congregationalist, Baptist, and other Protestant churchs by nearly 10,000 new members in the mid-1830s, a time when Vermont's population was about 285,000.

As the 1830s wore on, however, Vermonters seemed to feel less attracted to the excitement of the revival wave. From 1837 to 1838 a brief Canadian outburst of independence from British rule—called the Patriots' or Papineau's War in Lower Canada (Quebec) and Mackenzie's Rebellion in Upper Canada (Ontario)—held the interest and fired enthusiasm in some Vermonters. Money, arms, and men swelled the Patriots' ranks during 1838, when Canadian rebels massed in Vermont at Alburg. Their force of reportedly nearly 10,000 French and English Canadians, spiced with Vermonters and other Americans, thought they saw a repeat performance of the American War of Independence in the offing for Canada. Visions of a little Canadian plunder most likely had some appeal. United States federal troops under General John Wool soon dampened American enthusiasm for a Patriot sortie against Canadian militia and British regular infantry in the nearby townships of the Richelieu Valley. In the final years of the 1830s Vermonters looked to internal affairs, as the Panic of 1837 brought on economic depression.

An appealing almost emblematic figure for the social movements of the 1830s was Orson Murray, a onetime Baptist preacher from Orwell and frequent advocate of a variety of social improvements and reforms throughout the 1830s and 1840s. Even during his years of closest alliance

75 Young Women

From 15 to 35 Years of Age,

WANTED TO WORK IN THE

COTTON MILLS!

IN LOWELL AND CHICOPEE, MASS.

I am authorized by the Agents of said Mills to make the following proposition to persons suitable for their work, viz:—They will be paid $1.00 per week, and board, for the first month. It is presumed they will then be able to go to work at job prices. They will be considered as engaged for one year, cases of sickness excepted. I will pay the expenses of those who have not the means to pay for themselves, and the girls will pay it to the Company by their first labor. All that remain in the employ of the Company eighteen months will have the amount of their expenses 'to the Mills refunded to them. They will be properly cared for in sickness. It is hoped that none will go except those whose circumstances will admit of their staying at least one year. None but active and healthy girls will be engaged for this work. as it would not be advisable for either the girls or the Company.

I shall be at the Howard Hotel, Burlington, on Monday, July 25th; at Farnham's, St Albans, Tuesday forenoon, 26th, at Keyse's, Swanton, in the afternoon; at the Massachusetts' House, Rouses Point, on Wednesday, the 27th, to engage girls,---such as would like a place in the Mills would do well to improve the present opportunity, as new hands will not be wanted late in the season. I shall start with my Company, for the Mills, on Friday morning, the 29th inst., from Rouses Point, at 6 o'clock. Such as do not have an opportunity to see me at the above places, can take the cars and go with me the same as though I had engaged them.

I will be responsible for the safety of all baggage that is marked in care of J. M. BOYNTON, and delivered to my charge.

I. M. BOYNTON,

Agent for Procuring Help for the Mills.

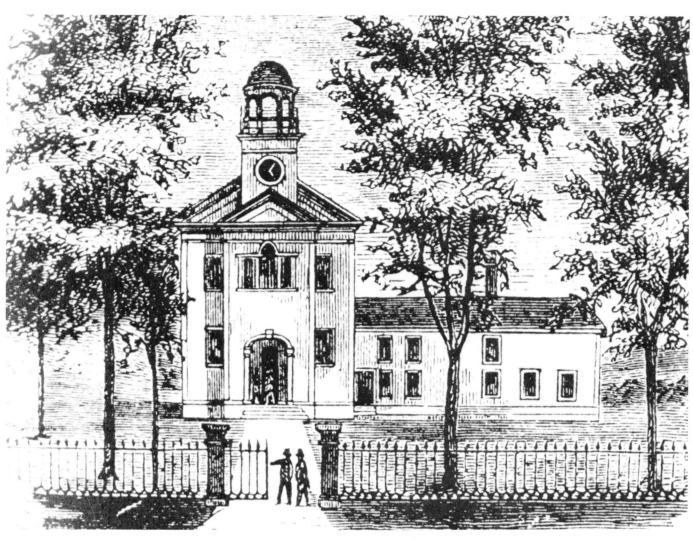

Facing page
As early as 1821 Massachusetts mill owners began recruiting Vermont women to work in the new textile centers. Mill agents drove up to Vermont on "long, low, black, wagons," and packed in as many recruits as possible for the southward-bound trip. Broadsides advertising for "healthy and active girls" between the ages of fifteen and thirty-five alerted young women to the availability of jobs and the terms of employment. In the pre-Civil War era, the Massachusetts mills offered Vermont women higher wages than they could earn at home. *Courtesy, Baker Library, Harvard University*

Top
Castleton Medical College was the first medical school in Vermont. The building was constructed in 1822 at a cost of approximately $2,300. Its interior contained lecture rooms, laboratories, and a dissecting room, with student housing in the wing. After Castleton Medical College ceased its operations in the 1860s, the building was moved to the Castleton Seminary, where it became known as "Old Chapel." *Courtesy, Vermont Historical Society*

Right
Revival preacher Jedidiah Burchard swept through Vermont in 1835, holding a series of "protracted meetings" at churches, including the First Congregational Church in Woodstock, pictured. *Courtesy, Woodstock Historical Society*

with Vermont's Baptists, Murray's efforts were often more broadly social than individually spiritual. In 1838, for example, he inspired the Baptist Association of Addision County, a hotbed of religious emotions, to adopt a resolution that struck at the double moral standard prescribed for sexual matters:

. . . we must labor so to reform public opinion, that licentious males shall occupy the same ground with the licentious female.

At one point in 1836 Murray dashed off to New York City where he briefly assisted William McDowell in the work of the American Society for the Observation of the Seventh Commandment, an organization devoted to the exposure of the social evils of prostitution. In an era when, as Charles Dickens observed on his visit to United States, conversation in mixed company would characterize chickens as walking on "limbs," not "legs," Murray aroused public outrage, especially from established church leaders, for even publicly alluding to sexual behavior.

Murray's apocalyptic language was consistent with a major stream of religious ranting for social reform. "Unless we do this work speedily," Murray warned, "God will destroy them and scourge us. There is no time to be lost . . . . The tempests of divine wrath are ready to be poured down." The approaching millenium was a compelling notion in the pre-Civil War era. In Vermont and the nation it came in two forms. These were religiously evangelical campaigns to organize new communities of saints or rationalistically planned missions to inhabit modern Utopias.

Millenarianism promised a reorganization of society. Evangelical millenarianism warned that only through returning to the purist first principles of the Holy Scripture would life be set straight again. Rationalistic social planners, on the other hand, sought a system of living based on their construction of society's "natural laws." Both kinds of millenarianism found followers in Vermont through the 1830s and 1840s. Perhaps the most memorable of the evangelical millenarians was William Miller of Poultney. Through reputedly careful calculations based on his study of the Bible, Miller first said that the millenium would come around 1843. His followers began to appear in various parts of the state. Then he spelled out his doctrine: Christ was coming for a second time, but to Vermont! When 1843 approached, faithful Millerites in Castleton and elsewhere wove white robes to wear when they met Jesus. One Castletonian, dressed in the white robe, sat silently for three days in his front hall waiting for Jesus to walk in the door. A sadder story is that of Mrs. Ira Young of Jamaica. She and her husband and their Millerite friends, who had given away all their worldly goods, awaited the Second Advent in the Youngs' parlor while an unruly crowd of unbelievers stoned the house, fired guns at the windows, and in other ways disturbed the meetings. Mrs. Young died in the midst of this excitement and a hastily convened (and perhaps illegal) coroner's jury found she had suffered and died from the fatigue and excitement of waiting for the Lord, compounded

by her lung disease. When 1844 passed without a Second Coming, a Millerite friend of Mrs. Young's took her own life in depression. More fortunate Millerites simply came down from the barn roof, where they had awaited Jesus' arrival, to find that their houses and furnishings, clothes, and other valuables they had dispensed to their doubting neighbors were now indeed someone else's property. Miller seldom found an audience after 1844.

John Humphrey Noyes of Putney found an increasingly attentive audience in Vermont after 1836 and eventually carried his Perfectionist philosophy to central New York. There he founded the long-lasting Oneida Community based on his conviction that Christ had spiritually come already in the time of the Apostles and established the millenium. Christians could attain the high-

est holiness—Perfection—as the New Testament had promised. Noyes concluded that sexual competition, unwanted pregnancies, and unfair divisions of labor were the great evils to be corrected. Birth control, community partnerships, and an easier load of labor were the bedrock of Noyes' Putney community. Some of his neighbors suspected commune residents of violating Vermont's statutory prohibition against extramarital sex. When Noyes and his followers left Vermont in 1847 for New York, he concluded ten years of a social experiment that remains to be equalled in Vermont for its thoughtful attempt to organize social and sexual relations to ameliorate the conditions of life.

Vermont's slim contribution to America's longest lasting reign of evangelical millenarianism, the Mormons, was to serve as the birthplace of

Facing page, top, right
The Mormon prophet Joseph Smith spent the first ten years of his life on a rocky farm in Sharon. His first vision occurred in 1820, five years after his family had moved to the "burnt-over" district of western New York. He published The Book of Mormon, *which he claimed to have translated from ancient plates of gold, in 1830, the year in which he founded the Church of Jesus Christ of Latter-Day Saints. Courtesy, Vermont Historical Society*

Facing page, top, left
John Humphrey Noyes was founder of the radical religious group called the "Perfectionists," who lived communally in Putney in the 1840s. Members of this sect put out a newspaper, ran a community farm and store, and lived peaceably with their neighbors until rumors broke out that they were practicing communal marriage. In 1848, Noyes and his followers moved to Oneida, New York, where they established a self-supporting community that lasted for forty years. Courtesy, Putney Historical Society*

Facing page, bottom
The female followers of John Humphrey Noyes, founder of the Oneida Community, worked on an equal basis with men, though often at sex-stereotyped jobs. Because they believed that long skirts were confining and made women look "like churns," female Oneidians cut off their skirts and wore trousers underneath. They adopted short hairstyles that were unheard of in the mid-nineteenth century. Courtesy, Vermont Historical Society*

Above
Brigham Young, the second president of the Mormon church and colonizer of Utah, was born in Whitingham. Although his formal schooling amounted to two months, he displayed genius as a scientific city planner and as a religious, social, and economic organizer. A social pragmatist, he worked to carry out his belief that the kingdom of God must be built on earth before it could be built in heaven. As a practitioner of polygamy, he was husband to seventy wives and father to fifty-six children. Courtesy, Vermont Historical Society*

In the early decades of the nineteenth century temperance workers regarded Vermont as fertile territory for reform. The state's early settlers reputedly drank on every possible occasion, from barn raisings to husking bees. In the view of temperance reformers, one sip of hard cider could start the descent down the Fatal Ladder towards drunkenness, poverty, sickness, and death. After 1828 crusaders for sobriety joined forces in over 200 chapters of the Vermont Temperance Society. Courtesy, Brooks Memorial Library

Throughout the nineteenth century each Vermont town was supposed to provide support for those members of the community who were too old, handicapped, or demented to provide for themselves. The poorhouse, like the one pictured here, was a place of last resort, where care was custodial, and from which inmates might be shipped off to the insane asylum to save the town a few dollars. With the coming of the New Deal, the state and federal governments began contributing welfare assistance to the poor, the elderly, and the handicapped. Courtesy, Mark Skinner Library

the founders. Joseph Smith was born at Sharon in 1805 and Brigham Young in Whitingham in 1801. With the great Vermont exodus of the 1840s, 232 Vermonters made their way into the Census of 1850 as residents of Utah, the seat of Mormonism, nineteenth-century America's most successful religious communal enterprise.

Other Vermonters in public life had also foreseen the coming of a paradisical millenarianism. Governor Ezra Butler, who was also a clergyman, declared in his Inaugural Address of 1826 that Vermonters had "just cause to consider ourselves the most favored of the human family, and nothing can or will stop the current of [God's] favor, unless it is obstructed by our own vice and folly." The economic chaos following the Panic of 1837

seemed to some Americans more a symptom of folly than vice. A variety of social improvement plans were proposed to correct society. Utopian schemes like the communitarian experiment at Brook Farm (1841) in Massachusetts appeared to some to be one way. The French Associationism of Charles Fourier was expounded in America by journalist Arthur Brisbane in the pages of native Vermonter Horace Greeley's *New York Tribune*. Brisbane found friendly readers in Vermont. In July 1843 a series of meetings in Randolph, Brandon, Middlebury, and Ferrisburg, first advertised as abolitionist meetings, drew speakers who harangued the crowds to leave Vermont and follow them to model communities in New York, Ohio, and further west. John Collins of Ben-

nington took a group to Skaneateles, New York; and John Wattles took a group, including the ever-zealous Orson Murray, to Prairie Home Community, in Ohio. Murray eventually campaigned for vegetarianism as the ultimate social curative, carrying raw carrots in his pockets to offer as a substitute for tobacco to smokers he encountered in his travels.

Important social acts of the 1830s and 1840s included a land reform campaign calling for the breakup of large tracts owned by farmers pursuing the sheep craze; the reform of public schools—the common school movement; the organization of labor into Working Men's Societies; prison reform that abolished imprisonment for debt and confined capital punishment to only murder convictions; and improvements in treating the mentally ill and the poor. One of the longest-lasting effects of these movements is perhaps best illustrated by the Brattleboro Retreat, a psychiatric hospital founded in 1834 with a grant

Above
The Vermont Asylum for the Insane, today the Brattleboro Retreat, was founded in 1834 largely through the generosity of Anna Marsh, a widow who left the sum of $10,000 for "a hospital for the relief of insane persons." This print shows the asylum ten years after its founding. Since fresh air and exercise were believed to have curative powers, the patients often worked outside on the grounds. Courtesy, Vermont Historical Society

Facing page
Newspaper editor Clarina Howard Nichols of Townshend crusaded for women's rights in mid-nineteenth-century Vermont. As editor of the Windham County Democrat, *a Brattleboro newspaper, she wrote a series of outspoken editorials in which she deplored the legal and property restrictions on married women. Largely through her efforts, legislation was passed in Vermont that granted property rights to married women. Courtesy, Vermont Historical Society*

of $10,000 from Anna Hunt Marsh, a New Hampshire doctor's widow. Patterned on the concept of "moral treatment," the Brattleboro Retreat pioneered great strides in the care of the insane with, for examples, the first dairy farm, which supported the philosophy of meaningful work; the first continuously published patient newspaper; a gymnasium; outdoor therapeutic camping programs; a swimming pool; and a golf course.

Assistance for the poor became an increasingly serious matter in Vermont as the effects of the expanding industrial revolution were felt even in this decidedly rural region of the eastern United States. The famines of 1846 to 1850 in Europe, especially in Ireland and Scotland, led many to Vermont. From 1849 to 1850 over one-third of the 3,600 recipients of public charity were immigrant Irish laborers and French-Canadian migrant farm workers. The cost of public relief was $120,000 in 1850, a year when approximately one percent of the population received this form of assistance.

Educational reform in the 1840s was led by Thomas Palmer and William Slade, the latter a prominent leader in the abolition movement, as well as a congressman in the 1830s and early 1840s and the governor from 1846 to 1848. Horace Mann's fervent mission to reform education, first in Massachusetts and then throughout the country, found ardent allies in Palmer and Slade. By their impetus a convention at Middlebury in 1845 reported that Vermont's educational system was backward in three major areas: teacher qualifications, teacher supervision, and textbook quality. The 1845 *Rutland Herald* urged the General Assembly to tackle school reform immediately because "the system of common schools in Vermont has become a farce." "An Act for the Regulation of Common Schools," passed by the General Assembly in late 1845, brought Vermont into line with Massachusetts, causing Horace Mann to cry, "We rejoice with unspeakable joy." The most important effect of the law was to provide for a centralized system of supervision of education, with a hierarchy of town district school boards, district superintendents, and a state superintendent. Horace Eaton was appointed the first state superintendent, and his first annual report revealed just how true the *Rutland Herald*'s criticism had been. Among the worst of the problems was parents sending their children to school with books the parents had selected, thus no

uniform texts were used. School boards had also hired inadequately trained teachers for as little as possible: twelve dollars a month plus room and board, for a man; four dollars and seventy-four cents for a woman. Actual school attendance was very light; the school session lasted only three months, but only 51 percent of Vermont's school-age children attended any school. "Appalling," said Eaton.

A profound impulse to reform society and assure equality for all vibrated through Vermont from the 1820s until the Civil War. As in the rest of the nation, education was seen to have a central role in assuring equality, a principle heard most directly in Superintendent (at the same time, governor) Horace Eaton's first annual report:

Let every child in the land enjoy the advantages of a competent education at his outset in life—and it will do more to secure a general equality of condition, than any guarantee of "equal rights and privileges" which constitutions or law can give. And if we would pre-

Above
In 1852 Clarina Howard Nichols, editor of the Windham County Democrat, *became the first woman to address the state legislature. She spoke in favor of a petition requesting that women be allowed to vote in school district meetings. Her speech was greeted by jeers and foot stomping. It took almost thirty more years for the school suffrage bill to pass. Courtesy, Madeleine M. Kunin. Taken from "Clarina Howard Nichols: Green Mountain Suffragette,"* Vermont Life, *winter, 1973*

Facing page
The typical Vermont schoolmarm of the nineteenth and early twentieth centuries presided over children of all ages in a one-room school. Despite the starkness of this schoolroom in West Dummerston, this teacher in 1919 reflects a dignity befitting her position. From the Porter Thayer Collection. Courtesy, Brooks Memorial Library

serve this life giving spirit, as well as the form, of our republican institutions, we must rely mainly upon popular education to accomplish our purpose.

Another complex and curious expression of the "life giving spirit" in Vermont's political life is found in the rise and brief success of Vermont's Anti-Mason Party during the late 1820s and early 1830s. The national Era of Good Feeling in politics that succeeded the internally disputatious years around the embargo and the War of 1812 came to a close with a heated contest between John Quincy Adams and Andrew Jackson for the presidency in 1824. Though Jackson led the four-

way race, the contest was finally resolved when thrown into the House of Representatives. The House, Vermont's delegation included, voted in the majority for John Quincy Adams. Jackson ran again successfully in 1828, but not a county in Vermont voted for him. Only Burlington gave him a few winning precincts.

From the War of 1812 until 1828 Vermont elected candidates of the Jeffersonian Democratic Party for governor. Around 1828 expressions of intense dislike for the Masonic Order began to be heard around the country, first in western New York and coming soon thereafter to Vermont. Anti-Mason feelings in New York were triggered by the mysterious disappearance of an ex-Mason, William Morgan. Speculations about Morgan's disappearance soon led to accusations that local Masons had kidnapped and murdered Morgan for his efforts to expose the secret society's reputedly evil purposes. Vermonters soon felt the impact of anti-Masonic sentiments. Randolph be-

came the center of Vermont's anti-Masonic campaign with "General" Martin Flint at its head.

Anti-Mason attitudes in Vermont grew into a complex tissue of religious, social, and political feelings, postures, and platforms. Especially among Vermont's spiritually democratic Baptists, Freemasonry had long been regarded, in the words of the church's historian, "with undisguised suspicion by many." From the earliest days of the Vermont Republic, the Masonic Order had enrolled members from among the leaders of Vermont society, including Thomas Chittenden, the first governor. Particularly in north-central and northeastern Vermont, among free-spirited and intensely democratic Baptists and some Congregationalists, the Masons were accused of elitism, exclusivism, and generally anti-democratic purposes. The secrets of the Masonic ritual further offended other Americans who professed the value of an open society. From 1828 to 1831 the Anti-Mason Party grew steadily,

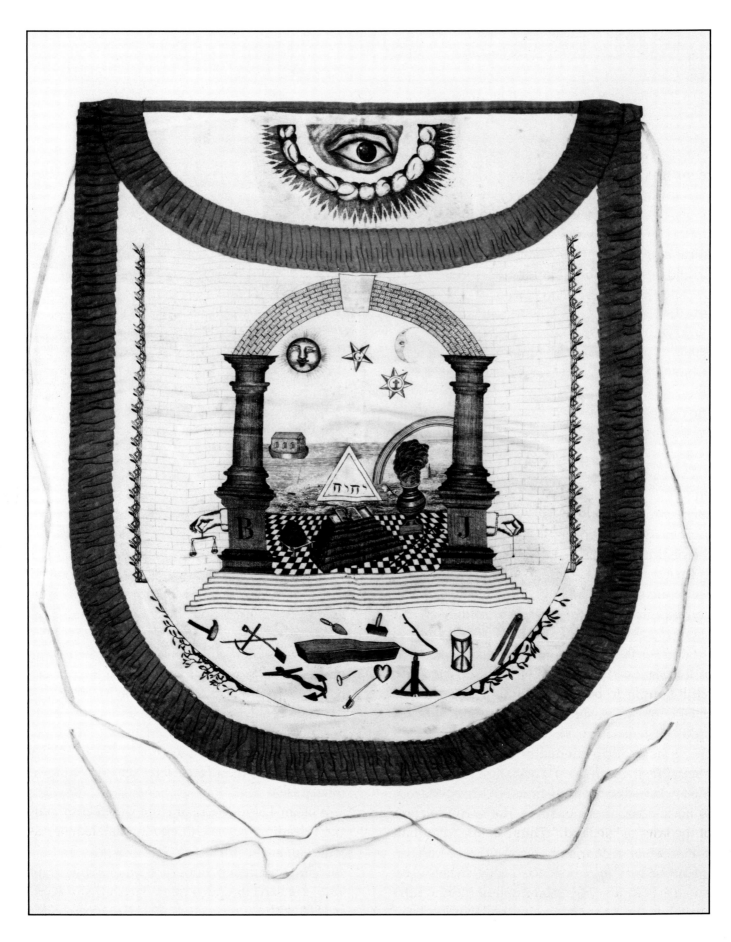

finally achieving the election of Vermont's only anti-Mason governor, William Palmer, for two terms until 1835.

In 1832 the presidential election pitted Andrew Jackson against Henry Clay, the National Republican candidate, and William Wirt, a former Attorney General, for the Anti-Mason Party. Vermont was the only state to cast a majority vote for Wirt in the national election. In these excited times, Vermont's electoral oddities on the national scene simply reflected the instability of political affairs within the state. In fact, successful candidates for gubernatorial office seldom won majorities. The election of 1835 best illustrates this. In that election Silas Jenison, the first native-born Vermonter to hold the office of governor, failed to gain a statewide majority at the polls. With the election thrown into the legislature, three days and thirty-five ballots later finally gave the office to Jenison, the first in a series of Whig Party candidates who would control Vermont politics until 1856.

The rise of the Republican Party, the construction of a modern rail transportation system, a successful temperance crusade, and the increasingly louder call for the abolition of slavery were the distinctive marks of the 1840s and 1850s.

The story of anti-slavery in Vermont is the preface to the state's role in the Civil War. Anti-slavery took its ideological foundations in Vermont from a long tradition beginning with Article I of the Declaration of the Rights of the Inhabitants of the State of Vermont, which declared that no adult "ought to be holden by law, to serve any person, as a servant, slave or apprentice." In 1786 the legislature resolved that "the idea of slavery is totally exploded from our free government," that the Vermont constitution liberated all slaves within the state, and the transportation of blacks from Vermont was "in open violation of the laws of the land." Thus slavery never had a legal basis in Vermont. There was also not an economic basis for constructing a defense of slavery in an economy built on small farms and little capital or the need to acquire the labor resource

Facing page
In the early nineteenth century many Vermonters regarded the rituals of the Freemasons with suspicion. Anti-Masons accused the secret society of being elitist, exclusive, and anti-democratic. The symbols on this Masonic apron were engraved on silk by Oliver Eddy of Wethersfield and published by Lewis Robinson, a native of Reading, sometime between 1814 and 1822. Both men produced aprons for Masonic Lodges throughout Vermont. Photo by John Miller Documents. From the Collection of the Museum of Our National Heritage

Above
Silas Jenison of Shoreham was the first native-born Vermonter to become governor. Although Jenison failed to gain a majority of votes in the election of 1835, the General Assembly finally gave him the office after thirty-five ballots. In 1836, when the Patriots' War broke out in Canada, Jenison issued a proclamation in which he warned Vermont sympathizers with the rebel cause against violation of the neutrality laws. Courtesy, Vermont Historical Society

slaves provided in large southern agricultural enterprises.

William Lloyd Garrison, the nineteenth century's leading journalistic abolitionist, led his nationwide attack on slavery from the pages of his Boston newspaper *The Liberator*, beginning in 1829. He had begun his campaign in Bennington in 1828 with a newspaper called the *Journal of the*

Times. With Garrison's encouragement nearly 2,500 Vermonters petitioned Congress to abolish slavery in the District of Columbia. Other Vermont journalists followed Garrison's lead in the 1830s. Chauncey Knapp, the anti-Masonic editor of the *State Journal,* forcefully expressed the abolitionist position after 1832. Orson Murray also threw himself into the abolition movement in the 1830s. While working for other reform causes he helped to form numerous town chapters of the Vermont Anti-Slavery Society in 1834. Garrison called Murray "one of the earliest . . . and most successful advocates of emancipation in New England."

Yet Murray and his fellow abolitionists frequently met resistance. In October 1835 Samuel May, a Unitarian minister from Connecticut, addressed a meeting in Montpelier on the abolitionist cause, only to see the meeting break up in a near riot. Timothy Hubbard, May's harshest critic that night and president of the Montpelier Bank, so offended other Vermonters for denying May's freedom to speak that Hubbard soon lost his position in the bank. By the mid-1840s, the *Rutland Herald* generously estimated that four-fifths of the inhabitants of Vermont were opposed to the continuation of slavery in the United States.

The full thrust of anti-slavery feelings running through Vermont brought near unity to the great mass of Vermonters by 1850. Yet opposition to the abolition movement also had its spokesmen,

Above
In 1828 William Lloyd Garrison moved to Bennington to become editor of the anti-Jackson newspaper, the Journal of the Times. *Under Garrison's editorship, the* Journal *crusaded for the causes of temperance, moral reform, peace, and antislavery. Garrison urged Vermonters to become leaders in the abolitionist movement. As the result of his efforts over 2,300 Vermonters signed a petition to Congress requesting the abolition of slavery in the District of Columbia. Courtesy, Vermont Historical Society*

Top, left
Rokeby, *the home of Rachael and Rowland T. Robinson of Ferrisburg, was an important station in the Underground Railroad in the decades preceding the Civil War. Fugitive slaves making their way toward freedom in Canada traveled secretly northward over two main routes in Vermont. At Rokeby, on the western route, the slaves were housed in a room above the kitchen. Drawing by W. Hofstetter. Courtesy, Rokeby Museum and Rowland E. Robinson Memorial Association*

Facing page
The Robbins & Lawrence Armory and Machine Shop in Windsor became world famous in 1851 when its displays at an industrial exhibition in London demonstrated to the world the system of interchangeable parts. This "American System," which Robbins & Lawrence developed in the manufacture of rifles, marked a turning point in the evolution from craft manufacture to modern industrial methods. Courtesy, American Precision Museum

though their positions seemed more in fear of a rupture in the national Union than a defense of the "peculiar institution" of slavery itself. In Burlington, for example, John Henry Hopkins,

Stephen Douglas, a native of Brandon, failed to win the hearts of fellow Vermonters when he remarked that Vermont is a good state to be born in, providing a man leaves it in his youth. Following his own advice Douglas moved west to New York, Ohio, Missouri, and Illinois, where he became famous as a United States Senator. By the election of 1860 the majority of Vermonters were united in their opposition to slavery. Douglas won 20 percent of their votes, while Lincoln captured 74.8 percent. Courtesy, Vermont Historical Society

the democratic urges in Vermont life. After the war, however, he led the move to reconcile the divisions in northern and southern branches of the American Episcopal church.

By the 1850s the three political parties seeking to control Vermont—Whig, Free Soil, and Republican—were resolving in their platforms to work for abolition by constitutional means. When Carlos Coolidge was elected governor in 1848, he stressed Vermont's moral stamina for pursuing the cause of freedom for slaves:

In performing their part of the work of destroying slavery, her people will not falter at that which they can rightfully do.

Just as the *Rutland Herald* noted in the 1840s and Governor Coolidge's speech suggested, Vermont's unanimity on the abolition issue spoke loudly. In the presidential election of 1860, 75.8 percent of the vote went to Lincoln, the Republican candidate. Pro-slavery candidates John Breckinridge of Kentucky and John Bell of Tennessee received less than 5 percent of the vote. Illinois Senator Stephen Douglas, a native of Brandon, Vermont, who once quipped that "Vermont is the most glorious spot on the face of this globe for a man to be born in, *provided* he emigrates when he is very young," managed to win less than 20 percent of the vote in Vermont.

Political stability had grown in Vermont during the years prior to Lincoln's election. The stabilized focus of political life in Vermont after 1856 was the Republican Party, an organization that was, as one historian noted, "both an expression of intense moral conviction on the slavery issue and a hostile reaction to the fractious maneuvering and sparring for votes and patronage seen in the Whig, Democrat, and Free Soil parties in the 1840s." With the ascendancy of the Republican Party after the election of Governor Stephen Royce in 1854, a measure of calm fell on Vermont politics as the nation moved on to the most destructive four years of bloodshed it has ever experienced.

Bishop of Vermont's Episcopal Church, first attempted to justify slavery in 1861 by reference to its appearance in scripture. An Irish immigrant and erstwhile ironmonger, Hopkins was ordained in Pittsburgh and came to lead Vermont's Episcopal flock in 1828 with his beautiful Irish tenor voice. From the 1830s until the Civil War, however, Hopkins never showed sympathy for

Stowe, "ski capital of the East," is also one of Vermont"s beauty spots. Here a lucky bus load of tourists glimpses the Green Mountains in that magical but brief time between late autumn and early winter. Rust-tinted foliage merges into snow-capped mountaintop. Photo by Andre Jenny. Courtesy, Vermont Department of Tourism and Marketing

Right

Right
"Naulakha riding on its hillside like a boat on the flank of a far wave" are the words Rudyard Kipling used to describe his Dummerston home. The broad porch led to flower gardens, that the writer had laid out himself. Naulakha *was Kipling's home between 1893 and 1896. It was here that he finished the* Jungle Book *and* Captains Courageous. *From the Wilbur Collection. Courtesy, Bailey/Howe Library, University of Vermont*

Center
On July 8, 1777, the first Constitution of the "free and independent State of Vermont" was adopted at a meeting of the delegates held at Elijah West's tavern in Windsor. The historic building pictured here later became known as the Old Constitution House. By initiating a government under authority of the 1777 Constitution, Vermont became a republic, independent of both Great Britain and the colonies and states of North America. Vermont retained its status as an independent republic until 1791, when it was admitted to the Union as the fourteenth state. From the Wilbur Collection. Courtesy, Bailey/Howe Library, University of Vermont

Right
The front hall of Robert Todd Lincoln's Hildene estate in Manchester reflects an elegance far removed from his father's humble log cabin origins. After Lincoln's assassination, Robert became an attorney in Chicago and eventually a millionaire as president of the Pullman Palace Car Company. In 1912 President William Howard Taft was a guest of the Lincolns at Hildene. Courtesy, Historic Hildene

106

Described by John Gunther as perhaps the "most charming" of all state capitols, the Vermont State House was designed by Thomas Silloway of Newburyport, Massachusetts. Completed in 1859, the present State House replaced the 1837 State House, which had been destroyed by fire in 1857. Vermont's first State House, a simple frame building, was constructed in 1808. Courtesy, Vermont Travel Division

Above
In Eric Sloan's **Vermont Hill Farm** *storm clouds hover above the hills as the farmer and his "hand" hurry to bring in the hay. The stone wall in the foreground is testimony to the fact that tilling Vermont's rocky soil has always been back-breaking work. Courtesy, New Britain Museum of Art. Gift of Dr. and Mrs. Colter Rule*

Facing Page
Vermont has benefited from an increasing desire among urban Americans to seek their relaxation in the outdoors. Vermont has it all—snow-shoeing in Brookfield, snow-boarding at Mt. Snow, sailing at Basin Harbor, canoeing on the Winooski, and bicycling at Groton State Forest. Photo by Bruce Chrisner. Courtesy, Vermont Department of Tourism and Marketing

Top
The modest increase in using draft horses for farming and logging in Vermont is partly based on the fact that they can maneuver steep or rough terrain better than tractors. At this farm in Brownsville two teams that know the lay of the land are used for raking hay. Photo by Carolyn Bates

Above
A star-studded field of dandelions means that spring has finally come to stay. Though some may disparage them as "common" flowers, a field full of dandelions is a cheerful and welcome sight to most Vermonters. Here they make their appearance at Pleasant Valley in Underhill. Photo by Carolyn Bates

Above
October Light *is the title of a novel written by John Gardner, who lived in Old Bennington until his death in 1982. Vermont's October light is admired by painters and photographers who appreciate its clarity and ability to sharply delineate objects. In this scene a group of barns form an almost abstract composition.*
Photo by Carolyn Bates

Right
The Bread and Puppet Theatre, started in the 1960s by Peter Schumann of Glover, is representative of various grassroots political and cultural activities that have grown and thrived in Vermont for more than thirty years. Using homemade puppet masks and superhuman effigies, Bread and Puppet productions deal with social, political, and religious themes. Courtesy, Vermont Department of Tourism and Marketing

Above
Storm clouds hover above Enosburg on a cold November afternoon. In 1840 Enosburg had a population of 2,022 people, 2,101 head of cattle, and 5,220 sheep. In 2000 Enosburg's population is 2,876. Photo by Carolyn Bates

Right
This View of North Dorset by an unknown artist was painted sometime after the railroad came through the valley in 1853. Courtesy, Vermont Historical Society

Facing page
Picking out the perfect pumpkin is no small task when one is confronted with an abundant harvest. A red-stockinged girl at the Huntington vegetable stand comes up with the makings of a pie or jack-o-lantern. Photo by Carolyn Bates

Facing page, top
As far as Vermonters are concerned, there's only one "World's Fair"—the one at Tunbridge. Started by the directors of the Union Agricultural Society in 1867, this four-day event attracts crowds of over 20,000 people every September. Annual events include horse racing, a midway and animal displays. In addition, the fair emphasizes history by providing demonstrations of contra dancing, spinning, weaving, shingle-shaving, log-hewing and iron forging. Photo by Carolyn Bates

Facing page, bottom
Jack Delano was one of a team of Farm Security Administration photographers who recorded typical scenes of rural life during the New Deal Era. As the United States began to pull out of the Depression and hovered on the brink of entering World War II, a few FSA photographers began experimenting with newly-invented Kodachrome film. These remarkable photos were misfiled at the Library of Congress and only rediscovered in 1978. This photo is entitled **Barker** at the Grounds of the Vermont State Fair, Rutland, September, 1941. Courtesy, Light Gallery and the Library of Congress

Above
A dairy farm in Fletcher with Mount Mansfield, Vermont's tallest peak, in the background. Dairy farms, though decreasing rapidly in number in recent years, still symbolize Vermont's rural character. Photo by Andre Jenny. Courtesy, Vermont Department of Tourism and Marketing

Above
Polo is played in Waitsfield.
Photo by Carolyn Bates

Right
Barre is home to an extensive Italian community. Italian stone cutters came to Barre in the 19th century to work in the granite industry and quarrying has been the mainstay of its economic life. From here granite is shipped all over the U.S. Rock of Ages is probably the best known of Barre's granite companies. Courtesy, Vermont Department of Tourism and Marketing

Above
This ski patrol in Killington is always on the lookout for anyone who might need assistance. Photo by Carolyn Bates

Left
Vermonter's enjoy canoeing on the Winooski River. Courtesy, Vermont Department of Tourism and Marketing

For forty-seven years the side-wheeler S.S. Ticonderoga cruised Lake Champlain, carrying passengers, freight, and automobiles. In 1954 the aging steamboat was retired to a permanent berth at the Shelburne Museum near the Colchester Reef Lighthouse which had been moved from its position on the lake. Courtesy, Vermont Department of Travel and Tourism

In the 1990s Vermonters worried that the family farm, like this one in Danby Four Corners, might become a thing of the past. In 1900 there were about 32,000 farms in the Green Mountain State, but only about 6,000 by 2000. Courtesy, Vermont Department of Tourism and Marketing

Shaping Modern Vermont: 1860 to 1940

*S*eldom is the story of a place and its people as neatly bracketed by two such powerful events as the Civil War and the Great Depression of the 1930s as is Vermont. The saga of Vermont in that roughly seventy-year period is, of course, not simply enclosed by those events. In a number of important ways the happenings of the 1860s shaped life in Vermont until the eve of the Second World War.

Vermont's role in the Civil War was as a generous contributor of men—nearly half of whom gave their lives—to defend the Union and help abolish slavery in the nation. In order to meet the deep moral and political commitment Vermonters felt for the northern cause, will and technology needed to coincide. The principal technology by which Vermont met its commitments was the railway system that had developed in the state beginning in the 1840s and connected it with the rest of America by 1860. If Vermont had had to rely on the transportation system that preceded the development of the railways, its role in the war would have been less

opened Vermont's doors to transport goods and people by steam and canal boats to New York and Montreal. America's second steamboat appeared in 1808 when the *Vermont* was launched on Lake Champlain. With a top speed of five miles per hour, however, the *Vermont* could barely keep up with sailing schooners running from Whitehall to Burlington on a twenty-mile-per-hour south wind. Running against the wind became close to a walk. The *Vermont* sank on the Richelieu in 1815. Captain Dick Sherman then took the *Phoenix* on the lake in 1815, until it too burned and sank off Colchester Point in 1819. In 1824 the Champlain Transportation Company (CTC) was chartered. Captain Sherman—known in ballads of the era as "Dandy Dick" for his style of command—plied the lake at the helm of the luxury liner *Burlington,* carrying passengers from Whitehall to Burlington and St. Jean for the CTC with such style that Charles Dickens in 1845 had to "praise the *Burlington* very highly, but no more than it deserves . . . a perfectly exquisite achievement of neatness, elegance, and order."

Boat traffic on the Connecticut was important for freighting goods, especially milled lumber, down river to Connecticut and Massachusetts. Despite canals constructed soon after 1800 at Bellows Falls, Sumner's Falls below Hartland, and the White River Canal above the confluence of the White and Connecticut rivers shoal waters inhibited development of the Connecticut as a major transportation route. Samuel Morey of Fairlee had pioneered the steamboat on the Connecticut at Fairlee in 1793. Some of his ideas for a steam engine appeared later in Robert Fulton's *Clermont* on the Hudson River in 1807. Dreams of connecting the Winooski with a canal to the White River and thus the Connecticut with the Champlain, however, were nothing more than that.

The completion of rail connections between Boston and White River Junction in the 1840s and then on to Burlington and Montreal in the same decade established the bases for a modern transportation system for Vermont. By 1860 the Ver-

substantial. A smaller war role would probably have also provided less experience on which to draw, as the people of Vermont moved beyond that tragic event into the 1870s. It was that experience that contributed in a broad sense to the postwar organization and development of Vermont into a society that could successfully adapt itself to its environment.

Until 1823 when the Hudson-Champlain Canal was opened, Vermont's transportation connections, both internally and with the rest of America, had been primitive, hard-going turnpikes and wagon tracks, some of them based on military roads cut for the Continental Army during the Revolution. The canal to the Hudson from Lake Champlain and a later canal around the Chambly Rapids on the Richelieu River in Quebec fully

mont Central Railroad ran from the southwest corner of the state north to Burlington. Spur lines did not run off to Montpelier and Barre until the 1880s. The Rutland and Burlington line ran from a Bellows Falls connection to Boston west to Rutland and north to Burlington. The Vermont and Canada line ran from Essex Junction north to the border and a connection with Montreal. The Rutland also ran southwest to Albany and beyond to New York City. The rail lines of northeastern Vermont—the Connecticut and Passumpsic, the Grand Trunk, and the St. Johnsbury and Lake Champlain—connected those regions of the state with Portland, Maine, as well as the lines to Boston, New York, and Montreal.

Vermont's railway system demonstrated its value for moving people both within and out of Vermont as it developed through the 1850s. Americans—no less Vermonters—were on the move after 1840. In Vermont people drifted from small hill farms into villages and towns, a movement that grew substantially after the Civil War and continued well into the twentieth century. Even greater numbers of Vermonters moved west in the great migration accelerated by the Gold Rush to California in 1849. The railroads of the

1850s carried settlers from Vermont and other eastern states to rail heads in Missouri. From there the winding wagon trains carried them further west to the far side of the Pacific slope. Vermont's population reached 314,000 in the 1850 census. It never went above 350,000 until World War I.

To some students of Vermont's past the stable population level sustained between 1850 and 1920 indicates a community having reached a socioeconomic dead end. Others see instead a Vermont that had established a population base adequately supportable by the topography, technology, and market access of the seventy-

year period ending in the 1930s. On either end of that seventy years stands a momentous event in the nation's and Vermont's history—the Civil War and the Great Depression.

On April 12, 1861, the newly formed Confederate States of America opened a four-year-long war on the United States by attacking the federal Fort Sumter in Charleston Harbor. Seven thousand Confederate troops beseiged seventy federal officers and men for five days. Two days after the fall of Sumter, President Abraham Lincoln issued a call for 75,000 volunteers for three months' service in the United States Army. Vermont was assigned a levy of one regiment of

riflemen consisting of 780 officers and men. George J. Stannard of St. Albans, the colonel of Vermont's Fourth Regiment of Militia, was the first man to volunteer himself and his regiment's services. Governor Erastus Fairbanks concluded, however, that the first regiment should be called from throughout the state. Command was given to John W. Phelps of Brattleboro, a West Point graduate and veteran of the Mexican War.

General William Tecumseh Sherman observed after the war that "no people on earth were less prepared for it than those of the United States." Vermont's war-readiness mirrored the nation's. By 1850 the legislature had ceased appropriating funds for the militia. The few militia companies still in existence by 1850 were merely social clubs that met once or twice annually and paid all of their own expenses, including the purchase of arms, uniforms, and, despite the alcohol prohibition law of 1853, large amounts of rum. June training sessions were more often drinking parties than military exercises. Common jokes re-

Above
Erastus Fairbanks was born in Brimfield, Massachusetts, and emigrated to Vermont in 1812. After his brother Thaddeus invented a platform scale, Erastus became chief executive of their rapidly expanding scale factory. In 1852 he was elected Governor of Vermont by the Whigs. In 1856 and again in 1860 he was elected governor on the Republican ticket. Courtesy, Vermont Historical Society

Top, left
Born on a hillside farm near Woodstock, Hiram Powers became famous as a sculptor. He began his career by doing portrait busts of such personages as

Andrew Jackson, John Calhoun, and Daniel Webster. Aided by loans from patrons, he was able to go to Florence in 1837, where he spent the rest of his life. His Greek Slave (1843) was the most renowned sculpture of its time. Engraving after a painting by Alonzo Chappel. From the Wilbur Collection. Courtesy, Bailey/Howe Library, University of Vermont

Facing page
A construction gang of Irish railroad workers paused to have their pictures taken on the Boston & Main railway bridge south of Brattleboro in the early 1900s. Courtesy, Brattleboro Photos

ferred to militia as "floodwood" companies for their jumbled appearance on parade. Modest attempts to revive the militia in the late 1850s brought Brigadier Alonzo Jackman, professor of military science at Norwich Military Academy, to command a Vermont militia brigade of only 900 men in 1860. Twenty-one towns claimed ability to mount militia companies in the same year, the Adjutant General reported, but there were

George Perkins Marsh, a native of Woodstock, created the concept of modern ecology. His book Man and Nature, *a pioneering study of the interrelationships between organisms and environment, predicted many of the crises in resources, overpopulation, and environment that confront the world today. In addition to his contributions as a conservationist, Marsh was a lawyer, congressman, diplomat, and an outstanding scholar who spoke twenty languages. He was one of the early workers on the* Oxford Dictionary, *a writer of encyclopedia articles, and a collector of reptiles for the Smithsonian Institution. Courtesy, George Perkins Marsh Papers, University of Vermont*

insufficient arms to supply more than 700 men in the entire state.

Despite their unpreparedness companies of volunteers from eleven towns gathered at Rutland on May 2, 1861, were mustered into federal service on May 9 and entrained that same day for the defense of Washington. On the 10th of June five companies in that first regiment under the command of Colonel Peter Washburn, a successful lawyer from Woodstock in civilian life, engaged Confederate troops at Big Bethel, Virginia, in one of the first battles of the war. The first regiment of seven hundred men was the initial wave of a flood of Vermont volunteers and draftees sent south in defense of the Union. With a population of 315,000 in 1860, Vermont sent 34,238 men, out of 37,000 military eligibles, to federal service before the war ended at Appomatox, Virginia, in 1865. The mortality rate was 40 percent—13,695 men by wounds, disease, or accidents.

The cost to the state's economy in taxes collected for war purposes was also heavy. In characteristic Yankee precision on tax matters, the record shows that $9,087,353.40 of public monies were expended by Vermont. Of that sum towns in Vermont raised $5,215,787.70 for war expenses.

The deep feelings stirred in Vermonters by the war, as one contemporary remarked, drew men to the federal army who "are a Cromwellian sort . . . who make some conscience of what they do." The average age was twenty-four. The first regiment to go south in May 1861 for the defense of Washington struck onlookers in the mid-Atlantic states for the extraordinary number of tall men in their ranks. John W. Phelps, their commander from Brattleboro, was well over six feet tall and wore an enormous campaign hat with a large black ostrich plume. A Manhattanite saw Phelps in uniform standing on a corner of Broadway and wondered aloud, "Who's that Vermont colonel?" Invoking a homegrown heroic tradition, one of Phelps' men replied, "Oh, that's old Ethan Allen resurrected!"

Vermonters participated in all of the major battles in Virginia, Maryland, and Pennsylvania. Some also served in the Deep South under the notorious General Ben Butler in Louisiana. After a promotion to Brigadier General in 1861, John Phelps was sent to the Gulf of Mexico where he organized the first Negro troops in federal service at New Orleans in 1862. When Butler ordered Phelps to organize the ex-slaves into labor companies, the Vermonter resigned his commission, rather than become a slave driver himself.

The exploits of the Second Vermont Brigade under General George Stannard at Gettysburg earned the highest praise. On July 3, 1863, Robert E. Lee's push into the North through Pennsylvania appeared ready to turn out a crushing victory for the South with the driving force of a final charge by Pickett's Confederate brigade. The battle had been waging for three days when the Vermont Brigade came to aid Meade's Army of the Potomac, a force outnumbered two-to-one by the Confederates under Lee. After receiving one-and-a-half hours of heavy cannon bombardment, Stannard's Vermonters executed a series of disciplined, regimental-sized maneuvers more likely to be accomplished on a dress parade field than a field of mortal combat. The Vermonters advanced in three regimental flank attacks and completely broke the rebel army's back at Gettysburg. Stannard's battle report recounted the extraordinary behavior of his men and concluded with Stannard's own recognition that he had led exceptional men in a devastating display of skill and power:

The movements I have described were executed in the open field, under a heavy fire of shell, grape, and musketry, and they were performed with the promptness and precision of battalion drill. They ended the contest on the center, and substantially closed the battle.

Officers and men behaved like veterans, although it was, for most of them, their first battle, and I am content to leave it to the witnesses of the fight, whether or no they sustained the credit of the service, and the honor of our Green Mountain State.

Total Union and Confederate casualties at Gettysburg reached nearly 8,000 killed and 35,000 wounded, rivaling the carnage of Napoleon's defeat at Waterloo. Robert E. Lee's drive north into Pennsylvania cost him half of his army. Had he won at Gettysburg, then Baltimore, Philadelphia, and New York would have been seriously threatened. Washington would most likely have fallen to the Confederacy in a few days and a Confederate government recognized by European powers. Stannard's aide-de-camp, George

Left
"When will this cruel war be over?" is the caption that photographer G.H. Houghton of Brattleboro wrote to accompany this 1862 picture of three dejected-looking Yankees somewhere in Virginia. The war went on for three more years and by the time it was over Vermont had lost 5,237 of its men. The man seated on the right may have been Brattleboro artist Larkin Mead, who nearly had his hat shot off while sketching an enemy fortification. From the Houghton Collection. Courtesy, Vermont Historical Society

Facing page
The St. Albans Raid was the only Civil War engagement fought on Vermont soil. In 1864 twenty-two Confederate soldiers came down from Canada, held up the St. Albans banks, and absconded to Canada with over $200,000. Only one Vermonter was killed in this action. The outlaws were later tried in Canada and acquitted on the grounds that the raid was an "act of war." Courtesy, Vermont Historical Society

Left
On April 4, 1862, several regiments of Vermont Volunteers took possession of stockaded Confederate fortifications at Young's Mills, Virginia, that had been abandoned by the enemy the day before. Twelve days later, at Lee's Mills, they made an assault on Confederate lines. Here, in the process of capturing enemy rifle pits, the first Vermont casualties were incurred. From the Houghton Collection. Courtesy, Vermont Historical Society

G. Benedict, observed in 1870 that Lee's failure at Gettysburg was "the rebellion's failure." The Second Vermont Brigade's precision flanking attacks on Pickett were the decisive blow to cause that failure.

Vermont's generous response to repeated calls to defend the Union between 1861 and 1865 was accomplished through the efficient civil organization of the community. Governors Frederick Holbrook and then John Gregory Smith were given responsibility by the legislature for raising, outfitting, and sustaining Vermont's volunteers and draftees with funds from the state treasury until they officially entered federal service. In addition the state paid relief monies to families who suffered economic hardship from the loss of male labor. Soldiers were carried on a state payroll while on federal service.

Despite the low military readiness of Vermont

in early 1861, state government raised the first and every subsequent levy by drawing on the state organization into towns, or little republics, as some Vermonters liked to call them. Governors appointed the selectmen of each town to act as recruiting agents. With an efficient telegraphic communication system in operation since the mid-1850s and a railway network linking the larger towns, men were moved quickly from even the most remote mountain villages in the northeast sections of the state to troop gathering places at the railways in St. Johnsbury, Brattleboro, Rutland, and Burlington.

The highly effective organization of Vermont in support of the federal army was not an experience lost on Vermonters after the war in a community politically stabilized by Republican control. The state also had good communication and transportation systems to move information,

Left
Hetty Green, seated here on the front porch of her house in Bellows Falls, managed her inherited fortune so shrewdly that she was considered to be "the richest woman in the world." To her Bellows Falls neighbors, however, she was an eccentric penny-pinching woman who wore shabby clothes, haggled over prices, and refused to give to local charities. Courtesy, Rockingham Free Public Library

Facing page
The neo-Romanesque Billings Library was designed for the University of Vermont in 1883 by H.H. Richardson, the most famous American architect of his time. It was the last and largest library designed by Richardson, who died in 1886 at the age of forty-seven. Photo by John F. Smith. Courtesy, I C Photo Service, University of Vermont

men, and material. These factors would provide valuable experience in the development of Vermont for the next seventy or more years.

The consolidation of power in central state government during the Civil War, in fact, increased as Vermont moved on into the twentieth century. The development of a usable highway system, broad-based funding for education, and a number of other measures related to agriculture are among the most evident examples of centralization in Vermont. Yet the dynamics of consolidation occurred within a lively ideological context that professed greater value in local town government than in any centralized government. It was often argued that the small scale of town government adequately met the citizens needs

and assured freedom from control by a faceless, distant tyrant.

With a population that grew by less than 10 percent between 1870 and 1945, leaders of government frequently maintained that "small is better." Annual sessions of the legislature, for example, were replaced by biennial sessions in 1870 because many believed that annual sessions passed too many laws. In 1894 Governor Urban Woodbury believed "it is better to do too little than too much." Similarly, a part-time legislature of "simple citizens," not professional politicians, was supposed to produce "the best legislation . . . by the combined judgment of average men," according to Governor William Stickney in 1900. Popular wisdom believed that the town meeting was the purest form of local control and the very essence of democratic liberty. The town unit was so sacrosanct as a governmental unit that each town had a representative in the Vermont House of Representatives until 1964.

Yet even as the small population of Vermont increased at only a snail's pace, some regions of the state experienced sufficient growth while others regressed. Significant disparities had developed in population and wealth by 1900. In 1902, for example, Burlington's grand list value totaled $135,000 and its population had reached 18,500; Glastonbury's grand list, on the other hand, made only $353 in a town populated by forty-eight residents. Both towns had one vote in the legislature nonetheless.

By 1900 towns with less than 900 in population controlled a majority of votes in the Vermont House of Representatives. Until the 1960s every effort to reapportion the legislature closer to a one-man-one-vote proportion of representation was defeated by the small-town majority controlling the House of Representatives. Finally when Vermont's small towns could not provide the public services required by their residents, such as a reliable road system to transport milk to market or schools that graduated literate children, the praises of local control gave way, and Vermonters voted for central government to provide the service.

As historian Samuel Hand convincingly argued, Vermont initiated centralized public services earlier and, in some cases, more thoroughly than other states because of its predominantly agricultural economy. During the first seventy years of the nineteenth century, Vermont's agriculture developed through a series of stages in which various crops were grown and marketed up to a point when the activity became unprofitable due to western producers outstripping Vermont's capacity. Grain, sheep, beef, pork, cheese, and butter were all important at some time from 1800 until the 1870s. The sheep in the 1840s totaled 1,680,000, with Rutland and Addison counties containing nearly the majority. By

1860, however, Vermont no longer produced sheep for market, though it remained an important source of breeding stock for Merino sheep, the breed that William Jarvis had first brought to his Weathersfield farm in 1811 from Spain. By the mid-century dairy farming dominated the agriculture of Vermont. In the late 1850s refrigerated railway cars carried cheese and butter to Boston and New York year-round. When Wisconsin and Minnesota cheeses captured the national market, Vermont's dairymen turned to fluid milk, an easily marketed product after the development of pasteurization.

Moving milk from St. Johnsbury or St. Albans to Boston or New York required, first, good roads in Caledonia and Franklin counties over which farmers could carry their milk to the railways headed for the metropolitan market. Road maintenance in the mid-nineteenth century rested on the town's shoulders, and by 1880 the roads of Vermont were in sad condition. Vermont's dairy farmers went to the legislature for relief and assistance in marketing their product. The first Dairymen's Association in the nation, in fact, was formed in 1869 in the Senate Agriculture Committee room of the Vermont State House. The Association quickly developed a legislative program for which it lobbied throughout the 1870s and 1880s. Laws were sought to impose state restrictions on the sale of oleomargarine and Canadian milk imports and to regulate freight rates. The association worked vigorously throughout the 1880s for state government to improve the roads over which dairymen carried their milk to market. The Highway Act of 1892 taxed town grand lists for highway maintenance. A redistribution formula for this tax assured that poorer towns would benefit from the tax on richer towns. In 1898 the legislature appointed a state highway commissioner and extended state authority for establishing road standards. In 1917 Vermont was among the first states to propose a state highway system under federal guidelines and thereby qualify for federal highway assistance.

In addition to its support for highway legis-

lation, the dairy industry sought state creamery inspection laws to assure healthy milk products on the market. In 1880 dairymen lobbied intensely for a state law to require imitation butter—oleomargarine—to be dyed pink before it was sold. In the area of federal laws, again, they strongly supported Vermont Congressman William Grout's bill to regulate the sale of oleomargarine in interstate trade, a law that became known as the Grout Act.

The rhetoric of local control also gave way to

Copper mining began in Vershire in 1853. By 1880 a mining boomtown called Ely had grown up around the mines. The majority of miners, pictured here near the company blacksmith shop and entrance to the mines, were natives of Cornwall, England. The boom ended in 1883, when copper prices dropped and the Vermont Copper Mining Company refused to pay its employees. When the miners rioted for back wages, the state militia was called in and mob leaders were arrested. Production continued sporadically until 1905, when the mines closed and the former boomtown became a ghost town. From the Dexter Photo Collection. Courtesy, Bailey/ Howe Library, University of Vermont

Tourism flourished in Vermont in the post-Civil War era. By 1867 a local historian was complaining that "city cousins" had corrupted Vermont's work ethic by importing the "seductive fashion of doing nothing and doing it elegantly." In this stereoscopic view, taken about 1870, two dignified "flatlanders" launch their boat from the banks of Long Island in Lake Memphremagog. From the Dexter Collection. Courtesy, Bailey/ Howe Library, University of Vermont

Right
Seated atop the "Rock of Terror" on the "Nose" of Mount Mansfield, a solitary figure contemplates the sublime view. In 1864 Ralph Waldo Emerson climbed the "Nose" by means of a stout rope. After "many sharp looks at the heavens and the earth," he descended to breakfast at the Summit House. From the Dexter Collection. Courtesy, Bailey/Howe Library, University of Vermont

Facing page, bottom
Photographer Frank F. Currier's stereoview of a party of mountain climbers titled Chin from the Nose, Mansfield, Mt., *was taken sometime between 1860 and 1870. The fashionably-dressed tourists in this picture were probably guests at the nearby Summit House. From the Dexter Photo Collection. Courtesy, Bailey/Howe Library, University of Vermont*

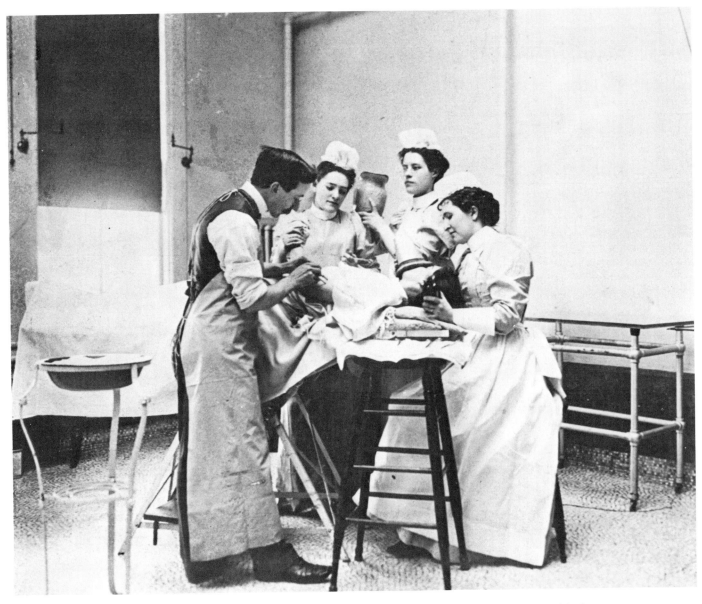

the reality of consolidated government in order to secure adequate funding for education, a goal still pursued by Vermont state government in the last quarter of the twentieth century though it was a political issue as early as 1880. In 1850 Vermont contained 239 towns and 2,594 school districts funded by a fee system paid by parents and a small supplementary tax on the town. Uneven quality and irregular attendance requirements were the norm by 1880 when Governor Roswell Farnham reported:

The large villages and cities of the State are well provided with schools, but many of the sparsely inhabited portions of the State have schools but a few months a year, and those of an inferior kind.

Farnham went on to observe that the small towns of Vermont were so lightly inhabited "or so strained in circumstances that they could not support good schools." Centralize was the solution and thus "have the expense of schools fall to a greater extent upon the whole state."

Nearly one-quarter of Vermont's school districts enrolled twelve or less students in 1886 when Govenor Ebenezer Ormsbee complained that "the people of our commonwealth are increasing in illiteracy" because of the system of numerous small districts. But if the state wanted to impose larger districts, with commensurately

Facing page
Three graduates of the Mary Fletcher Hospital School of Nursing in Burlington assist a University of Vermont medical student in the operating room in 1900. Linda Richards, who grew up in Derby and Lyndon, received the first American diploma in nursing in 1873. Nellie Gray Barnes of Coventry became the first graduate of the Mary Fletcher School in 1882. Courtesy, Medical Center Hospital of Vermont

Above
Chansonetta Emmon's carefully arranged photograph of a teacher and her students in front of the Edson Hill School in Stowe, circa 1910, showed the influence of Winslow Homer's painting, Snap the Whip. *Such idealized views are nostalgic glimpses into the past, but do not reflect the fact that district schools were often drab learning environments in which female teachers were paid approximately half the amount that male teachers earned. Courtesy, William A. Farnsworth Library & Museum*

the legislature then consolidated school districts into town districts, and in 1894 raised the state school tax to eight cents. Debate on the state road and school taxes in 1896 pointed out that road improvements, because they aided an agricultural economy, will always "profitably use more money" and "the poorer communities have a right to equality in school burdens." The rhetoric of local control and the reality of consolidated governmental powers apparently did not even recognize each other in a debate where the price was right and the principle noble.

The fate of direct primary elections for selecting candidates for statewide and national offices after 1900 provides another view on how local control gave way to centralization. During the Progressive Era, direct primaries were promoted for their reputedly democratic character. Repub-

larger expenses, it was argued, then the state should help to meet those expenses. So, in 1890, with only twelve opposing votes, the legislature approved a tax of five cents on the grand list of each town to be redistributed by formula. In 1892

lican, Democrat, and Progressive platforms all called for direct primaries by 1914 after a popular referendum on the question carried 18,934 to 5,132. But the legislature in 1915 defeated a direct primary bill, 103-115. The bill's main opponents were Democrats, who disliked the provision that ballots contain only candidates of a single party, and Republican House members from small towns, who recognized that direct primaries would cost them their influence in selecting their party's candidates. Small town members knew the caucus system then in use gave them power in their party far beyond the number of votes in their towns might suggest.

Under the urgings of Governor Charles Gates, the House reconsidered and passed a primary bill with a referendum clause, 149-25. As many expected, the popular referendum approved the primary by 24,500 to 21,000 votes, with the large Vermont towns providing the margin for passage. Not surprisingly, the town vote, as opposed to the popular vote, produced 134 towns against and 102 for the primary. One major result of direct primary was that small towns lost control of senatorial delegations in their counties. In 1918, for example, Windham County's two Republican candidates for the Vermont Senate resided in Brattleboro; Chittenden County's senators that year were also both from Burlington. The general result of these shifts in the Senate was to reduce the power of agriculture in favor of commerce. Despite vigorous support from agrarian interests, the 1923 income tax bill, for example, was defeated by senators representing commercial interests from the larger towns of Vermont.

Efforts to increase the powers of the executive branch of Vermont's government were seldom given serious consideration during the nineteenth century; a single two-year term was the norm for twenty-nine governors beginning in 1870. A brief flurry of interest in strengthening the executive's powers occurred after World War I when the scientific management craze was sweeping America. In 1921 James Hartness was

elected governor with just 40 percent of the vote. He was the only trained engineer to have held the office. In 1922 Hartness called for an appointed manager to serve for six years as the state's senior administrator. Apparently Hartness's message was not heeded. Only after a great natural disaster, in fact, did Governor John Weeks serve more than two years. Weeks served two terms, 1927 to 1931, with the middle point of his first term marked by the powerfully destructive Flood of 1927, from which Vermont recovered under Week's leadership in an unprecedented second term for a modern governor of Vermont.

The seventy-year period after the Civil War provided a number of other illustrations in the story of Vermont's development into a modern society. The chapters modern historians have written about that development include accounts of the struggle by Vermont's women for the right to vote in the twentieth century and their role in the temperance crusade of the 1870s and 1880s. They also include Vermont's various ethnic groups: the French, who came to work in Vermont's dairy industry and textile mills; the Swedes and Finns, who migrated to America for work in Vermont's lumber industry; the Italians, Scots, Irish, and Spaniards, who came for the work in marble and granite; the Welsh and Poles, who came to work in the slate quarries; the Cornish, who came to mine copper; and the Staffordshire English, who came to work in the Bennington potteries.

In his 1798 *History of Vermont* Ira Allen said of the young state's inhabitants, "They are all farmers, and again every farmer is a mechanic in some line or other, as inclination leads or necessity requires." Even as recent historians remind us that Vermont is not a homogeneous ethnic or religious community, so Vermonters have been employed, as Ira Allen's early observation suggests they might, in other fields than dairy farming or producing maple syrup. For example, after the European famines of the 1840s Irish immigrants were widely employed in constructing more than five hundred miles of Vermont's rail-

way system by 1870. After the first wave of rail-road construction subsided, many of Vermont's new Irish population found jobs quarrying and cutting marble, especially after Redfield Proctor organized a group of marble extractors into the Vermont Marble Company at Sutherland Falls, a village soon renamed Proctor and fitted out with company houses, a store, and later a hospital. Other extractive jobs were filled by Italians who came to Barre, Rutland, and Proctor to cut

In 1880 the first Scottish stone-cutters arrived in Barre. During the next two decades other ethnic groups who immigrated to Barre to work in the granite industry included Swedes, Irishmen, French-Canadians, Italians, Poles, Spaniards and Germans. By 1900 more than 90 percent of Barre's multi-cultural work force belonged to one of fifteen local labor unions. In 1903 the Quarry Workers' International Union of North America was formed, with national headquarters in Barre. Courtesy, Aldrich Public Library

granite and marble in the 1870s and 1880s. By 1900 Swedish marble workers in Proctor had also come to form a significant group.

Efforts to organize into unions began as early as 1880. Irish marble workers in Rutland formed a chapter of the Knights of Labor and attempted to elect their members to public office in the name of good government. Unlike Barre granite workers—Scots, Italians, and Spaniards who were 90 percent organized by 1889 when Samuel Gompers, President of the American Federation of Labor, came to speak to them—the marble work-

ers of Rutland County faced a powerful opponent in the Proctor family. In the 1880s and 1890s, marble, Proctor, and Vermont seemed almost synonymous. Redfield Proctor, Governor of Vermont from 1878 to 1880, headed the largest corporation in the state. His son Fletcher assumed control in 1891 and also later served as governor from 1906 to 1908, as would the grandson Mortimer R. Proctor from 1945 to 1947. Redfield served as United States Secretary of War in 1891 and represented Vermont in the United States Senate for four terms. The contrast between the Proc-

tor's wealth and power and the wages of Vermont's labor force is instructive. In 1910 when Redfield Proctor completed his fourth and final term in the Senate, he was the richest member in the United States Congress. The approximately 4,000 Vermonters employed in the marble industry, most of them working for the Proctor firm, ranked thirty-sixth in the nation for wages paid to them.

In an era when the owners of Vermont's businesses and industries expected, and usually got, docility and hard work from their employees in return for small pay, Vermont's labor force nonetheless left a record of their struggle to improve their position in the work place and the quality of their lives through their collective efforts in a union. The methods and aims of the union movement in Vermont were encompassed in collective bargaining, but conditions sometimes required the ultimate measure—a strike. The Bolton War of 1846 is probably the first major work stoppage in the story of Vermont labor. Two hundred Irish

laborers on the Vermont Central right-of-way construction site near Richmond walked off the job in early July after three months without pay. Burlington's Light Infantry militia company and a musket-armed volunteer fire brigade quelled the Irish riot. In 1883 Cornish and Irish copper miners struck in Ely when the Vermont Mining Company worked them for two months with no pay. The railroad built nearly forty years earlier by Irishmen quickly carried state militia to put down the copper miners strike. Copper mining came to a full stop in Vermont after the Ely strike.

The piece rate pay of the Vermont Marble Company became increasingly unsatisfactory to workers at the beginning of the twentieth century, bringing a strike in 1904. Only 10 percent of the workers participated in the strike, but the Proctors heard the message in the workers' actions and attempted to improve relations with a cooperative company store and free company hospital. During the Great Depression of the 1930s, however, Vermont Marble Company

Left
In 1870 Redfield Proctor of Rutland and Sutherland Falls succeeded in merging various small individually-owned marble quarries into the Sutherland Falls Marble Company. This merger marked the beginning of what became the Vermont Marble Company, the world's leading producer of marble. Proctor was prominent in public affairs, serving as governor of Vermont from 1878 to 1880, as United States secretary of war during Harrison's administration, and as a United States senator from 1891 until his death. Courtesy, Vermont Historical Society

Below
Skilled artisans working for the Vermont Marble Company in Proctor were the principal producers of statuary for national

monuments during the late nineteenth century. This picture shows a group of Proctor carvers at work on elaborate capitals for the Arlington Memorial. The choice Danby marble they used continues to be favored by architects for its beauty, strength, and durability. From the Wilbur Collection. Courtesy, Bailey/Howe Library, University of Vermont

Facing page
Redfield Proctor began hiring Swedes to work in his marble quarries in the 1880s. Ten years later there was a large Swedish settlement in Proctor. This group was photographed at a Swedish Lutheran Sunday school picnic in 1908. Courtesy, Vermont Historical Society

withdrew the benefits of the free hospital, with-held house rents and cooperative store bills from paychecks, and paid workers reduced wages of 40 cents to 60 cents for an hour's work. In 1935 Vermont Marble Company workers organized and struck. Despite national attention and sup-port, the eighteen-month-long strike proved dis-couraging to the workers. Frank Partridge, president of Vermont Marble, held the compa-ny's original position until the workers returned in July 1936.

The ready supply of water and energy at Bel-lows Falls invited paper manufacture to that spot from Vermont's earliest years. International Pa-per Company opened a paper mill on the Con-necticut in 1898 and employed 500 workers at its peak. Unfortunately International's twenty-seven-year residency at Bellows Falls was a rec-ord of frequent disagreements between labor and management, resulting in frequent strikes. Fi-nally in 1925, in a move the company repeated at a number of its mills in the northern tier states, International Paper closed the Bellows Falls mill

and moved its operations to Canada.

Barre, "The Granite Center of the World," be-came the home of Vermont worker solidarity by 1890. Barre served as the national headquarters for the Quarry Workers' International Union of North America after 1903, having drawn skilled Italians, Scots, Spaniards, and Swedes to that industry in the last quarter of the nineteenth cen-tury. Granite workers fought for shorter work days, improved wages, and exhaust systems in their cutting sheds to remove the dust that caused the deadly lung disease called silicosis. The battle with employers over dust removers continued into the 1930s.

After granite workers in Barre suffered a 33 percent wage cut in the 1930s, they struck. Vio-lence erupted briefly and national guardsmen patrolled Barre's streets for a while. When the granite workers finally returned to work, they had accepted only a dollar per day wage cut in-stead of the three dollars over which they had originally struck.

Between 1870 and World War I, Vermont was

Above
Half a century ago most of the finishing work at the Vermont Marble Company in Proctor was executed by sculptors who employed tools and methods that had been in use since the Renaissance. Today tools and methods are far more modern. Now in its second century of continuous operation, the Vermont Marble Company is the world's largest producer and fabricator of marble. From the Wilbur Collection. Courtesy, Bailey/Howe Library, University of Vermont

Facing page
This buxom beauty of the late 1800s unabashedly shows off her hourglass figure while weighing in at 150 pounds. Such subliminal advertising undoubtedly helped sell more scales. Those who wished to order a copy of this color-lithographed poster could receive one by simply mailing fifteen cents to the Howe Scale Company on Rutland. Howe claimed to be second only to the E.T. Fairbanks Company in St. Johnsbury, the world's largest platform scale manufacturers. From the Wilbur Collection. Courtesy, Bailey/Howe Library, University of Vermont

well on its way to establishing itself as the most rural state in the nation. By World War I its rural character was secured, and each post-war census further underlined that, of the forty-eight contiguous states, Vermont was indeed the most rural. Dairy farming, mainly producing fluid milk for the Boston and New York markets, was a leading industry. By the eve of World War I, however, Vermont's non-agricultural work force had grown to over 10 percent of the population of this very rural state. Vermont was number one in the nation by 1910 in the production of marble, granite, and asbestos, and number two for slate, talc, and soapstone. Including workers in the lumber and timber industry, by 1920 around 18,000 worked in enterprises drawing on the natural resources of Vermont.

From 1910 to 1940, however, Vermont saw little positive change in factors of life such as population or economic growth. Population grew by only .9 percent, hardly a noticeable change. Rural farm population between 1920 and 1940 declined from 35.3 percent to 29.4 percent of the general population of Vermont. While population remained static for nearly thirty-five years, the Great Depression took its toll by reducing the industrial work force to 15,000 from the peak of 18,000 reached on the eve of World War I. The period from 1940 to 1980 gives a useful contrast. During that more recent forty-year span, population grew by 42 percent, 359,000 to 511,000, and the employed industrial and service work force grew to 150,000—35,000 of whom were members of labor unions in 1985.

A new nation developed as the United States proceeded from the Civil War through the turn of the century. The original rural-agricultural American society passed through a violent moment that crystallized moral and political energies given since Andrew Jackson's time to working out an equalitarian social structure.

America, on the other hand, would henceforth be urban-industrial. Vermont as an agricultural society in the post-Civil War period seems, at first glance, to run counter to the national trend. Yet another view of Vermont taken from the perspective of the 1980s might instead say that this region's development as a "milk shed" is an obviously natural development for a piece of geography that grows grass so splendidly for forage and is only three to six hours away from millions of milk drinkers by rail, first, and, more recently, by interstate highway trucking. Moreover, even during the violent economic cycles of inflationary booms and deep recessions in the late nineteenth century, Vermont continued and improved its production of milk for the seaboard markets with only the slightest growth in agricultural production capacity. The average twenty-five-cow farm actually remained the norm until the 1960s.

Historians such as Deborah Clifford of Cornwall and Marshall True of Burlington have re-

minded us that the evolution of Vermont as a society in the late nineteenth and early twentieth centuries was not simply a matter of political campaigns to provide government's assistance in marketing milk or improved school systems in order to graduate literate sons and daughters of Yankee dairymen or immigrant stone cutters. Vermont's women, for example, participated in the two major campaigns of the modern women's rights movements prior to World War II that organized the intelligence,

Facing page, bottom
In the early twentieth century men working on Pike's farm in Berlin used traditional reaping methods. Earning a livelihood on Vermont's backcountry farms has always been a struggle. Unable to compete with the large mechanized farms of the West, small-scale farming has been declining in Vermont ever since the nineteenth century. In 1945 Vermont had 26,490 operating farms. By 2000 there were fewer than 3,000. *Courtesy, Vermont Historical Society*

Above
In the early years of the twentieth century, Vermont began developing its potential to produce electrical power as a means of stimulating industrial growth. The construction of Vernon Dam, which spanned the Connecticut River between Vernon and Hinsdale, New Hampshire, was completed in 1911. Historian Walter Crockett hailed it as "one of the greatest water power developments of the East." The power it generated, however, turned more wheels of industry in Massachusetts that in Vermont. *Courtesy, Vermont Historical Society*

Left
"The woods are full of women just like me. We want to vote on the spending of our taxes," wrote Elizabeth Van Patten of Burlington in the December 28, 1912, issue of the Woman's Journal. *At approximately the same time, this sign advocating "A Square Deal" for women appeared on a building in Grafton. Courtesy, Vermont Historical Society*

Facing page
A group of dignified old Civil War veterans gathered in front of the Newfane Courthouse in 1916 for the dedication ceremonies of a soldier's monument honoring the fighting men of the Civil War. From the Porter Thayer Collection. Courtesy, Brooks Memorial Library

emotions, and energies of many American women between 1870 and the ratification of the Nineteenth Amendment to the Constitution of the United States in 1920, making women's suffrage national. Ratified in January 1920, the earlier Prohibition amendment had outlawed alcoholic beverages. Both amendments were linked in the national and Vermont stories of women struggling for their rights.

Beginning with legislative efforts from 1870 to 1872 to grant women full suffrage, the early campaign in Vermont to enfranchise women was fought with a number of near successes, reaching its final goal when the new century completed its second decade. In 1917 the first law in New England to allow women to vote in school district elections was passed in Montpelier by the Vermont legislature. As early as 1886 the Vermont House of Representatives had passed a similar municipal suffrage bill, only to see it defeated by eight votes in the Senate. Opponents had objected to giving the ballot to "such a dangerous class as the women of Vermont." When both chambers of the legislature passed a presidential suffrage bill in 1919, Governor Percival Clement, a perennial opponent of women's rights, refused to sign the act on the grounds that he believed

it was unconstitutional. Clement later refused to even cooperate with women and men supporters of women's rights when Vermont's turn came around to ratify the amendment. He resisted all urgings to call a special session of the legislature for that purpose. World War I had helped to convince most Americans of women's right to vote. In Vermont, for example, when the total work force fell from 52,000 to 42,000 as Vermont sent nearly 17,000 men into the military services, industrial and agricultural production increased to meet war demands after the legislature passed amendments to the labor laws that permitted women to work for longer hours than the progressive prewar labor laws had allowed. Women and even some children (in textile mills) made extraordinary contributions to the war effort. Vermont's politicians, except for the hidebound Clements and like-thinkers, finally came around to support women in the struggle for their civil rights.

Vermont had followed Maine in passing temperance laws before the Civil War. Later local options statutes were adopted. By the 1870s it was evident even in rural Vermont that alcoholism was violently tearing at the American social fabric. By the 1870s and 1880s, local option towns

had their share of saloons. Even dry towns had hotels or restaurants where whiskey and beer could be easily obtained. With only the usually feeble town constable to enforce local regulations, few places in Vermont were really dry. Moreover, in nearly every town with a railroad connection and hotel, pre-Mann Act Vermont offered a brothel not far from the bar and the whiskey barrels. The suffrage and temperance campaigns were closely allied from the 1870s to the passage of the Nineteenth Amendment.

Yet opposition was strong and widespread. As Burlington flourished through the lumber boom years of the 1870s, it offered a variety of saloons and brothels to citizens and visitors in a busy town of over 13,000. An attempt to stop the illegal sale of alcohol in Rutland during 1871 caused a riot. In St. Albans there were over forty stores, hotels, and restaurants serving alcohol despite legal prohibitions. St. Albans' notorious name

for drunkeness and its well-known and plentiful suppliers caused a group of three-hundred women to gather for the first Vermont Temperance Crusade meeting on March 9, 1874, to hear Dr. Diocletian Lewis lecture on "The Duty of Christian Women in the Cause of Temperance."

The nineteenth-century temperance crusade and the subsequent prohibition movement leading to the Volstead Act and Eighteenth Amendment were not simply responses to the great amounts of alcohol being consumed by Americans. Widespread alcoholism and attendant poverty and violence, often damaging families, were significant aspects of disturbing and dislocating developments in American life generated by expanding industrialization and commercialization. In as much as Vermont was American, it was not immune from either the symptoms or the cause. Attempts to dry up a notorious drinking town like Middlebury, for example, though

legally dry in 1877, failed to convince the sheriff of Addision County to close even one of Middlebury's three hotels known to sell liquor or even to discover the names of liquor sellers from arrested drunks. The symptoms themselves were epidemic in proportions. By 1900 Americans were per capita consuming annually nearly three gallons of absolute alcohol, when reduced from beer, whiskey, and wine. Various state and local prohibition laws reduced that amount to 1.96 gallons per capita, for fifteen-year-olds and above, during the period from 1916 to 1919—the lowest level since 1870. President Herbert Hoover called the Eighteenth Amendment "a noble experiment," but he never learned how to fully enforce it. Since the repeal of Prohibition in 1933, the consumption of alcohol has been controlled by enforcement authorities ranging from a Liquor Control Commission to the Vermont State Police. The per capita absolute alcohol consumption today is not even close to the socially destructive levels of 1870. In fact, reactions to drunken driving in the

'80s and '90s generated public opinion against excessive consumption of alcohol so that legal and other sanctions against destructive behavior induced by excessive alcohol have risen once again to a prominent position on Vermont's political and legal agenda.

The willingness of three hundred Vermont women to attend a temperance meeting in St. Albans in the late winter of 1874 was not easily evoked in an era when women's public roles, especially in a rural region of the country, were still ruled by traditional expectations of domesticity. The public activities of Vermont's women in the temperance movement and in the suffrage campaigns, efforts that perhaps never drew more than 2,000 women at a time to their ranks, were important contributors in shaping modern Vermont. The skills of organizing and speaking in public—sometimes to hostile audiences—and of marshalling energies and emotions to a socially valuable purpose were acquired in ways that defined such skills thereafter as standard equipment in the arsenal of any campaign for women's rights.

The world war fought in by Americans in Europe from 1917 to 1918 and a natural disaster at home—the Great Flood of 1927—were two events of the early twentieth century that stand out in the story of Vermont. Vermont produced no military folk heroes in World War I. During the Spanish-American War almost twenty years earlier, however, naval power proved that Vermont, even without a coastline, could produce prominent naval leaders. Admiral George Dewey, a Montpelier native, gave a command to his chief executive officer—"Fire when ready, Gridley"—on August, 13, 1898, and American warships reduced the Spanish fleet to junk without losing a single man at the Battle of Manila Bay. Admiral George Clark of Bradford, meanwhile, steamed at flank speed around Cape Horn to join the Atlantic Squadron and smash the Spanish again at Santiago, Cuba.

Though no international fame or glory came to Vermonters later in the First World War, Ver-

Right
A photographer shot this store window in Montpelier in the early 1900s. Back in those days health-conscious Vermonters were urged to take "the road to Wellville" by eating Postum and Grapenuts. Today they are more likely to eat tofu and granola. Courtesy, Vermont Historical Society

Facing page
John Dewey was born in Burlington, where his father was proprietor of a grocery store and tobacco shop. Dewey began his study of philosophy at the University of Vermont, and later went on to obtain a PhD from John Hopkins University. He taught for forty years at the University of Chicago and Columbia University, eventually achieving renown as a pragmatic philosopher whose educational theories laid the foundation for the twentieth century progressive education movement. Original of portrait by Edwin B. Child (1929) in Billings Library, University of Vermont. Courtesy, Vermont Historical Society

Above
Vermonters' hearts swelled with pride when Admiral George Dewey, a Montpelier native, moved his squadron to the Philippines and destroyed the Spanish fleet in the Battle of Manila Bay in August 1898. Every Vermont schoolboy could quote the admiral's famous command to his chief executive officer, "Fire when ready, Gridley!" Dewey was treated to a hero's welcome on his return home. Bands played, flags waved, and crowds cheered all over the state. Courtesy, Hathaway & Turner

Facing page, top
Admiral George Dewey of Montpelier was acclaimed a hero in Vermont when he defeated the Spanish fleet in the Battle of Manila on August 15, 1898. On the same day Vermont infantry-

men who had sat out an incredibly hot summer in Georgia, suffering from dysentary, food poisoning, and malaria, rejoiced when they received orders to return home. Courtesy, Vermont Historical Society

Facing page, bottom
Farm work that would ordinarily have been done by men was performed by members of the Woman's Land Army during the First World War. This picture of the "Brattleboro Unit of Farmerettes" appeared in a 1919 issue of The Vermonter *magazine. Courtesy, Brooks Memorial Library*

mont as a community responded to the nation's call with the same commitment it had shown during the Civil War. Anticipating Washington's call for men in early 1917, Governor Horace Graham instructed the listers of Vermont's towns to enroll all able-bodied males between the ages of eighteen and forty-five as liable for military duty. The method was the same as that Governor Erastus Fairbanks employed at the beginning of the Civil War. Fairbanks' successors, Governors Frederick Holbrook and John Gregory Smith, continued using the structure of town governments to raise troops for the federal army throughout the Civil War, even resisting efforts of the federal government to impose a provost marshall system to conduct the federal levy. In World War I, however, the federal government took some of its first giant leaps of expansion. In a single day, June 5, 1917, under the national direction of Provost Marshall General Crowder in Washington, Governor Horace Graham in Montpelier supervised by telephone and telegraph the Selective Service registration of 27,244 Vermonters.

With the call-up of Vermont's National Guard regiment, in addition to volunteers and draftees, a total of 17,000 of Vermont's men and women served in World War I, most of the army personnel with the Twenty-Sixth or Yankee Division, and others in the Marine Corps and Navy. Vermonters also served in foreign armies during the First World War, with almost 150 of them in the Canadian Army. Vermonters experienced 2,000 casualties. Many succumbed after the Armistice of November 10, 1918, from the influenza epidemic that swept Europe and America in 1919.

In less than twenty months Vermont raised a war effort of substantial size in materials as well as manpower. Agricultural productivity increased and, except when national building industry declines cut into demands for marble and granite, Vermont's industrial production grew— especially in textiles and munitions manufactured for war supplies.

When Johnny came marching home again after

Above
Poet Robert Frost considered Vermont and New Hampshire to be "the two best states in the Union". Born in California, he became famous as a New England sage. He wrote of endurance, toughness, loneliness, and compassion, expressing profound ideas in the simple colloquial speech of rural New England. Frost moved to Vermont in 1919, living first in Shaftsbury and later in Ripton. Photo by Clara Sipprell. From Moment of Light by Clara Sipprell. Courtesy, Harper & Row, New York, and Special Collections, University of Vermont

Facing page, top
After he became President of the United States Calvin Coolidge still enjoyed visits with old friends and relatives in Plymouth Notch. In this picture "Cal" and his wife Grace relax with some of the locals on the front steps of the Plymouth Post Office and General Store. Courtesy, Vermont Historical Society

Facing page, bottom
On August 3, 1923, a milk train with one private Pullman car attached to it pulled into the North Bennington station. A large crowd turned out to catch a glimpse of the new President, Calvin Coolidge, on his way to Washington. Courtesy, Vermont Historical Society

the war, he came to a Vermont characterized in American popular culture by W.D. Griffith's silent film *Way Down East*. Though its title suggested Maine, Griffith shot the film starring Lillian Gish on location at White River Junction in 1919. Vermont was presented to the American moviegoer of the 1920s as a place of "solid Yankee farmers" who lived by a harsh moral and social code based on Holy Scripture.

Robert Frost first lived in New Hampshire after returning to New England from self-exile in old England. The 1914 publication of his *North of Boston*, a landmark in the history of American poetry, brought laconic New England idioms and understated rhythms to the center stage of American poetic practice. The character Silas, in Frost's 1904 *Death of the Hired Man*, for example, is a sensitive treatment of the New England hired hand of the turn of the century and, in Silas's blend of pride and dependency, a perceptive image of the working man in general. Frost brought young poets to the meadows and mountains of Vermont, though, by being an active early participant in the Breadloaf writers conference at Middlebury. Vermont, he admitted, was also a good place to live. Frost later moved to Ripton, where he starred annually at the summer Breadloaf School.

After the death of President Warren Harding and the full exposure of his scandal-ridden administration in 1923, the United States was ready to "Keep Cool with Coolidge." Vice-President Calvin Coolidge took over the presidency of the United States in early August 1923, after Harding died of an embolism in San Francisco. Coolidge, on vacation at his father's farm in Plymouth Notch, Vermont, was sworn in as president by his own father in the parlor of the family homestead. Taking Stephen Douglas' advice to heart, Coolidge had left Vermont as a young man to attend Amherst College. He then became a lawyer and the mayor of Northampton, Massachusetts. As Governor of Massachusetts during the Boston police strike of 1919, he attracted national attention and earned a place on the Republican

ticket with Harding in 1920. Coolidge's rise to the peak of American political power was a series of calculated moves in which he cunningly exploited his reputation for frugality and few words, sometimes with an obviously contrived image of the Yankee farmer. He frequently visited Vermont in the summer, returning to the family farm in Plymouth where he primly displayed for photographers and journalists his rusty farming skills in haying and milking. Under his overalls or farmer's smock, a sharp eye could nevertheless detect a fine linen shirt, city trousers, a pair of lawyer's wingtips, and sometimes even a tie. "Silent Cal's" personality seems to have been what the nation wanted after the ugliness of the Harding scandals, for the Republicans nominated Coolidge unanimously in 1924 and the American people turned him into one the most popular presidents they ever selected.

Chester A. Arthur, an earlier president (1881 to 1884), had also been born in Vermont, but young Arthur's brief stay in his Fairfield birthplace in 1830 was only slightly shorter than his presidential tenure. A New York City lawyer in the post-Civil War era, Arthur's loyalty to the Republican Party earned him the Vice-Presidential running mate's position with James A. Garfield. When President Garfield was shot and killed four months after the inauguration, Arthur

brought his charming married daughter as hostess to the White House and enjoyed a taste of champagne and elegant dinners for the remaining forty-four months of his tenure.

American political life found Vermont allied with the Republican Party from the Civil War until the post-World War II era. On the national scene a figure like Coolidge, though he left Vermont at a young age, caused popular wisdom to connect Vermont with quiet independence and the Grand Old Party. Coolidge's concise statement in 1928 when he declined renomination— I do not choose to run for President in 1928— seemed to many a perfect emblem of the Vermont way.

Two long-serving Vermont members of the United States Congress in the last half of the nineteenth century seem in retrospect more closely allied with the political and social values at work in Vermont well into the twentieth century. George Edmunds of Richmond served in the Senate from 1866 to 1899, and Justin Morrill of Strafford served in the House from 1854 to 1864 and the Senate from 1867 to 1898. Edmunds and Morrill stood in the American political scene as figures of solid respectability. Many of his contemporaries believed Edmunds saved the nation from another Civil War during the Hayes-Tilden presidential election controversy in 1876. Morrill early in his career mastered the rules of Congressional strategy. His record included gaining successful passage of the Land Grant Act of 1862, on which today's American public university system is based, and persistence in completing both the Library of Congress and the Washington Monument, the latter according to the original obelisk design of George Perkins Marsh of Woodstock, Vermont. In Morrill's later years as Senator from Vermont, he opposed the Spanish-American War and the annexation of Puerto Rico and the Philippines. His conscientious resistance to the imperialistic impulses of national Republican Party leadership led him into conflict with fellow Vermonter Redfield Proctor.

Natural skepticism ought to exact a reasonable

Above
This fine example of Gothic Revival architecture, located in the village of Strafford, was designed by Justin Smith Morrill, who served forty-four years as a United States Representative and Senator. In 1857 Morrill became chief sponsor of the Land Grant Act. Passage of this significant act in 1862 led to the establishment of a system of state-supported agricultural, scientific, and industrial colleges. Courtesy, Vermont Travel Division

Facing page
A replica of the small parsonage in Fairfield in which President Chester A. Arthur was born in 1830 was erected by the state in 1954. Although Arthur came into office burdened by the scandal of Garfield's assassination, his administration was an honorable one. He refused to bring the spoils system into national government, and backed a civil service reform bill that passed in 1883. Courtesy, Vermont Historical Society

Right
Republican legislator Justin Morrill of Strafford served twelve years in Washington in the House of Representatives and almost thirty-two years in the Senate.
From the Wilbur Collection. Courtesy, Bailey/Howe Library, University of Vermont

discount on the image of modern Vermont Republicans as taciturn mossbacks. In the case of Coolidge, we need only remember that he was the first President in the age of public relations and image creating. Morrill, on the other hand, while no rhetorical wizard, bluntly opposed the expansion of American power on moral grounds. As Tom Bassett remarked, Morrill, whose Strafford home stands today as one of Vermont's best examples of domestic Gothic architecture, was for fifty years of public life Vermont's premier Victorian. During the boom times of the 1920s, Coolidge, though never himself a business leader, was favorably disposed to business in America. Morrill as Vermont's tower of moral respectability criticized President William McKinley's intentions in 1898 "to take them all [from Spain] and to educate the Filipinos, and uplift and civilize and Christianize them." Unlike his President, the Senator from Vermont knew that the Philippines had been Christian for 300 years.

The fact that Vermont remained loyal to the Republican Party for nearly 100 years, even in the face of Franklin Delano Roosevelt's landslide of 1936, is not a simple issue. The pre-World War I development of an increasingly influential dairy industry, the growth of various state agencies—in agriculture, education, highways, and wildlife conservation—all led to an increasingly powerful centralized government at the expense of local autonomy. Ironically, in a one-party state a variety of interests were served.

After World War I the Great Flood of 1927 exercised profound and long-reaching effects on the economic, social, and political makeup of Vermont. In 1927 New England experienced one of the rainiest Octobers on record. Two days of especially heavy rainfall through November 3rd and 4th caused flooding throughout Vermont's river valleys. Houses were destroyed, whole herds of cattle drowned, thousands of acres of agricultural land spoiled, and much of the state's

transportation network ruined. Eighty-five people died, including Lieutenant Governor Hollis-
ter Jackson, who was swept from his feet by the
flooded Potash Brook in Barre.

Faced with a monumental rebuilding job,
Governor John E. Weeks called the General Assembly into special session and requested an appropriation of over $8,000,000 to reconstruct
roads, bridges, and other government facilities
throughout the state. As in World War I and the
Civil War, state government played a role that
de-emphasized the traditional idea of local autonomy in dealing with disasters or emergencies.

Above
*Turbulent waters ripped up
roads, railroad tracks, and
bridges in the 1927 flood, leaving behind heaps of rubble and
immobilizing transportation for
months. One thousand two
hundred fifty-eight bridges were
destroyed or severely damaged.
In the flood's aftermath, millions of state and federal dollars
went toward building new
bridges and an improved highway system. Many of the state's
railroads, which had to rely on*

*private investors to finance re-
pairs, were never rebuilt. Courtesy, Vermont Historical Society*

Facing page
*Fifty-five lives were lost in the
basin of the Winooski River and
its tributaries during the flood
of 1927. This picture was taken
on Webster Avenue in Barre,
where four people drowned.
Rescues were made by throwing
ropes from the top of the oil tank,
visible at left. Courtesy, Vermont Historical Society*

The State Highway Board, not town selectmen, decided to reconstruct Vermont's road and highway system with hard-surfaced roads. Destruction to Vermont's railway system, on the other hand, received less attention from state government. While the St. Johnsbury and Lake Champlain Railroad received a state loan for repairs, other rail lines either went without repairs and were abandoned, or they sought private funding to rebuild bridges and roadbeds. The highways, moreover, were funded for the first time by long-term bonds. Giving up "pay-as-you-go" policies and turning to bonds, Vermont established another public policy that strengthened central government. Even the office of governor was affected. John Weeks, after shifting 180 degrees on "pay-as-you-go" in order to secure immediate funding to repair flood damages, also broke with the long-standing single-term tradition. He was the first governor to serve two terms since 1841 and the first two-term governor since the biennial term act of 1870.

Maintenance of new hard-top roads required a state income tax, passed in 1931 in the very depths of the Great Depression. When in 1933 the General Assembly passed the "worthy debtor" law to provide debt relief to small business and farms, as historian H. Nicholas Muller pointed out, it should have been apparent to political observers that "moss-backed conservatism" was not the order of the day in Vermont. Myths die hard, however, and sometimes they are kept alive even when reality has left them far behind. Though she served in the 1931 General Assembly as Vermont's only female Senator, Consuelo Northrup Bailey said in 1976 that Governor Weeks had told President Coolidge in 1927 that despite the widespread destruction of·the flood, "Vermont wants nothing. She will take care of herself." Bailey omitted noting that Weeks had asked and received from the federal government $2,600,000 in assistance at the same time

Right
Civilian Conservation Corps enrollees lived according to a somewhat spartan military regime, yet generally seemed to enjoy "roughing it" in Vermont. In return for building roads, dams, parks, ski areas, and bridges, they earned thirty dollars per month. In the depths of the Depression, the Vermont CCC program provided 40,868 young men from all over the United States with job-training, employment, and comaraderie. Courtesy, Vermont Historical Society

Facing page, right
Registered and practical nurses of the WPA Nurses Project extended nursing care to many rural communities. Although many Vermonters remained hostile to Roosevelt's New Deal programs, federal relief agencies stimulated a new awareness of pressing needs within the state in the fields of welfare, health, and education. Courtesy, Vermont Historical Society

Facing page, left
This Farm Security Administration photo from the 1930s is titled simply, Son of Woodcutter, Vermont. *During the 1930s there were those who claimed that Vermonters were so used to hard times that they never even noticed when the Depression set in. F.S.A. photo by Mydans. Courtesy, Vermont Historical Society*

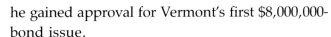

he gained approval for Vermont's first $8,000,000-bond issue.

As the Great Depression of the 1930s wore on Vermont found itself increasingly dependent on federal assistance for providing the social and public services its citizens needed. Yet to admit that its 350,000 people could not generate sufficient public monies to underwrite a modern society and government was not easy for some Vermonters. During his campaign for the United States Senate in 1934, for example, Warren Austin fiercely criticized the whole panoply of New Deal legislation. Still, some Vermonters saw that they could benefit from federal programs. Despite Austin's Senate vote against Roosevelt's Social Security Act, the first federal check issued by the Social Security program, in the amount of $22.54, went to Ida M. Fuller of Ludlow, Vermont. When the forester Perry Merrill of Montpelier saw that Vermont's forest and parks program could benefit from Civilian Conservation Corps (CCC) crews planting new forests, constructing park buildings, and erecting flood control dams to prevent another Flood of 1927,

he energetically coordinated state efforts to bring CCC camps and workers to Vermont. Nearly 70 years later, Vermonters profit from and enjoy the state's wise use of New Deal programs in which unemployed young men came from around the country to construct facilities at the ski area in Mount Mansfield Park and the Sand Bar Park on Lake Champlain.

The social, economic, and political processes that shaped Vermont from the Civil War to the 1930s seem, with the benefit of retrospect, inevitably to have produced a leader in the order of George D. Aiken. A successful horticulturist with a wildflower nursery serving a national market, Aiken was elected to the Vermont House from Putney, served as House Speaker, and then as lieutenant governor. In 1936 when Roosevelt beat Alf Landon in every state but Maine and Vermont, Aiken was elected governor. During his nine years in those state offices, Aiken ju-

diciously mixed the rhetoric of an "independent Vermonter" with a willingness to accept those federal programs that clearly benefitted Vermont. His early legislative work included a role in passing the income tax bill of 1931 and efforts on behalf of conservation and recreation. The frugality of his campaigns for office, even throughout his thirty-four years in the United States Senate, enhanced his image in Vermont. Yet Aiken knew that good roads were essential to Vermont's economic welfare, and he was willing to see the state spend money on them, especially if the federal government added its share. When the federal government proposed building the Green Mountain Parkway in 1935 down the backbone of the Green Mountains on the model of Virginia's Skyline Drive, however, Aiken carefully avoided the issue. Proponents claimed the Green Mountain Parkway would create much needed jobs and attract tourists. The federal government would pay 97 percent of the costs. Opponents said it would blight the landscape and be too expensive. Aiken saw the dispute over this issue not worth his risk. When questioned on it he was decidedly neutral: "I am sure it would not do the harm its opponents claim it would, nor would it do as much good as its proponents claim." Soon a popular referendum settled the issue: 12,500 more Vermonters were against the Parkway than were for it.

The general election of 1936 posed Burlington Democrat Alfred Heininger against Republican Aiken. Federal vs. state control was a major issue. Aiken showed he could calculate the best interests of Vermont. Suspecting that a federal land retirement plan had little chance of success as it was then proposed, Aiken attacked it on the grounds that the federal government might gain too much control over Vermont affairs. His support for the Old Age Pension, however, was a foxy attack on the pension bill in the Vermont Senate for its niggardly provision for weekly payments of $2.75. Heininger was the bill's author. Instead Aiken wanted the "federal government [to] bear a much larger proportion of the expense."

George Aiken extended his prominence from Vermont to the nation after his election to the United States Senate in 1940, an office he held until 1975. He represented, like the state that lifted him to leadership in the 1930s, a combination of intelligence and values that continued to assert the importance of the individual in an increasingly complex world. Aiken's remark about the Vietnam War—we should declare victory and go home—is often quoted in discussions of the war and the 1970s. As a Vermonter whose service to his town of Putney, his state, and the nation spanned over fifty years, he might be best remembered for his work in designing the Federal Food Stamp Program, in his mind a way both to help individuals in need of aid and to provide assistance to farmers in selling their products. The idea was Aiken's. The source of his experience was Vermont.

Facing page
The flooding of Vermont's rivers in 1927 caused over thirteen million dollars of damage. To assure that such a disaster could never happen again, Vermont embarked on a federally-funded flood control program. Throughout the thirties the Army Corps of Engineers and the Civilian Conservation Corps built a series of seven dams. Workers at Wrightsville Dam are pictured constructing a rock spillway in March 1935. Courtesy, Vermont Historical Society

Above
Perhaps more than any Vermonter of this century, George D. Aiken embodied the values and qualities that have come to represent the essence of Vermont. Aiken's independent thinking, commonsense wisdom, and down-to-earth humor earned the respect and affection of Republicans and Democrats alike. He served his state and country, first as Governor, then as United States Congressman and Senator from 1936 to 1974. When he retired at the age of eighty-two, the "Governor," as he was addressed in Vermont, claimed he wouldn't miss Washington at all: "Home's up on the mountains in Vermont." Photo by Sanders Milens

World War II
and the Mid
Twentieth Century

T he impact of World War II on Vermont was of the order of earlier powerful events such as the Civil War and the Flood of 1927. Human resources were efficiently mustered in response to urgent calls from Montpelier and Washington. Economic resources were also generously devoted to the cause of defeating Fascism in Europe and Imperial Japan in the far reaches of the Pacific Ocean. Lives were lost, as in those earlier events, and social arrangements, especially in political affairs, were revised when the veterans returned from the war.

Vermont entered the conflict even before Congress officially declared war on Japan, Italy, and Germany. In September 1940 President Franklin Delano Roosevelt called the National Guard into federal service. The Vermont National Guard's 172nd Infantry Regiment went to Camp Blanding, Florida, for training in March 1940. In order to pay a state bonus to guardsmen on federal service, the General Assembly declared a state of "Armed Conflict" on September 11, 1941. Assigned as a unit of the 43rd Division, the 172nd

Infantry Regiment sailed in late 1942 from California on the USS *Calvin Coolidge*, destination: New Zealand. Despite a mine sinking the *Coolidge* in the New Hebrides Islands, the 43rd, commanded by General Leonard "Red" Wing of Rutland, fought in New Georgia, Munda, and the bloody battle for Guadalcanal. Known as the "Winged Victory" Division for their commander, the 43rd, including the renamed 172nd Infantry Combat Team, which was reduced to 40 percent Vermonters by 1944, also caught the attention of the Japanese propaganda broadcaster "Tokyo Rose." She called them the "Munda Butchers." On January 9, 1945, with Vermonters by then reduced to 25 percent of their original strength in the 172nd, the "Winged Victory" 43rd Division participated in the battle for the Philippines, assaulting the beach at Lingayen Gulf.

Before the Japanese surrender on September 2, 1945, ended World War II, nearly 50,000 Vermonters had served in various branches of the

Above
The Phineas Smith house in Arlington, built in 1829, was designed by a Troy, New York, architect. The house was later purchased by the Canfield family and eventually became the Martha Canfield Library. Its stepped gables and four chimneys show the influence of the Hudson River Valley style. Various other examples of architecture that reflect the Dutch impact on Vermont are located in the southwest portion of the state. Courtesy, Vermont Historical Society

Facing page, top
Soldiers from the Tenth Mountain Division received rigorous training on the slopes of Mount Rainier in Washington before being dispatched to Europe in World War II. Between 300 and 400 of these men were Vermonters. On February 18 and 19, 1945, soldiers from the

85th, 86th, and 87th Regiments of the Division took Riva Ridge, then went on to the town of Monte Belvedere in Italy, and led the drive to eventual defeat of the Germans on May 2. In a three month period the three regiments suffered heavy casualties, with 993 men killed and 4,000 wounded. Courtesy, Sewall Williams and New England Chapter 10th Division Association

Facing page, bottom
Taking part in a 1945 celebration in front of the State House in honor of Major General Leonard Wing of Rutland were Mrs. Mortimer Proctor, wife of the governor (left), and Mrs. Wing (right). Major General "Red" Wing, recipient of the Distinguished Service Medal, had served as commander of the 43rd Infantry Division in some of the most bitter battles of the Pacific. Courtesy, Vermont Historical Society

Facing page, top
During the war years a number of popular movie stars made whirlwind appearances at War Bond rallies throughout the state. At this 1942 rally in Montpelier, participants included (left to right) Governor William Wills, actress Ann Rutherford, and actor Charles Laughton. At a similar rally in Brattleboro, fans were thrilled when film star Dorothy Lamour gave her lacy handkerchief to the purchaser of a $2,000 war bond. Courtesy, Vermont Historical Society

Facing page, bottom
Before boarding the bus that would carry them to a performance at the 1939 World's Fair, members of the Vermont Symphony Orchestra posed for a farewell picture. Violinist Lou Levy, pictured stifling a laugh in the center of the photo, was still playing with the orchestra at its Fiftieth Anniversary celebration in 1985. The Vermont Symphony Orchestra was organized by Dr. Alan Carter in 1934, and gained recognition and support from the Vermont Legislature in 1939, thus becoming the first "State Symphony" in the country. Courtesy, Vermont Symphony Orchestra

Above
Ernest W. Gibson is treated by Private Albert S. Tammario for a head wound received during a Japanese bombing raid on Rendova Island in the Pacific during World War II. This picture appeared in newspapers throughout the country with Gibson identified as a former United States Senator. Courtesy, Gibson Family Papers, Wilbur Collection, University of Vermont

armed forces in every theater of action. As a percentage of the state's population, Vermont's manpower contribution to World War II exceeded by 2 percent the enormous levy of men for the Civil War. In the Second World War, however, Vermont lost only 1,233 out of 3,870 casualties.

The homefront in Vermont was also heavily mobilized. Fort Ethan Allen in Colchester was a scene of busy war preparations, as it had been in World War I. Shelburne Shipyards was the construction site for patrol torpedo boats that were sent off to the Pacific theater. With an appropriation of $35,000 from the legislature, Governor William H. Wills organized twelve companies of home guard by June 23, 1941, consisting of 111 officers and 1,361 men.

When the GIs returned to Vermont after the war, changes began to occur in the Green Mountain State. A major revision in the political order of Vermont was effected by the election to gov-

Above
In April 1940 Governor George Aiken (center), with Company Commander Gerald Potts, reviewed CCC Company 1141 in Bellows Falls. Aiken frequently attacked New Deal philosophy, but "heartily" approved of the CCC program, which poured millions of federal dollars into conservation projects and development of state forests. Courtesy, Vermont Historical Society

Facing page
An antiquated machine at a southern Vermont mill malfunctions and spews out yards of wrinkled paper. Plants such as this struggle to survive in competition with larger more modern corporations. The small village mill is fast disappearing from the banks of Vermont's streams. Those still in operation are often owned by out-of-state companies. Photo by Jill Noss

ernor of war veteran Ernest J. Gibson, Jr., of Brattleboro. A long-time friend of Senator George Aiken, Gibson had briefly occupied the United States Senate seat left vacant by his father's death in June 1940 before entering the army in 1941. On November 5, 1940, George Aiken was elected to the elder Gibson's Senate seat, a position he held until retirement in 1975, as Ernest, Jr., prepared to go off to war. Back in civilian life five

years later, Gibson campaigned in 1946 against incumbent Governor Mortimer Proctor in pursuit of the Republican nomination for governor. Gibson defeated Proctor, the last of the marble dynasty to hold a major public office in Vermont, by attacking the Republican "establishment" as a lifeless elite—"a study in still life." Gibson's election to governor brought legislative actions on a minimum salary and a retirement fund for teachers, a graduated income tax, and a state police force. When offered a seat on the federal court bench by President Harry Truman in 1950, however, Gibson resigned halfway through his second term as governor.

By the 1950s certain developments began to indicate that Vermont was on the brink of a major departure from the patterns of life, economics, and politics that had organized the Green Mountain State since the Civil War. From 1910 to 1920 the United States Census returns had shown that Vermont had been losing its population by nearly 3,000 people. From 1930 to 1940 population again fell, by about 400. Migration and a low birth rate were taking their toll. From the end of World War II until 1950, however, Vermont's population grew by 15,000, the highest growth since before the Civil War. Most of this growth was attributable to the veterans' baby boom. From 1960 to 1980 the greatest expansion in modern Vermont's population came as the Green Mountain State reported 511,000 residents in the 1980 census.

As the population of the state grew toward a half million, patterns of work and employment changed. Where the extractive marble and granite industries, on one hand, and agriculture, on the other, once occupied most of Vermont's work force, by the last quarter of the twentieth century some of Vermont's largest single employers were now the state government, International Busi-

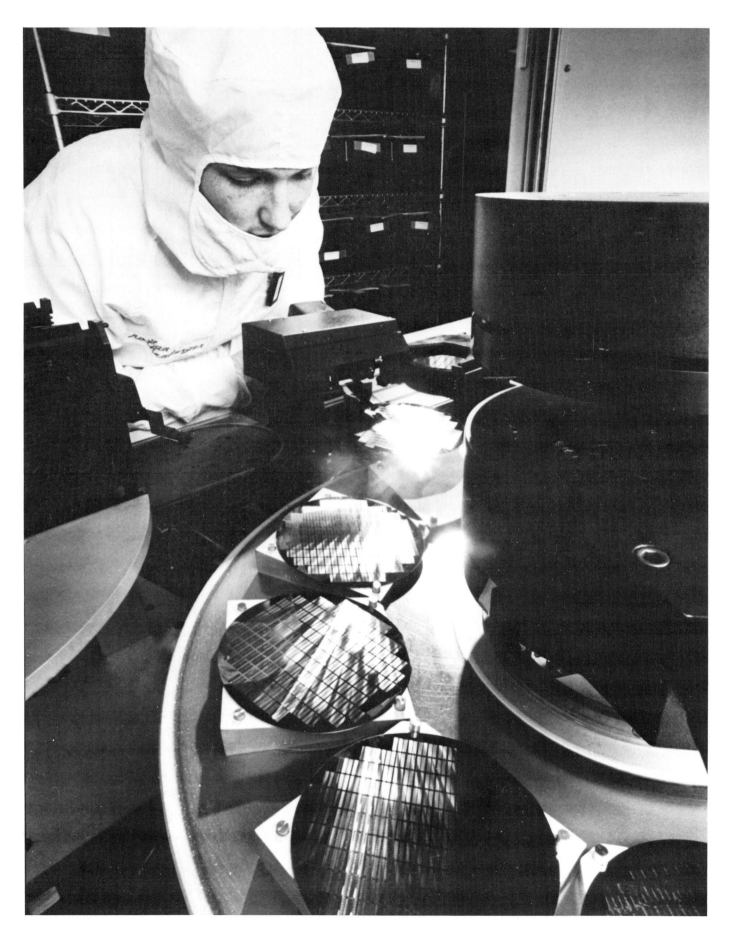

Facing page
An IBM manufacturing employee in Essex Junction checks the motion of a robotic arm as it positions silicon wafers that will become computer memory chips. Each of the new chips, which were developed at the company's Vermont facility, can store up to 256,000 bits of data. Courtesy, IBM Corporation

Right
Two dairy farm management students work toward fulfilling their required number of hours in Vermont Technical College's modern milking parlor. Although the number of dairy farms in the state has been declining ever since 1950, the average size of dairy herds and the production of milk has been increasing. Courtesy, Vermont Technical College

ness Machines in Essex Junction, the University of Vermont in Burlington, General Electric in Burlington and Rutland, and Digital in South Burlington. These public and private enterprises each employed from 2,000 to over 6,000 people. Vermont's dairy farms, meanwhile, declined to 11,000 units by 1950 at the beginning of a downward trend in the number of farms, though not in milk production. By 1985, in fact, Vermont contained fewer than 3,000 dairy farms, and the State Department of Agriculture predicted that 1,500 dairy farms would be operating by the year 2000. In 1985, however, Vermont's annual production of milk constituted 41 percent of all the milk produced in New England for the great Boston milk market. Even as the number of farms decreased, the size of dairy herds grew from an average of twenty-five cows to sixty, and the average dairy farm more than doubled its acreage between 1950 and 1985.

The greatest surge in population growth occurred between 1970 and 1980, a decade adding 121,391 people to Vermont. Equally distinctive of the post-World War II period, however, was the shift in areas of population density to the western side of the Green Mountains. In 1940 Burlington, Rutland, Bennington, Brattleboro, and Barre were the leading population centers. By 1980, the densest population centers had shifted to Burlington, Rutland, Bennington, Essex, and Colchester, and slightly over half of the state's population lived in the western counties.

Political changes in Vermont after World War II also distinguished the next forty years from earlier periods. Ernest Gibson's 1946 defeat of the last Proctor to hold public office marked the rise of a new crop of young Republicans, including Sterry Waterman, Winston Prouty, and Consuelo Northup Bailey, to prominent positions in the party. Bailey became the nation's first female lieutenant governor in 1955. Unlike the post-Civil War Republican Party in Vermont, however, these new faces and names in statewide political affairs exerted no singular force in directing Vermont's public agenda. The way was thus left open for the previously less powerful Democrats. As the fifties and sixties began, Democrats began to win major public offices, sometimes the first in over a century. William H. Meyer, for example, was the first Vermont

Democrat elected to the United States Congress in over one hundred years in 1958. That same year saw Republican Robert Stafford win the gubernatorial election from Bernard Leddy, a Burlington Democrat, by only 719 votes after a recount. In 1962 Philip H. Hoff of Burlington was elected the first Democratic governor of Vermont in 108 years. Patrick Leahy's election to the United States Senate in 1974 sent Vermont's first Democrat to the upper house of the Congress since the founding of the Republican Party in 1854.

The office of governor during the years 1950 to 1985 clearly reflects the major changes occurring in the life of Vermont during these years. In addition to electing the first Democrat to governor in over 100 years, Vermonters kept Hoff in office for three terms (1962 to 1968), an unprec-

An abandoned plow beside a sign advertising one of Vermont's resorts emphasizes the disparity between a vanishing agrarian way of life and the development of former farm acres for year-round recreational use. Tourism—the state's fastest growing industry—provides jobs for many Vermonters. As resorts develop, however, sharply rising property values mean that average wage-earners often find themselves unable to afford to continue living in their own towns. Photo by Jeff Axelrod. Courtesy, Vermont Natural Resources Council

edented modern tenure of office for a governor. Then in the 1970s Republican Richard Snelling of Shelburne was reelected for four terms (1976 to 1984). Of the nine governors elected between 1950 and 1985, six were Republicans and three were Democrats, clearly a break in the eighty-year hegemony of the Republican Party after the Civil War. Moreover, while for eighty years only eleven of thirty-four governors were lawyers,

Above
Between January and April of each year 150 members of the Vermont House of representatives convene in this Greek Revival chamber beneath an ornate Victorian chandelier. In 1985 nearly 30 percent of these legislators were women. Courtesy, Vermont Department of Tourism and Marketing

Right
United States Senator Robert Stafford is pictured holding granddaughter in Enosburg. Republican Stafford served as Vermont Governor from 1958 to 1961, as a United States Congressman between 1960 and 1971, and was a United States Senator until 1988. Courtesy, Senator Stafford's Office

Facing page
Philip Hoff, Democrat, of
Burlington was elected gover-
nor of Vermont in 1962. He
served as the first Democratic
governor of Vermont in over
100 years. Hoff's six years as
governor marked the entrance
of the Democratic party as a
force on the Vermont modern
political scene. Courtesy,
Philip Hoff

Above
Since its founding in Putney in
1932, the Experiment in Inter-
national Living now known as
World Learning, has excelled
in promoting international
understanding through cultural
exchange and educational
programs. In 1962 The Experi-
ment established its present
headquarters in Brattleboro
and subsequently added a

degree-granting academic div-
ision, the School for Interna-
tional Training, and a field
division, Projects in Interna-
tional Development and Training.
The convivial student group
pictured above exemplifies
founder Donald Watt's belief
that "people learn to live
together by living together."
Photo by Nanci Leitch. Cour-
tesy, World Learning.

since 1950 six governors have been lawyers, two came from industry, and one was a journalist. Two post-World War II governors have also been foreign born: Joseph Johnson (1954-1958) of Springfield was born in Sweden; Madeleine Kunin (1984-1990) of Burlington was born in Switzerland. Only three of Vermont's nine governors since 1950 were born in Vermont. Governor Kunin was the first woman to hold the highest elected office in Vermont.

The expansion of available leisure time and a huge recreation industry to satisfy America's vacation needs were two new factors in the development of post-World War II Vermont that marked a major departure from life in an earlier Vermont. Few Americans could have predicted in 1940 that thirty years later we would have constructed a national life providing large chunks of time devoted only to the pleasures of recreation and amusement. The formerly sleepy country villages of Stowe, Wilmington, Dover, Warren,

and Waitsfield had become major recreation centers for winter skiers and summer vacationers by 1970. As early as the 1870s Vermont had tried to attract city dwellers to the soft pastoral landscape of Vermont's summers and early autumns. Until the expansive popularity of skiing, however, the rugged Adirondacks of New York had drawn vacationers and hunting and fishing sportsmen from the southern regions of New York and New Jersey, while summer resorts in the White Mountains of New Hampshire attracted vacationers from eastern New England. Despite handsome and venerable inns like the Equinox House in Manchester and comfortable resorts on Lake Champlain, Vermont had only moderate success in developing itself into a major eastern vacation and recreation area until after World War II.

In 1934 when Vermont's first tow pulled two skiers up a hill in Woodstock the Vermont of 1985 was unimaginable. Indeed, the farming families of the Mad River Valley, for example, could not

Facing page
Governor Madeleine Kunin and Fish and Wildlife Commissioner Steve E. Wright are pictured on a canoe tour of the Winooski River. In 1985 Kunin broke new ground by becoming Vermont's first woman governor. She served as Lieutenant Governor from 1979 to 1983 and brought an outstanding legislative background to her position as chief executive of the state. Photo by Toby Talbot

Right
Street vendors, strollers, shoppers, and sidewalk cafes fill Burlington's Church Street Marketplace. Forming a backdrop to this busy scene is the First Unitarian Church, designed by Boston architect Peter Banner and built by local craftsmen in 1816. Courtesy, Church Street Marketplace District Commission

Above
The Ticonderoga *is the last re-maining vertical beam side-wheel steamer in the world. Built at Shelburne shipyard in 1906, this venerable steamer traveled the waters of Lake Champlain for nearly fifty years. The Ti-conderoga was retired from service in 1953. The 862-ton steamboat was carried two miles overland on a double set of rail-road tracks to its final destina-tion at the Shelburne Museum in 1955. Courtesy, Vermont Travel Division*

Far right
In January 1934 the first tow in the United States—a circulat-ing rope powered by a Model T Ford engine—began hauling

skiers up a 900-foot pasture slope in Woodstock. This ingenious invention, which eliminated the arduous ordeal of having to climb uphill in order to ski downhill, launched a new era in winter sports. Courtesy, Ken Miner and the Woodstock Historical Society

Facing page
Over fifty years later advanced technology has provided Ver-mont's thirty-one ski areas with easy uphill transportation. The four passenger gondola at Kil-lington (pictured), which spans three and a half miles, is the longest ski lift in North Amer-ica. Photo by Bob Perry. Cour-tesy, Bob Perry and Killington Photos

have suspected the changes they would see in the next fifty years. In the Mad River Valley towns of Fayston, Warren, and Waitsfield fewer than a dozen working farms operated in 1985 where over one hundred had once stood. Only two working farms remain within the town limits of Warren's 27,392 acres. Waitsfield is the valley's commercial center, containing a dozen gourmet restaurants, banks, stock brokerage offices, computer outlets, a cable television company, a movie theater, and a supermarket. Four of five residential units on the tax rolls of Warren belong to absentee owners who spend vacation time in Vermont for the winter skiing; the usual Vermont summer activities of hiking, fishing, and swimming; or the imported suburban pursuits of tennis and golf. Why do they come to Warren, Killington, Stratton, or Stowe—summer and winter? "I garden, hike, see friends, swim," said a New York clothing de-

signer who owns a house in Warren. "It's green . . . and the birds sing, and the sky spans from one end of the valley to another."

By 1970, however, it had become clear to Governor Deane Davis and others that the new and successful attractiveness of Vermont as a place for recreation also contained the seeds for destroying the very features of the countryside that drew rapidly increasing numbers of Americans and Canadians to the Green Mountain State. Problems developed that no one initially foresaw. Large second-home developments constructed in previously tiny rural communities needed waste disposal systems that would not pollute local water supplies. Above certain altitudes, the fragile soil structures of mountains faced destruction from road and other building work. Vacation cottages were soon converted into year-round residences with consequent expec-

Left
As long as the state's major ski areas continue to expand into four-season resorts, second-home construction promises to keep booming. Some critics view multi-unit condominium projects as inappropriate to the Vermont landscape. Environmentalists express concern that the pace of second-home development is testing the limits of Vermont's land use and water quality regulations. Photo by Jeff Axlerod. Courtesy, Vermont Natural Resources Council

Facing page, bottom
Vermont Yankee Nuclear Power Station, located near the Connecticut River in Vernon, began commercial operation in 1972. The nuclear facility produces approximately 80 percent of the state's total electrical generation. Vermont's private utility companies have claimed that the energy provided by Vermont Yankee is more economical and safer than alternative sources. Courtesy, Vermont Yankee Nuclear Power Corporation

Right
Construction of approximately 300 miles of interstate highway in Vermont by 1970 greatly increased the accessibility of the state's recreation areas to out-of-staters. I-89 (pictured), the Vermont portion of which was completed in 1969, crosses Route 2 in Bolton. As construction of ski areas, recreation centers, and condominiums increases, some Vermonters complain that the interstate system is turning the state into a suburb of New York and Boston. Photo by Donald Wiedenmayer, Vermont Department of Highways. Courtesy, Vermont Historical Society

tations for public services—schools, police and fire protection, health care, and road maintenance—in areas where such services had previously been minimal or nonexistent. Wildlife habitat, uncluttered roadsides, and open land began to shrink in some central and southern regions of Vermont. Population centers of western Vermont and the Connecticut River Valley in the east sprouted strip developments along highways feeding city centers.

Vermont's legislative effort of 1970, Act 250, was the initial step in protecting natural resources. Despite criticism from development interests, Act 250 continues to regulate the orderly use of Vermont's land, water, and scenic resources. Additional protection efforts, including a statewide cleanup each May on "Greenup Day" and a returnable bottle law, have helped to maintain Vermont as a clean and pleasant place. With only minor amendments to expedite its administration, Act 250 stands as Vermont's hallmark in social planning and environmental protection. Over three hundred years of exploration, settlement, exploitation, and development have been

nothing if not a continuous parade of change. The changes in the landscape may be the most obvious. Almost 90 percent of Vermont was forested when Samuel de Champlain first journeyed into the region. By the mid-nineteenth century the forests had been almost fully cut off. In the late twentieth century, however, the forest had returned to cover nearly 80 percent of the land. Within the framework of that forested landscape over half a million people pursue lives that depend for their sustenance on agriculture, recreation, and the services and products of high technology that commonly characterize modern American life.

Despite the extent and depth of changes on the face of Vermont and the increase in the number of Vermonters, the qualities of independence and endurance so necessary in establishing the communities on which modern Vermont is based remain active features in today's Green Mountain State. Although the colonial power of France lost its foothold in Vermont over two hundred years ago, in the late twentieth century approximately one-quarter of northern Vermont's pop-

ulation can trace their roots to Francophonic Quebec. The United States Census for 1970 reported that nearly 10 percent of Vermont's population grew up hearing French spoken at home.

After the Abenaki lost control of lands in the Missisquoi region in legal battles with the Allen family in the 1780s, those native people remained a quiet, almost underground community through the nineteenth and much of the twentieth century. Just as other ethnic communities across the country began to develop pride and a sense of individual and group dignity based in traditional values of their communities, so in the 1970s the Abenaki of Vermont (estimated at approximately 2,000) developed and asserted a presence demonstrating that they, too, had endured and indeed survived three hundred years of changes in Vermont. In the Swanton-Highgate region, for example, the elected Abenaki Tribal Council oversees a community development agency that has established a day-care center and promoted education for tribal members through a Native American Program in Franklin County schools, as well as a General Equivalency Diploma progam for adults. The Abenaki Selfhelp Association built and operated an attractive low and middle-income housing project in Swanton and won competitive contracts for roadbuilding and other projects. Retaining their identity as an

indigenous people, the Abenaki are constructing their own way of being independent Vermonters.

Independence of spirit in Vermont is sometimes heard in exotic languages. It may be in the Russian pronouncements of exiled author Alexander Solzhenitsyn who resided in Vermont from 1974 until returning to Russia in 1994, or in the Latin plain chants of Benedictine or Trappist monks or the Buddhist prayers of Tibetan monks in the peace of their respective monasteries.

The enduring spirit of independent thought continued in Vermont, as it had since the eighteenth century, in March at the town meeting. The town meeting remained a vital forum to discuss issues both large and small. While financing roads and schools have been, and will continue to be, the central issues for towns to decide each year, large moral issues, such as slavery back in the 1850s, can also get a hearing. In 1984 the agendas of town meetings brought thou-

Above
The 369-foot covered railroad bridge in Swanton is the longest of its kind in the United States. Built by the St. Johnsbury & Lake Champlain Railroad in 1898, the double lattice trussed bridge carried heavy freight and passenger trains across the Missisquoi River for seventy years until its destruction by a vandal's fire in 1987. Photo by Sanders Milens. Courtesy, Preservation Trust of Vermont
Facing page, top
Ladies' Aid Societies have been organizing suppers to raise money for church-related causes for over a century now. Baked ham, baked beans, chicken pie, or potluck are standard fare at these gatherings. Townspeople and tourists come together to enjoy a hearty meal at the annual Fall Harvest Supper in Cabot (pictured). Courtesy, Vermont Travel Division

Facing page, bottom
Participatory democracy thrives in Vermont. Snow or shine, most villagers wouldn't think of missing the politics and sociability of their local town meeting, held annually in early March. Here oldtimers and newcomers assemble to discuss and vote on issues ranging from school budgets to road maintenance to environmental concerns. Debates are often lively and spiced with Vermont witticisms. Courtesy, Vermont Historical Society

sands of Vermonters to speak out for a freeze on the development of nuclear arms.

In his *Natural and Political History of Vermont* (London 1798), Ira Allen told us that he "contemplated the extent of the New Hampshire grants, and probable advantages that might arise by being contiguous to Lake Champlain, and determined to interest [himself] in that country as soon as able to ride." When Allen finally reached his destination on the banks of the Onion River after a skirmish with New York land agents he said:

I went up the open meadow where the blue joint grass . . . was thick till in sight of a large and lonely elm. Computing the open field about fifty acres, I was much pleased with this excursion, promising myself one day to be the owner of that beautiful meadow.

Modern archaelogists have taught us that the meadow Allen coveted was probably cleared by Abenaki who had maintained settlements on the river's banks in the centuries before Allen's ar-

rival. The blue joint grass and the lonely elm, the soft pastoral scenery of Vermont that excited Allen in 1773 continues to exert its appeal. As the New York clothing designer at her Mad River Valley home had described Vermont: "It's green, green, green!"

(Left) Brattleboro's Main Street has undergone significant changes since the mid-nineteenth century. An early stereoview shows a muddy street running through what appears to be a deserted town. (Below) By the 1880s Brattleboro's business district was prospering. The earlier elm was gone and the wooden buildings had been replaced by three- and four-story "blocks" sporting striped awnings. (Facing page, top) The automobile helped turn Brattleboro into a busy regional commercial center. Cars brought with them paved streets, traffic congestion, and parking problems. Courtesy, Brattleboro Photos (Facing page, bottom) Today's downtown Brattleboro, designated as an Historic District, retains many architectural features of a century ago. Photo by Harold A. Barry

Continuity and Change

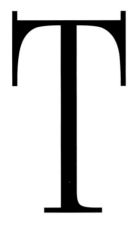

The rapid growth in Vermont's population, so noticeable in the decades following World War II, continued on to the end of the century. From 511,456 people in 1980, to 562,758 in 1990, the state grew to an estimated 605,068 residents in 2000. In each decade since 1960 the addition of another 50,000 people produced a robust population increase of 55.2 percent by the end of the century. Clearly, Vermont was changing.

What brought about these changes? Most important, and probably the least commented on, was the completion in 1977 of an interstate highway system linking Vermont to the large population centers in Massachusetts, Connecticut and New York. In 1960 a resident of Boston wishing to spend a long weekend at a vacation resort in northern Vermont had to drive for six or seven hours over two-lane country roads that twisted and turned with the contours of the mountains. The drive was beautiful, but daunting. Ten years later that same trip took only three and a half hours. People's perception of distance changed. Harried Boston office workers could jump in their

The Woolen Mill in Winooski, built as a textile mill in 1882 and renovated into 150 luxury apartments in the early 1980s, perhaps exemplifies what has been taking place in Vermont in the last quarter of the 20th century—a blending of old and new habits, occupations, styles, and values, creating a dynamic and innovative society. Courtesy, Vincent Feeney

The I-89 interstate highway near South Royalton passes through Vermont's unspoiled countryside, connecting New York City, Hartford, Connecticut, and Springfield, Massachussetts with north-western Vermont. Nearby I-91 brings visitors from the greater Boston area to north central Vermont. These two highways form the background for most of the changes which have taken place in Vermont in the last thirty years. Courtesy, Vermont Department of Tourism and Marketing

car on Friday evening and be at their mountain cabin in time for a late-night dinner. Or, they could move to Vermont and still easily get down to Hartford or New York City to visit friends or aging parents. For a number of years in the 1980s one enterprising academic taught filmmaking on Fridays at New York University, but lived the other six days of the week in South Burlington. This modernization in transportation revolutionized Vermont.

Another force bringing about change was the transformation in the way many people worked. The advent of personal computers, modems and faxes meant that increasingly some people could live and work wherever there was a phone line. By the 1990s it was not uncommon to find an investment counselor with clients all over the United States working out of a log home nestled in a brook-defined valley outside of Stowe or Killington. Just as the change in travel-time changed Vermont, so too did the new technology.

Yet, the changes in travel and technology would not have impacted Vermont as much without another factor at work—the growing perception in America after 1960 that the quality of urban life was declining. People increasingly frustrated with traffic jams, long lines at banks, bureaucratic government officials, and the everyday inconveniences

of big-city life, sought wistfully for a simpler way of living. For many of these restless urbanites moving to Vermont, with its picture post-card beauty, small villages, and relatively affordable real estate was the answer to their frustrations.

There is nothing more apparent in the Vermont population figures than that growth came more from migration from other states—and even other countries— than from births over deaths. Vermont is rapidly becoming a state inhabited by people from "away," as the old Vermonters say. In 1960, 79 percent of Vermonters were born in the state, a figure that dropped to 59 percent in 1990. There is even a small, but significant, Asian population in the Green Mountains as the state has actively participated in the federally-sponsored Refugee Resettlement Program. Today Asians make up almost one percent of the state's population, with most of them concentrated in and around Burlington. Bosnians have also recently come into Vermont in sizeable numbers.

Growth, however, has not been uniform. Chittenden County, home to the state university, the Fletcher-Allen Medical Center, St. Michael's College, and a number of the state's largest private employers, has witnessed the greatest growth. In 1960 the county had 74,425 residents, 131,761 in 1990 and an estimated 147,372 in 2000—

Right
Shoppers browse the farmer's market at City Hall Park in Burlington. With nowhere to expand, Burlington's population of 39,000 has changed little over the past few decades, but dramatic growth in the surrounding communities has made the "Queen City" the hub of a dynamic community. Courtesy, Vermont Department of Tourism and Marketing

an increase of almost 100 percent in 40 years. Counties surrounding Chittenden—Franklin, Grand Isle and Addison—have seen similar rates of increase, as better highways have made them a short commute away from Burlington-area jobs. But further away from Chittenden County, in the more remote corners of the state, particularly the fabled "Northeast Kingdom," population has either stagnated, or in some cases actually decreased. In those areas, where a hardscrabble

Below
Peter Clavelle, five-term mayor of Burlington, greets visitors at Waterfront Park. For years Burlington's shoreline on Lake Champlain was an eyesore collection of derelict buildings, old train tracks, and weed-choked

fields. Through public and private initiative this area has been turned into a scenic attraction, with public parks, restaurants, a boat house, sailing facilities and offices. Courtesy, Burlington City Hall

Below
Population growth in Chittenden County has brought new vitality and enthusiasm to the area. The Champlain Mill in Winooski, an old textile mill which ceased operations in the

1950s, was outfitted for adaptive reuse by local businessman Raymond Pecor, and in 1981 opened with numerous restaurants, shops and offices. Courtesy, Vincent Feeney

A bicyclist rides by the shores of Lake Iroquois in Hinesburg. Beginning in the 1980s Vermont became a popular destination for bicycle touring groups. Photo by Andre Jenny. Courtesy, Vermont Department of Tourism and Marketing

farming existence has been the norm rather than the exception, the lifestyle of an older Vermont continues to exist. Burlingtonians, with their close ties to Boston and New York, like to joke that the nicest thing about their city is that it's so close to Vermont.

There is some irony associated with this growth and this has not been lost on many Vermonters. While population increase and a robust economy through most of the 1980s and 1990s has meant more and better paying jobs, there has been a downside. Big-box retailers like Wal-Mart and Home Depot, watching the growth areas around the country, discovered Vermont in the 1990s. Within a few years, despite efforts in some communities to dissuade them, malls sprang up on the outside of traditional downtowns. Strip development, which began in the 1960s, has became commonplace in the more urban areas of Vermont. The Barre-Montpelier Road, Route 7 leading out of Burlington, and Route 7 in Rutland and Manchester, have the appearance of Anywhere, USA.

Vermonters have responded in a number of ways to this threat to their traditional lifestyle. Financed by a grant from the Orton Family Foundation in Rutland, concerned citizens organized the Vermont Forum On Sprawl to investigate its causes and the means to combat it. The conservation

movement has also stepped in to stem the tide of exploding development. In the last 20 years organizations like the Vermont Land Trust, the Vermont Nature Conservancy, and the Vermont Housing and Conservation Board, have put hundreds of thousands of acres either in the public domain, or restricted their use to agriculture or other low-impact activities. In the most notable recent acquisition, in 1998 the Conservation Fund of Arlington, Virginia, working with the Vermont Land Trust, acquired 133,000 acres of land in the Northeast Kingdom from Champion International, a logging company. The purchase guaranteed that this vast area would never be clear-cut, and that it would be forever open to the public for recreation.

But all the efforts by a concerned citizenry have been unable to stop a longstanding trend: the decline in working farms. In 1964 42.6 percent of the Vermont countryside was farmland. In 1992 that figure had declined to 21.6 percent. The landscape was changing, although it's worth pointing out that the production of milk—Vermont's principal agricultural product—has increased over the years. Larger herds of more efficient, and oftentimes smaller farms, were turning out more milk than ever. What was being lost was the small family farm.

Vermont dairy farmers, large and small, faced a serious crisis in the 1980s and early 1990s—the price which they received for milk in 1995 stood at the same level as in 1980, while costs had risen dramatically. Unless radical action was taken, Vermont was destined to go out of the dairy business. In 1996 Congress provided some assistance, allowing the six New England states to join in a dairy compact to set the price that milk processors were required to pay farmers for milk sold in the northeastern market. Despite protests from dairy states in the Midwest, the law went into effect in 1997. Beginning in August 1997 the average Vermont dairy farm's income increased by $1,500 a month. As long as the Dairy Compact continued, Vermont farmers could expect a reasonable return on their investment.

There has been one positive result in the reduction of farms: an increase in forest land. In the 19th century, farming increased at the expense of the wilderness. Old photographs from the 1860s and 1870s show whole mountainsides bared as a result of clearcutting. In 1870 only about 20 percent of the state was covered with forest, while in 1990 that figure had grown to 80 percent.

Increased forest land created an environment in which wildlife could thrive. The story of Vermont's moose population is one example. According to the Fish and Wildlife Department there were only about 20 moose in Vermont in 1960, all located in the northeastern county of Essex. In those days the sighting of one of these lumbering animals was a rare occurrence. By 1980 this number had increased to 200, although still primarily confined to Essex County. The estimate for the year 2000 is that there are 2,500 to 3,000 moose in the state, found everywhere except for Grand Isle County. They are now so abundant that signs are posted to warn speeding motorists of their presence.

Another animal that has made a dramatic comeback in recent years is the Eastern wild turkey. This once numerous bird had disappeared from the Green Mountains by 1920. To rectify this, in the late 1960s the Fish and Wildlife Department introduced a small flock of wild turkeys from upstate New York to the area around Pawlet, in west-central Vermont. Officials hoped that the turkeys would increase and spread to their traditional habitat in Bennington, Rutland, Windsor and Windham counties. The program far exceeded the expectations. Soon turkeys were visible every-

Above
In the late 19th century widespread logging and extensive farming cleared much of the forest from the Green Mountains. Today, as this Brookfield scene shows, Vermont is again blanketed with lush forests. Courtesy, Vermont Department of Tourism and Marketing

Bottom
Congressman Bernard "Bernie" Sanders campaigning in White River Junction, 1992. An Independent, Sanders' mayoral victory in Burlington in 1981 ushered in a dynamic era in the city's history, and eventually led to a seat in the U.S. House of Representatives. Photo by Chris McKinley. Courtesy, Congressman Sanders' Office

where. One could hardly pass a field in summer without noticing a few dozen gobblers pecking away. By the late 1990s there were an estimated 30,000 turkeys roaming the countryside.

While Vermont's landscape underwent subtle transformations, there were changes also taking place on the political scene. Possibly the most important was the coming to political prominence of Bernard "Bernie" Sanders. A native of Brooklyn, New York, in the 1970s Sanders was the perennial also-ran of Vermont politics, twice unsuccessfully running as a left-leaning candidate for the offices of governor and senator. In 1980, however, he was

In 1991 Lieutenant-Governor Howard Dean was suddenly called to be Vermont's chief executive when Governor Richard Snelling died unexpectedly of a heart attack. Dean subsequently won re-election four times, becoming one of Vermont's most popular governors. Photo by Jamie Cope. Courtesy, Vermont Department of Tourism and Marketing

the surprise victor over long-time incumbent Gordon Paquette in Burlington's mayoral race. A tireless and innovative mayor, he was re-elected three more times before becoming Vermont's sole congressman in 1990. An Independent, Sanders generally sides with the Democrats and leads a caucus of its more progressive members.

In 1983 Sanders supporters in Burlington organized the Progressive Party, with the hope of winning more influence at the state level. But in fact, with the exception of the Congressman himself, the Progressive Party has garnered little attention outside of Chittenden County, although there it remains quite strong. Two state representatives, Terrill Bouricius and Dean Corren, represent Burlington in the legislature, and Peter Clavelle, another Progressive, has been the mayor of Burlington for all but two years since Sanders left city hall. According to a number of polls, under the inspired leadership of the Progressive movement in the 1990s, Burlington emerged as one of the most desirable places to live in the United States.

Another "outsider" who has made a strong impact on the political scene is Howard Dean, governor since 1991. Like Sanders, Dean was born and raised in New York, was then educated at Yale, and in 1978 received a medical degree from Albert Einstein College of Medicine in New York City. A residency at the Medical Center Hospital of Vermont brought him to the Green Mountain State

where he and his wife, also a doctor, eventually settled.

While still practicing medicine, Dean was elected as a Democrat to Vermont's part-time legislature, in 1982. In 1986 and 1988 he was elected lieutenant-governor during the last two Kunin administrations. He was again re-elected to the number two position in 1990, this time during the Republican administration of Richard Snelling.

On the morning of August 14, 1991, Governor Snelling died of a heart attack. When Dean took the oath of office to succeed Snelling, Vermonters knew little about him, other than that he was a physician. His position on a broad range of issues was unknown, as the position of lieutenant governor was largely ceremonial.

At the time, Vermont was in difficult straits. A recession beginning in 1989 had left the state awash in red ink. In fact, Richard Snelling, with a reputation as a no-nonsense businessman, had come back to again serve as governor in 1990, specifically to put the state's finances in order. What would the new Democratic governor do? To everyone's relief, especially Vermont's creditors, Dean proved himself a fiscal conservative, moving quickly to retire the state's deficit. He also cut the income tax and initiated welfare reform. At the same time he established Vermont as a national leader in the area of children's issues and health care reform. Vermonters appreciated his efforts, and have continuously re-elected him to office. In 1996, in his third campaign, he won 71 percent of the vote, and in 1998 he became the first modern Vermont governor to serve four terms.

While Vermonters have shown no hesitancy in electing outsiders to high office, they have been remarkably consistent in the last two decades in returning two native sons to the United States Senate: Patrick Leahy and James Jeffords. Leahy, a native of Montpelier and the grandson of a Barre quarry worker was first elected to the Senate in 1974 at the age of 34, and remains the only Democrat elected to this office from Vermont. With over 25 years of seniority, by the late 1990s he was one of the most powerful members of the U.S. Senate.

At a clinic in Vietnam supported by the Leahy War Victims Fund, Senator Leahy, on the right, and former Senator John Glenn (D-Ohio) help a Vietnamese man into his first wheelchair.

The clinic and the Leahy program aid landmine victims and other civilians wounded in war. Courtesy, Senator Leahy's office.

Like Leahy, Republican James Jeffords has served Vermont for many years in Washington, but not all of them in the Senate. From 1975 to 1988 Jeffords was Vermont's lone congressman, but was elected to the Senate in 1988 on the retirement of Robert Stafford. In 1997 he became chair of the powerful Senate Health, Education, Labor and Pensions Committee, which oversees 1,000 Federal programs. Chairmanship of this committee pushed him to the forefront of national education issues.

The combination of Leahy, Jeffords and Sanders has given Vermont a unique congressional delegation. With one an Independent, and the other two

from the Republican and Democratic parties, they represent the broad diversity of political opinion in Vermont, but they are not ideologues. Perhaps they are best described as Vermonters in the progressive tradition of George Aiken—individuals who put the interests of all Vermonters before the demands of party. And with their combined total of 60 years experience in Washington, Vermont's delegation brings the Green Mountain State influence well beyond its size.

There have been many political issues that have concerned Vermonters in the last decades of the 20th century, but none has been as controversial as education finance reform. Prior to 1997 local property taxes were the principal source of public school support in Vermont, with the state supplying only a small amount of money—in 1995 Vermont ranked 45th in state share of funding of education. Poor towns, where property values were low, had to pass high school-tax rates to pay

Senator James Jeffords, left, celebrates Dewey Day in Montpelier, October 9, 1999. Dressed as the admiral is Dennis Malloy, a local resident. This celebration commemorated Dewey's triumphal return to his native Montpelier in 1899 after his victory in Manila Bay. Senator Jeffords has a special relationship to the armed services, having been an active duty naval officer in the 1950s, and a member of the naval reserve until retirement in 1990. Courtesy, Senator Jeffords' office

for even a minimum level of public education, while towns with high property values could provide a superior educational experience with a low school-tax rate. By the mid-1990s this disparity was blatant to everyone concerned with education.

In the mid-1990s Amanda Brigham, an elementary student in the little township of Whiting, brought suit along with the school districts of Brandon and Worcester, against the state, claiming that over-reliance on the property tax led to inequities and violated the state constitution's equal protection and education clauses. The issue eventually went to the Vermont Supreme Court and on February 5, 1997, it decided in favor of Brigham, ruling that the state, not local districts, was responsible for education and funding, and ordered that the legislature remedy the situation.

The ruling went to the legislature, which was then in session. Proponents of the Brigham decision introduced House Bill 257, which allowed for a statewide school property tax to fund education equally for all students throughout the state. Under its terms, money from property-rich towns would be redistributed to poorer towns. The bill also gave responsibility for setting educational standards to Montpelier.

Opposition to the bill was widespread, coming principally from what were called "gold towns," and from towns with traditionally low property taxes. The "gold towns"—often resort communities like Stowe, had high property values, and generously supported their local schools. They pointed with pride to the quality of their schools, and feared that if they were forced to contribute to a shared pool—critics called it a "shark" pool—their own schools would suffer. A few towns—Strafford in Orange County is the best example—had so few young people living in them that they had no schools, and a very low property tax. They resented having to pay increased taxes to support schools elsewhere in Vermont. Critics also charged that the bill took away local control of education, and would hurt Vermont's important second-home real estate market.

In the end the proponents won, and House Bill 257 became Act 60, signed into law by Governor Dean on June 26, 1997. This created a statewide property tax of $1.10 per $100 of valuation (in 1997 dollars), which gave every public school student in Vermont $5,000 for education. So that the tax would not be regressive there was a rebate system for families who earned less than $75,000 a year. The act went a long way towards eliminating disparities in educational opportunities, but opposition to it continued.

Another problem that nagged at Vermont in the 1990s was the cost of electrical power. In the 1980s as Vermont's population and industries grew, concern was widespread that there was insufficient electrical power available to sustain this growth. Quebec, however, having just completed the James Bay hydroelectric facility, had power to spare. In 1984 a number of Vermont utilities, including the two largest, Central Vermont Public Service Corporation (CVPS) and Green Mountain Power (GMP), signed long-term contracts with Hydro-Quebec, guaranteeing that Vermonters would have a supply of electrical power for years to come.

There was some opposition in Vermont to these contracts at the time, but it was focused mainly on the impact of the James Bay facility on the environment, and on the lifestyle of the Cree Indians. In the mid-1990s criticism shifted as it became apparent that prices charged by Hydro-Quebec were above those of other suppliers. More importantly, the Hydro-Quebec contract put GMP and CVPS in a financial straightjacket, as they could only pass their increased costs on to their customers with the approval of the Public Service Board—the state agency regulating utilities. This, the Service Board was reluctant to give. Both GMP and CVPS tottered on the brink of bankruptcy. In 1997 *The Burlington Free Press* said, "...the Canadian hydro contract may have been Vermont's worst business decision of the decade," and Senator Jeffords in 1999 unsuccessfully attempted to have the contracts abrogated. As the century came to a close, the question of Hydro-Quebec and the financial health of Vermont's utilities continued unresolved.

In the international arena a resident of Putney received one of the world's most prestigious awards for her humanitarian work. In 1997 the Nobel Committee gave its Peace Prize to 47 year-old Jody Williams for her efforts to ban the use of landmines worldwide. An activist since her days in the Vietnam anti-war movement, the folksy but fearless Williams joined the Vietnam Veterans of America Foundation in 1991. The Foundation was deeply committed to ending the use of landmines—a cause which was espoused by another Vermonter, Senator Patrick Leahy. By the mid-1990s Williams was the coordinator of an organization called the International Campaign to Ban Landmines, and it was for this work that she won the Peace Prize.

Vermonters are used to the hardships of weather—temperatures can range from a frigid 30° below zero in winter to a high of 100° degrees in summer. Winters are so severe that there is even a small institute for arctic studies in Wolcott. But even the crustiest old Vermonter was surprised by two events in the 1990s: the Montpelier Flood of 1992, and the Ice Storm of 1998.

The Montpelier Flood caught the capital city unawares. It was brought about by a combination of weather, geography, and bad luck. In early March 1992 there was a thaw in the Northeast; on Tuesday, March 10, the temperature climbed to 52 degrees in Montpelier. Ice on many Vermont rivers broke up and began moving downstream.

Above
Ice breaking up on the Winooski River caused the flooding which inundated Montpelier, March 11, 1992. Courtesy, Russell Smith

Below
Main and State streets, the principal intersection of downtown Montpelier, at the height of the flood. It took weeks to clear the water and mud out of basements. Courtesy, Jane Walker Richmond

Even in adversity Vermonters look for a silver-lining. Here two young men canoe around Montpelier at the height of the flood. Courtesy, Jane Walker Richmond

did cause minor flooding downstream in Bolton, Jonesville, and Richmond.

Montpelier was devastated. The state's leading newspaper, *The Burlington Free Press*, under headlines reading "Capital Catastrophe," said it was Montpelier's worst natural disaster since the great flood of 1927. Two hundred and eighty people were forced from their homes. Damage to streets and bridges was put at $1,000,000, and losses to homes and businesses was estimated at $5-10

With some of the money received from the federal government to revitalize Montpelier after the flood, the city created Stonecutter's Way along the Winooski River, just visible on the right. In the 19th century this area was lined with massive sheds where stonecutters worked on the granite brought from quarries in nearby Barre. By the middle of the 20th century the area had been abandoned and become an urban eyesore. Now it is a pleasant pathway, popular with walkers, joggers and bicyclists. Courtesy, Vincent Feeney

Montpelier, with its capital buildings and 8,000 residents, is shaped like a bowl, with two rivers—the Winooski and the North Branch—flowing through it. Early on the morning of Wednesday, March 11, chunks of ice jammed against the Bailey Street Bridge on the southwestern edge of the city. The effect was to back up water into the city. By 7:30 A.M. the capital's main thoroughfare—State Street—was knee deep in water, and by 8:00 A.M. it was waist deep. The bowl was filling up.

There were bizarre scenes everywhere. Some people fled to the high ground of the State house where they watched river water lapping at the front steps. The state police patrolled downtown on a skijet and in a camouflaged duck hunting boat. Two 18 year-old boys canoed around town, at times riding waves down Main Street. Everywhere business people and citizens tried to save their possessions. At the Kellogg-Hubbard Library water poured into the basement where the children's books were shelved. Librarians quickly mobilized a group of 30 volunteers and moved 20,000 books upstairs in an hour. By noon that day the capital was under 3 to 5 feet of water.

The immediate crisis ended at 5:30 P.M., when a crew of state workers using a heavy beam as a battering ram broke up the ice jam. Water levels quickly dropped, although the onrushing water

million. Bill Shouldice, owner of downtown Montpelier's popular Country Store, put his losses at $100,000. No one had flood insurance. As Mayor Ann Cummings surveyed the extent of the damage, she feared that few businesses would recover, and Montpelier might become a ghost town.

Fortunately, her fears were unfounded. Even before the floodwaters subsided help was on the way. National Life of Vermont, an insurance company that is also Montpelier's largest private employer, set aside $200,000 for relief, and within days every business in town that was affected by the flood received a check for $2,000. Local people donated clothing, bedding and appliances. Senator Leahy, a Montpelier native, pushed through a HUD grant earmarked for downtown reconstruction.

In an ironic twist the flood turned out to be a boon for Montpelier. It actually promoted downtown revitalization. A number of businesses that had been forced out of their former premises relocated to a newer building called City Center which had been only partially occupied. And part of the HUD money received by the city went to building and landscaping a pedestrian path called Stonecutter's Way along what had been an urban eyesore adjacent to the river. Only two businesses permanently closed as a result of the flood, and that had more to do with retirement plans than with the devastation.

The Ice Storm of 1998, however, was a different story. Here the damage was more severe, the area affected more widespread, and its consequences long-term. Its cause was the rare convergence of two weather patterns. Cold air from Canada came down and settled in the Champlain and St. Lawrence valleys. At the same time warm, moist air from the Gulf of Mexico came in and rode over the cold air. The warm air produced rain, but when the precipitation passed through the shallow cold layer it turned to ice, turning the landscape into a slippery, silvery, wonderland.

The storm began Wednesday afternoon, January 7, 1998, with ice coating the roads. Police advised motorists in Chittenden, Addison, Grand Isle and Franklin counties to stay at home. By that

Ice-laden branches turned trees into strangely beautiful ice sculptures in the Champlain Valley during the ice storm of 1998. Unfortunately, many of those limbs eventually broke, creating transportation problems and power outages. Courtesy, Fred Stetson

evening only the occasional vehicle ventured out. But worse was yet to come.

That night ice-laden tree limbs began snapping: one or two at first, then hundreds, and finally, thousands. Residents of South Hero likened the sharp crack of the crashing trees to the sound of a cannon. Tom Dunn, the chief engineer of the state Public Service department, after surveying damage in Grand Isle County said, "It's like a bomb. It's like a war zone." By Thursday morning downed trees littered every community in the Champlain Valley. Worse, falling trees severed electrical lines throughout the region. On Friday, 35,000 people were without power.

Burlington, the state's biggest city, virtually shut down. Many residents, whose heat source was electricity-dependent, huddled around fireplaces and woodstoves, or moved to makeshift community shelters in churches and schools. Dairy farmers who used electric milking machines were in a difficult fix. Cows left unmilked for two days became sick. Something had to be done.

On Thursday, January 8th, Governor Dean

declared Grand Isle County in a state of emergency; this was followed on the 9th by Chittenden, Franklin and Addison counties. This allowed the Governor to call out the National Guard to clear roads of fallen trees. The main push, however, was to get power restored. To help the already over-burdened local utility workers, crews from as far away as Virginia and Arizona flew in to help. Gradually the lights went back on in the Champlain Valley. By Monday, January 12, those without power were down to 7,250. Although residents of Isle La Motte went without power till the 17th, the crisis was over.

Those who saw the destruction in the Champlain Valley described it only in superlatives. Meteorologists called it the "state's worst ice storm in the 20th century." Surveying the damage in hard-hit Grand Isle County a shocked Senator Jeffords called it "massive destruction, the worst I've ever seen." In all, the storm toppled or tore off limbs on trees over 700,000 acres, or about 15 percent of Vermont. Repairs, cleanup, damages, and lost productivity cost the state tens of millions of dollars. Foresters said that until damage to Vermont's forests could be assessed—something that could not be done for years—the real cost of the ice storm was unknowable.

Despite the vagaries of weather, as the 20th century drew to a close, Vermont came to occupy an almost mythical place in the American imagination. Though it was rapidly changing, it was still a place of quiet beauty, of small villages, of narrow dirt roads and low crime rates. This was an image supported by fact, but also one nurtured by self-promotion and by Hollywood. The 1940s film "Holiday Inn" with Bing Crosby portrayed Vermont as the idyllic place for those wishing to escape the woes of the big city, a theme carried on in television's "The Bob Newhart Show" in the 1980s.

In the popular imagination Vermont conjured up images of rural beauty, environmental purity, craftsmanship, hard work, frugality, and healthy living. In the minds of many, Vermont stood for what America used to be, and this idea was not lost on those interested in marketing the Green Mountain State. Dynamic agencies like the State

Tourism and Marketing Department, in alliance with local entrepreneurs, aggressively campaigned to sell Vermont products around the country—with much success.

Though a number of companies have capitalized on Vermont's image, the most successful was Ben and Jerry's Ice Cream. Its story is a metaphor for Vermont in the 1980s and 1990s. Two young Long Island hippies, Ben Cohen and Jerry Greenfield, captured by the Green Mountain mystique, moved to Vermont in the late 1970s, took a mail order course on ice cream making, and opened an offbeat ice cream parlor in an old gas station in Burlington. In beards and ponytails, they did things differently. On Wednesday nights they showed free outdoor movies against a brick wall

In the 1990s the Ben and Jerry's Ice Cream factory on the main road leading to Stowe became the single most visited tourist attraction in Vermont. Every day hundreds of adults and delighted children stopped to see this premium ice cream being made. Courtesy, Vincent Feeney

Despite the influx of new residents, much of Vermont still looks like this peaceful farm scene in Pomfret, enticing a steady stream of tourists from *out-of-state. Photo by Andre Jenny. Courtesy, Vermont Department of Tourism and Marketing*

next to the gas station. And it worked. Their zany business style appealed to a new generation of Vermonters. Within a few years their shoestring operation grew to a business that sold ice cream across the country, and in the American consciousness came to symbolize Vermont. In 1999 Governor Dean described Ben and Jerry's as Vermont's "signature" company.

Not surprisingly, as the century wore on tourism came to play an increasing role in Vermont's economy. According to the most recent figures available, tourism in 1997 brought in $2.2 billion, or about 15 percent of the Gross State Product (GSP), putting it behind only manufacturing and retail/wholesale in economic importance. What is surprising about this growing industry is its diversity. Forty years ago tourists came to the Green Mountains either to downhill ski or to relax at a lakeside resort. Now the winter sports enthusiast could cross-country ski, snowshoe, snowboard, or ride a skimobile through the woods.

Summer sports fans had even more options, including bicycle touring, canoeing, kayaking, hiking, road running, fishing and hangliding. And when the day was done, the tired visitor had hundreds of quality restaurants and inns from which to choose.

The natural beauty and small village flavor of Vermont has not only served business well, it has also lured artists to the Green Mountain State. Writers, particularly have found the serenity of Vermont attractive. This is an old phenomenon. At the turn of the century Rudyard Kipling lived and wrote from his dowdy retreat Naulakha in Dummerston. In the 1920s Robert Frost made South Shaftsbury his residence for a number of years, and had a summer home in Ripton in the

Vermont residents and tourists alike enjoy snow-shoeing in Brookfield at the Ice Harvest Festival. Photo by Andre Jenny. Courtesy, Vermont Department of Tourism and Marketing

1940s and 1950s, while teaching at the nearby Breadloaf Writer's Conference. Even Wallace Stegner, usually thought of as a western writer, had a summer home in Greensboro from the late 1930s until his death in 1993. One of his last novels, *Crossing To Safety*, is partially set in Vermont.

This tradition of attracting writers continued into the 1980s and 1990s. Perhaps Vermont's most famous literary resident was Alexander Solzhenitsyn. The author of *One Day In The Life of Ivan Denisovich* and *The Gulag Archipelago* lived in the remote mountain township of Cavendish from 1976 until 1994. Respecting the famous Russian writer's desire for solitude the owner of the local general store put a sign in his window stating, "No directions to the Solzhenitsyn home."

The playwright David Mamet, though born in Chicago, attended Goddard College in Plainfield in the 1960s, and since the 1980s has spent most of his summers at his Cabot home. His Atlantic Theatre Company, based in New York City, frequently performs in Vermont. Annie Proulx, the

As in the rest of America, road-running became a popular sport in Vermont in the 1980s and 1990s. The Burlington City Marathon has become one of the country's premier running events, attracting 5,000 runners every May. The Stowe 8 Miler, begun in 1982, brings in runners from around the world in July. Here, Andy Ronan of Ireland, number 1, leads Eric Morse of Vermont, number 2, and Abebe Boazza, number 8, and Rachid Tbahi, number 7, of Morocco. Courtesy, Larry Kimball and Lee Labier

Pulitizer Prize winning author of *Postcards* and the well-received *Shipping News* lived and wrote in Vershire for many years before moving to Wyoming in the mid-1990s. Edward Hoagland, the naturalist writer, maintains a summer home in Barton. Resident writers include the activist Grace Paley, Antigua-born Jamaica Kincaid, and the Hispanic writer Julia Alvarez. Howard Frank Mosher, who lives in the northern hamlet of Irasburg, has written a number of novels with Vermont settings, two of which—*Where The Rivers Flow North* and *Stranger in the Kingdom*—have been made into films by local director Jay Craven. All of these writers have found the near-isolation and smallness of Vermont conducive to their work.

With extensive mountains and abundant snowfall it's no surprise that Vermonters excel in winter sports. Vermont downhill skiers have been in the forefront of Alpine skiing since the 1930s. In recent years, however, some of the Green Mountain's best athletes have excelled in ice hockey, with John LeClair being the best of them all. After a successful but injury-ridden career at UVM, LeClair became the first Vermonter to play in the NHL, initially going to the Montreal Canadiens in 1991, and then to the Philadelphia Flyers in 1994 where he established himself as one of the premier power forwards in hockey. He was the first American player to score 50 goals in three

Actress Tantoo Cardinal as "Bangor," in the Jay Craven film of the Howard Frank Mosher novel, Where The Rivers Flow North. *The theme of this work, set in the 1930s, is one still close to the heart of Vermonters: how to maintain the old ways in the face of encroaching development. Courtesy, Jay Craven*

Middlebury College men's hockey player John Giannacopoulos clears the puck during Middlebury's 5-0 win over Wisconsin-Superior in the '99 NCAA Division III National Championship game. The win was the fifth straight NCAA Title for the Panthers, setting a new NCAA hockey record. Photo by Raj Chalwa. Courtesy, Middlebury College Athletic Department

John LeClair, Vermont's greatest hockey player, in his days at UVM. Photo by William Dilillo. Courtesy, University of Vermont Athletic Department

consecutive NHL seasons. In his hockey-mad hometown of St. Albans, LeClair is a revered hero.

At the team level, both the University of Vermont (UVM) and Middlebury College have produced noteworthy hockey programs in the 1990s. The 1996 Vermont Catamounts, led by All-Americans Martin St. Louis, Eric Perrin and Tim Thomas, went all the way to the Final Four before losing in overtime to Colorado College. It was UVM's finest hockey season. Middlebury College was a Division III powerhouse, winning five consecutive national titles between 1995 and 1999. But perhaps more surprising than Vermonters' excellence in winter

sports, was their success in sports not usually associated with the Green Mountain State: track and field, cross country running, and basketball. Moreover, the stars in these sports have been women, reflecting the new opportunities opened to them in the last 20 years through Title IX, the Federal law mandating that women have equal opportunity in collegiate athletics. Individually, a few names stood out. Lyndonville native Judi St. Hilaire starred at UVM in the late 1970s in track and field, and in 1991 placed seventh in the World Track and Field Championships in the 3,000 meter race, and in 1992 placed eighth in the 10,000 meter finals at the Olympic Games in Barcelona, Spain.

Perhaps one of the most surprising athletes produced in Vermont in the last 20 years was Erin Sullivan, a phenomenal cross-country runner. On a lark, after two years playing soccer, in 1997 the diminutive Sullivan turned out in her junior year of high school to run cross-country. Week after week she defeated all comers, capturing the state title, then the regional, and finally the national high school cross country championship. She won the national crown again in 1998, and as a freshman at Stanford University in 1999 won the

Shari Turnbull of UVM shoots from the free-throw line in a game against Rutgers, March 1993. For two years the Turnbull-led Lady Cats went undefeated in America East competition, losing only when they went to the NCAA play-offs. Photo by Sally McCay. Courtesy, University of Vermont Athletic Department

PAC 10 women's title and finished seventh in the NCAA championships.

For women's team performances in the last quarter of the 20th century little can compare to the accomplishments of UVM's Lady Cats basketball teams of 1991-92 and 1992-93. Under the inspired coaching of Cathy Inglese, the 1991-92 team went 29-0 in the regular season, only to lose in the opening round of the NCAA playoffs to George Washington University. The next year they

again went undefeated in the regular season, but again lost in the opening round of the playoffs. Despite these losses in the NCAA Tournament, they did set an NCAA record of 52 consecutive regular-season victories, and validated women's athletics in Vermont.

As the 20th century came to a close, Vermont was a place characterized by continuity and change. Old field patterns criss-crossing the countryside, villages huddled around dirt intersections,

Running sensation Erin Sullivan was unbeatable during her high school career, 1997-98. Running as a freshman for Stanford University in 1999, she finished seventh in the women's NCAA cross-country championships in Indianapolis and was named an All-American. Courtesy, Claudia Sullivan

wood-covered bridges spanning root-beer colored rivers, and wrinkled farmers hobbling in blue overalls, are all reminders of an older, agrarian culture. Because these vestiges have all but disappeared elsewhere in America, people flock to Vermont. Some to spend a weekend or two, others to make a home.

As the new century opened, the legislature passed a law that put Vermont on the front page of every newspaper in the country: Act 91 which allowed gay and lesbian couples to form civil unions. Like the controversial Act 60 the civil union bill grew out of a Vermont Supreme Court decision. On December 20, 1999, the court ruled in Baker v. State that the Vermont statutes uncon-

stitutionally discriminated against same-sex couples who sought to "establish a permanent, stable family relationship." It was up to the legislature, said the court, to remedy this situation.

The issue was the most contentious in the 1999-2000 legislative session. One hotly debated issue was whether the remedy would require a change in the laws relating to marriage, or could it be accomplished through the creation of an entirely new institution. Eventually the legislature decided that the marriage laws would not be changed, but that a new category—"civil union"—would be created, which would give gay and lesbian couples the same rights and guarantees as those enjoyed by married heterosexual couples.

City dwellers enjoy sailing at Basin Harbor. Courtesy, Vermont Department of Tourism and Marketing

As the civil union bill made its way through the House and Senate in February through April, 2000, feelings around the state ran high. Conservative forces, led principally by the state's Catholics, denounced civil union as an attack on marriage, while supporters of the bill defended it as a civil rights issue. Public testimony on the issue in the legislature was carried live by Vermont Public Radio to the most remote corners of the state. Many towns used their town meetings in March to gauge public opinion on civil union, and almost all of the towns that did so voted against civil unions. Clearly, many Vermonters, perhaps a majority, were uncomfortable with the notion of civil union.

With strong public sentiment against the bill legislators were on the spot. For some of them, a vote for the bill might mean their political future. In the end, however, the civil rights argument won out. On April 19 the Senate voted 19 to 11 in favor of the bill, followed by the House on April 25, with a favorable 79 to 68 count. The next day Governor Dean signed the bill into law. It was an historic moment. Vermont became the first state in the union to give gay and lesbian couples the same rights as married heterosexual couples.

Ironically, it has been Vermont's visible connection to the past that has been one of the greatest catalysts for change in the Green Mountains. Visitors see the barns, the sugar houses, the dairy cows—and dream of old Vermont. Perhaps it is a Vermont that never existed in reality, but one which lingers in the imagination. To capture the dream, people move to the Green Mountain State. For some Vermonters the coming of so many outsiders has been a disturbing trend. They should not be alarmed, however, for these new arrivals bring a new vitality—a vitality that may have been born and nurtured in another place, but which adds to the whole which is Vermont. They are the Ben Cohens, the Howard Deans, the Jody Williamses, the Madeline Kunins, and the Howard Frank Moshers who bring so much to life in the Green Mountains. Vermont proudly carries this mosaic of continuity and change into the future.

While Vermont changed dramatically in the last quarter of the 20th century, much of it remains the same as it was 100 years ago. The centuries-old craft of making maple syrup from the sap of the maple tree still takes place every spring in sugar houses like this one in Chelsea. Courtesy, Vermont Department of Tourism and Marketing

Chronicles
of
Leadership

Vermont women have been making their own quilts ever since pre-Revolutionary days. During the Depression they utilized their skills by participating in a WPA "Comforter Project" held in Montpelier. Courtesy, Vermont Historical Society

When Ethan Allen and his brothers came to Vermont in the 1760s, it was called the Hampshire Grants because the governor of New Hampshire claimed that King George had granted the land to him. However, because New York's governor made an identical claim, some of those who came here to farm bought their land from New Hampshire, others from New York. A colorful dispute ensued.

The Allens bought their land from New Hampshire. When New York insisted they pay for it *again*, a sometimes rowdy group of farmers calling themselves the Green Mountain Boys came into being. New York never quite recovered (the land or its aplomb).

Ethan stormed Fort Ticonderoga, capturing it "in the name of the Great Jehovah and the Continental Congress" in 1775, but Congress still refused to settle the disputes in the Grants. So the Green Mountain Boys declared independence!

For fourteen years they ran their own postal system, minted coins in Rupert, and ran Vermont as a Yankee republic. It was not until 1791 that Vermont's fiercely independent farmers ratified the U.S. Constitution, becoming the first state to enter the Union after the Revolution.

Vermont's industrial history is tied directly to its farmers. Gristmills and sawmills served farmers; village blacksmiths became brawny pillars of society by making spuds, axes, adzes, scythes, and everything else needed on farms.

William Jarvis brought a fine flock of 400 Merino sheep from Spain in 1811 and inspired Hubbardton to found the Farmers Cotton and Woolen Manufacturing Company. By the peak year—1840—Merino sheep outnumbered human Vermonters six to one. Between 1828 and 1834, eighteen cotton and woolen mills were established.

Farmers cleared the land, and thriving businesses in lumber, paper, potash, and charcoal grew up where the trees fell. At its peak over 80 percent of the forests had been clear-cut for farming.

That, of course, revealed another major resource: rock. The first use of the high-quality granite found in the hills around Barre was in stone fence posts, grinding stones, and doorjambs for local farms. When monuments and memorials came into vogue, Barre's granite industry became known around the world.

Thaddeus Fairbanks' platform scale was introduced in 1830 to weigh the load on a farm wagon. Shaftsbury's Silas Hawes put two saws together, making a carpenter's square in 1814 for farmers who built their own homes. In 1880 the Butterfields of Derby Line started manufacturing a tool to improve a wagon axle. The companies have tenaciously survived.

Asabel Hubbard invented a water pump in 1828 and founded the National Hydraulic Company in Windsor. Russell Jones and Ebenezer Lamson split off National Hydraulic in 1876 and moved to Springfield. Because the Jones & Lamson venture helped found three other tool companies, Springfield became the major manufacturing center it is today.

As is obvious throughout this book, while Vermonters have produced everything from stoves to machine tools, from maple syrup to microchips, from milk to insurance, they had the foresight to leave a beautiful state in the wake of all its industry. Much of those cleared farmlands are again in forest, and tourism is a bit more prominent than farming, but if Ethan Allen and the Green Mountain Boys were to return, they would find Vermonters still endowed with an enviable strain of fierce Yankee independence and their state the most rural in the Northeast.

The organizations whose stories are detailed on the following pages have chosen to support this important literary and civic project. They illustrate the variety of ways in which individuals and their businesses have contributed to the area's growth and development. The civic involvement of Vermont's businesses, institutions of learning, and local government, in cooperation with its citizens, has made the state an excellent place in which to live and work.

BELL-GATES LUMBER CORPORATION

When a West Coast architect was looking for some quarter-sewn maple, his long search finally ended in Jeffersonville at the Bell-Gates Lumber Corporation, a leading supplier of Vermont hardwood. Current company president Jerry Gates recalls, "He said he had called every sawmill in the country with no luck. We happened to be sawing some 5/4" maple at the time. We sent him about 600 board feet of it." That kind of personal attention is the hallmark of the company that evolved from the first sawmill built in Jeffersonville to survive fires, floods and the Great Depression, among other hardships. "We like to

B. E. Reynolds Mill on Brewster River in Jeffersonville, Vermont, circa 1930.

keep it small, I think it's better for the customers," says Jerry, who recently welcomed his son Tyler as the fourth generation to join the operations located at the intersection of Routes 108 and 15.

In 1877, Lucius Wheelock built the first sawmill, which was operated by water power from the Brewster River until it was lost in high water about 1898. The next owners were David and George Griswold, who ran the mill until 1920 when it was purchased by Bert Reynolds. He enjoyed successful operations due to "extensive logging operations, large supplies of local timber, adequate water and rail transportation," until the Flood of 1927 hit the mill and large quantities of lumber were lost.

At the end of 1927, Mr. Reynolds sold the mill to Abner A. Bell and the mill became known as Bell's Mill, one of the first mills to ship

Founders Jonathan Gates, left and Abner A. Bell.

Northeastern hardwood on a grade basis. The new owner first joined the lumber industry in 1906, when he went to work for the Webster Lumber Company of Swanton. A.A. Bell's daughter, Eunice Bell Gates, recalls that her father earned $1.25 per day for the first year. "As a hardwood lumber grader, he would travel by train and horse-drawn stagecoach to the smaller towns in Vermont to buy lumber from other mills. He bought and sold lumber all over the Northeast and Canada, earning an excellent reputation for honesty and fairness."

The Great Depression in 1929 made the early years a struggle for Bell's Mill. Another catastrophe struck in 1940 when the mill was destroyed by fire; operations were continued from East Fairfield. In

October 1943, A.A. Bell and Jonathan Gates formed the Bell-Gates Lumber Company. The 1960s brought another generation into the company as Jerry Gates, son of Jonathan and Eunice Bell Gates, joined the mill. In 1962 the mill was extensively renovated with the installation of up-to-date equipment.

Fire struck the Bell-Gates mill again in 1971, when the mill was completely destroyed, although no lumber was lost. Jonathan and Jerry worked quickly to rebuild the mill, and the first log in the new plant was sawn six months to the day from the time of the fire. Since that time, operations have continued to run smoothly, although availability of timber presents a constant challenge to lumber production.

Today, the Bell-Gates Lumber Corporation employs 18 workers to run a double-cut band mill and manufacture approximately three and one-half to four million board feet per year. Hard maple accounts for 50 percent of production, with ash, soft maple, beech, yellow birch, red oak, cherry and basswood also harvested and milled.

Bell-Gates Lumber Corporation, 1980s, at the junction of Routes 108 and 15, Jeffersonville, Vermont.

BEN & JERRY'S

Ben & Jerry's Homemade, Inc. was founded in 1978 in a renovated gas station in Burlington, Vermont, by childhood friends Ben Cohen and Jerry Greenfield. After completing a $5 correspondence course in ice cream making from Penn State—and receiving a perfect score because the test is open book!—they opened their business with a $12,000 investment ($4,000 of which was borrowed). They soon became popular for their innovative flavors, made from fresh Vermont milk and cream.

The early days were marked by unusual events, such as their free summer movie festival, when they projected movies on the outside wall of the old gas station. Their first anniversary was celebrated by a Free Cone Day, now an annual celebration at Ben & Jerry's Scoop Shops worldwide.

In 1980, two years after its founding, Ben & Jerry's began packing their ice cream in pints, to distribute to grocery and Mom & Pop stores along the restaurant delivery routes that Ben serviced out of the back of his old Volkswagen. The following year, only three years after its founding, the business opened its first franchise in Shelburne, Vermont. An attention-grabbing event occurred when Ben & Jerry's ice cream was used to build "the world's largest ice cream sundae" in St. Albans; the sundae weighed 27,102 pounds.

Original gas station, Burlington, Vermont.

By 1988, only 10 years after its founding, Ben & Jerry's annual sales exceeded $47 million, with more than 80 shops open in 18 states. That same year Ben and Jerry were named U.S. "Small Business Persons of the Year" by President Reagan in a White House Garden Ceremony. Neither were recognizable in the press photos which pictured Ben sporting an Italian waiter's jacket and Jerry in his only suit.

Ben & Jerry's operates on a three-part mission statement emphasizing product quality, economic reward and a commitment to the community. Ben & Jerry's gives 7.5 percent of its pre-tax profits back to the community through corporate philanthropy that is primarily employee-led. The company supports projects that are models for social change, focusing on those related to children and families, disadvan-

taged groups and the environment.

Ben & Jerry's is committed to using milk and cream that have not been treated with the synthetic hormone, rGBH. In keeping with its commitment to the environment, they introduced the ice cream industry's first pint container made from unbleached paperboard, reducing the company's use of all paper products that utilize a chemical process leading to toxic water pollution in this country.

Internationally, fans will find Ben & Jerry's products and social mission initiatives in Belgium, Canada, France, Ireland, Israel, Japan, Lebanon, the Netherlands, Peru, the UK and Sweden. In the states, Ben & Jerry's Ice Cream Factory Tour and onsite scoopy shop at the Waterbury plant is Vermont's #1 tourist attraction, and is open seven days a week year round.

Recognized for their innovation and dedication to social responsibility—as well as their infamously-delicious ice cream—Ben Cohen and Jerry Greenfield remain active participants in their communities, as well as noted authors and business leaders. Though these two childhood friends are the original creators of this legacy, the company and all of its associates continues strengthening the role of Ben & Jerry's as leader, innovator and entertainer.

Waterbury plant, Waterbury, Vermont.

BRATTLEBORO MEMORIAL HOSPITAL

Elizabeth Rowell Thompson, founder.

"Brattleboro Memorial Hospital Started With a Romantic Past"

Once upon a time, when a Boston millionaire named Thomas Thompson was traveling through Vermont in customary fashion by carriage, he chanced to meet one Elizabeth Rowell whom he later pursued to be his wife. Married in 1843, it was almost 20 years later when the couple was on one of many summer visits to Brattleboro. It was there that Mr. Thompson (considerably older than the young and beautiful Mrs. Thompson) announced that he was bequeathing his fortune to her. She is reported to have said, "Why do that? I am not wise in worldly ways, and I should not know how to expend your fortune as you might wish. I should be the prey of the designing and be caught in the meshes of the law."

However, at her husband's insistence, Elizabeth Rowell Thompson did make a decision about the inheritance. She decided to bequeath what would be left of Thompson's estate after their deaths "to the sewing women of Brattleboro" (and Rhinebeck, New York, but that's another story). While Mr. Thompson is said to have made little comment on his wife's suggestion, when he died eight years later it was found that he had honored her wishes.

Meanwhile Brattleboro was changing. The sewing lady numbers were dwindling, and with the river and railroad trade, the community was booming. At the turn of the last century, nearly 200 years after Fort Dummer was built on the Connecticut River as Vermont's first English settlement serving as both scouting post and trading center, Brattleboro's population continued to grow and flourish. There was, however, nary a nurse to be found in the area. Persons in need of surgical attention were obliged to go to Boston or other places with hospital facilities. At the beginning of the 1900s, the need for a hospital was clear.

To the benefit of residents of Brattleboro, the court ruled the phrase in the Thompson will—"kindred charitable purposes"—would allow beneficiaries other than the sewing women, including funds for the first hospital. Two years after Elizabeth Thompson's death in 1901, the fund known as the Thompson Trust gave $100,000 toward that cause.

Mr. Richard Bradley, as a trustee, bought the hilltop Hemlocks estate on Canal Street for the purpose of building a hospital. In 1904 the institution was incorporated under the name "The Hemlocks Hospital," but its Socratic suggestion did not meet with favor and it was changed to Brattleboro Memorial Hospital.

Brattleboro Memorial Hospital is a not-for-profit community hospital which has provided care to the people of greater Brattleboro and neighboring towns in New Hampshire and Massachusetts for nearly 100 years.

The area's only full-service healthcare facility, BMH provides a wide range of diagnostic and therapeutic services. The emergency room, the laboratory, and X-ray services at BMH are available 24-hours a day.

As a follow-up to the recent $7.55 million modernization project, BMH is renovating the Birthing Center and second floor Medical/Surgical Unit, enabling the hospital to more efficiently serve the community with both modern inpatient and outpatient health care. Its Birthing Center offers labor tubs, all-inclusive LDRP rooms, midwifery services, and an experienced staff.

Some of the services available are advanced surgical procedures and various endoscopic examinations and other state-of-the-art diagnostic equipment including MRI, CT and SPECT scanners, a bone densitometer, stereotactic breast biopsies, sonography, and mammography. BMH also offers same-day surgery, an oncology unit for cancer patients, physical and occupational therapy, cardiac rehabilitation programs, the family-oriented Birthing Center, and occupational health services. In addition, BMH offers physician sub-specialist clinics staffed in part by doctors from Dartmouth-Hitchcock Medical Center, with which the hospital is affiliated.

More than 50 board-certified physicians covering most specialties are on the medical staff at Brattleboro Memorial Hospital. Most physicians who have moved to Brattleboro to practice do so for the same reasons many area residents locate in Brattleboro—to escape the rigors of city and suburban living, providing Brattleboro with cosmopolitan professionals in a largely rural setting.

Brattleboro, which was recently selected as the fifth best small town in America, has much to offer even the most discriminating. And Brattleboro Memorial Hospital is counted among the excellent facilities available in this unique community.

Brattleboro Memorial Hospital as it looked in the early 1900s.

THE BURLEY PARTNERSHIP, ARCHITECTS

Robert Burley founded The Burley Partnership following his graduation from the Columbia University of School of Architecture and a seven-year association with the late Eero Saarinen in Michigan and Connecticut. Under Saarinen's direction, Burley was the designer-in-charge for the U.S. Embassy in London and the 630-foot high Gateway Arch in St. Louis.

Burley and his wife Pat, were avid skiers and had developed a love of the Green Mountains, and close ties with Vermont friends. In 1964, they chose to leave the metropolitan area and live in Vermont, establishing an architectural office in a 1900 schoolhouse in South Fayston.

Burley built a staff of talented architects and soon began playing an important role in Vermont's and Northern New England's architectures. In 1967, the firm was selected as architects for the State's Capitol Complex in Montpelier.

The Burley Partnership created a master plan for the buildings that responded to the changes in staff and space needs, as state programs continued to grow. Recognizing the need to preserve Vermont's heritage, Burley also argued for the preservation of the Pavilion Hotel and its adaptation into State office space and a museum for the Vermont Historical Society. After a long debate in the Legislature in the late '60s, the hotel was finally recon-

State of Vermont Capitol Complex.

Bailey-Howe Library, University of Vermont.

structed for State use. Most significantly, however, is that the debate sparked a new awareness of Vermont's architectural heritage and marked the beginning of Vermont's historic preservation movement.

William Gallup is also a principal of The Burley Partnership, having joined the firm in 1985. The firm's reputation has enjoyed continued growth throughout the country with new libraries at the University of Vermont and Colby-Sawyer College in New Hampshire; resort hotel projects for the Woodstock Inn, the Trapp Family Lodge, and the Carambola Resort in St. Croix, V.I.; an addition to the Vermont Statehouse; and residences in Vermont, Maine, and Florida. Historic preservation, resort planning, and institutional design are important strengths of the firm, as is its ability to produce modern projects that are in context with their environment— projects that are appropriate to the particular setting in which they are located. The firm's ability to innovate and create excellent projects has been recognized by many state and national design awards.

Burley served as executive director for the Taliesin Preservation Commission in Spring Green, Wisconsin from 1990-1994. On "loan" and with the support of his Vermont office, he established and directed the preservation program for TALIESIN, Frank Lloyd Wright's

Trapp Family Lodge, Stowe.

600-acre estate and a National Historic Landmark.

Burley has served as vice-chairman of the National Park System Board. Currently, he is chairman of the Architectural Advisory Panel for the restoration of Thomas Jefferson's Poplar Forest Plantation in Virginia, and the American Institute of Architect's National Committee on Historic Preservation.

CENTRAL VERMONT MEDICAL CENTER

The years following World War II were years of optimism and growth. Vermonters were imbued with the same sense of limitless possibilities that had captured the nation. Nearly every community of size felt justified in maintaining its own school, library and hospital to meet the needs of its own citizenry. And central Vermont communities were no different. In Washington and Orange counties, an area home to 45,000 people, two hospitals existed within seven miles of each other.

In 1895, Homer W. Heaton founded Heaton Hospital in Montpelier, Vermont's capital city. Following a serious accident, Heaton's medical condition convinced him that Montpelier needed "a public hospital for the reception and care of those temporarily sick or injured and in need of medical and surgical treatment." Responding to the health needs of a rapidly growing granite industry in the neighboring town, Frank E. Langley and a group of community leaders organized in 1904 "to maintain a public hospital, not for profit, in the City of Barre." Barre City Hospital opened three years later. The pride felt by both communities in their respective institutions initially created an impediment to merger discussions that

Montpelier's Heaton House, located on 10 acres in Vermont's capital city, admitted its first patient on August 6, 1898.

date back to 1947. By the early 1950s both hospitals had abandoned merger talks. Instead, they built new wings to their respective facilities in declaration of their intent to remain separate. Soon after, these two small hospitals found that they could not keep pace with acquiring the latest in burgeoning medical technology.

Attracting and retaining physicians was also at issue. Physicians were leaving central Vermont to practice elsewhere. By 1960 there were only 37 physicians in Washington County, down from a high of 58 in 1885. In fact, it was the physicians of Barre and Montpelier who, along with other community leaders, revived the movement toward merger as a way of preserving and expanding community-based medical care for central Vermonters. The intent to create a single, central Vermont hospital was further strengthened with support from the Vermont Association of Osteopathic Surgeons and Physicians Association who had tentatively planned to build a new 30-bed hospital of its own in the town of Berlin—located between Barre and Montpelier.

By March 1961 the medical staffs from Heaton Hospital and Barre City Hospital had voted to reciprocate staff privileges. This action was quickly followed by the State Health Commission's recommendation that the two hospitals merge to eliminate duplication and provide

a broader range of healthcare services to its citizens. Less than six months later, the medical staff of Mayo Memorial Hospital, a small, 29-bed hospital located 15 miles to the south, voted to join in the merger discussions.

In 1963, Central Vermont Hospital (CVH) was incorporated. Five years and nearly $5.5 million later, construction was completed. The new 175-bed hospital combined the boards of directors and the medical staffs of Barre City Hospital and Heaton Hospital. Also integrated were Mayo Memorial Hospital's physicians and the local osteopathic physicians.

In August 1968, CVH opened its doors on a beautiful 70-acre site in Berlin under the direction of Joel Walker, the former administrator of Barre City Hospital. Harold F. Shea, assumed the role of president, board of trustees of the Central Vermont Medical Center (CVMC), parent corporation to the hospital. Governor Philip Hoff and Vermont's senior U.S. Senator, George D. Aiken, presided at the opening ceremonies, which were attended by hundreds of supporters. The festivities ran as the lead story in the local *Times-Argus* on August 12, 1968.

The new hospital employed 395 local residents, making it one of the largest employers in the area. During its first year in operation, the hospital experienced an 83 percent

occupancy rate and 949 births. CVH discharged 7,600 patients, saw more than 9,000 people in the Emergency Room, provided more than 288,000 hours of nursing care, conducted more than 88,000 laboratory tests and extended more than $120,000 in charity care. The cost for a semi-private room was $40 a day.

The philosophy adopted in 1968 was for CVH to provide "the best possible care at the lowest cost." That philosophy continues to the present. Today Central Vermont Hospital is lauded as being one of the more efficiently run hospitals in the state. But while its philosophy has remained constant, much else has changed. In response to the changing incentives in the health-care field and an industry-wide trend toward outpatient care, Central Vermont Medical Center has made many changes. Over the years improvements have been

made to the physical plant, including the redesign of patient-care areas as well as the addition of several medical office buildings. Today CVMC operates a hospital facility with 122 licensed beds, serves a population of 65,000, and employs nearly 1,100 people. More than 25,000 patients are seen annually in CVH's Emergency Department and more than 164,000 outpatient treatments including more than 3,000 outpatient surgeries are provided. The hospital boasts a medical staff of more than 110 physicians representing a wide range of primary and specialty services. In 1993, CVMC extended the commitment it had made in the 1970s to provide long-term care locally, by opening Woodridge Nursing Home. This was built on the hospital's grounds to further ensure the availability of convenient, quality, long-term care in a home-like environment. Also

Area businessmen started a fund drive in 1913 to construct Barre City Hospital, which was completed in 1915 and served the community until August 1968.

significant was the affiliation CVMC entered into in 1996 with the Dartmouth-Hitchcock Alliance, a regional healthcare system comprised of 10 organizations. This affiliation strengthened the local hospital's ability to provide quality, compre-hensive care close to home while having the commitment and support of a larger organization behind it.

Today, CVMC and its medical staff work in close collaboration with other healthcare providers in the region to maximize locally available health services. To the credit of those who forged ahead with thoughts of merger in the face of skepticism, Central Vermont Medical Center continues to grow as a healthcare resource for the entire central Vermont community.

CLARA MARTIN CENTER

The Clara Martin Center was founded on October 27, 1966. The purpose of the organization was to assist those in the community who suffered from mental illness and were in need of care.

Clara Martin came to Orange County with her husband Brewster on August 3, 1953. Clara and her husband's family lived in Vermont for several generations. Clara's great grandmother came to Vermont from Germany in 1850. The Martin family resided in Vermont for several generations. After Brewster and Clara were married they moved to Chelsea, Vermont. Dr. Martin opened a physician's practice in the area and a small nursing home for local residents. Clara Martin, who assisted Brewster in his practice and helped many of the patients in the nursing home, was concerned about those she saw that were suffering from mental illness.

During this period many who suffered from mental illness were sent to the state hospital and ended up living there for several years. This institutional setting often robbed the spirit from their lives. Dr. Martin was reluctant to sign someone into the State Hospital knowing that the impact on his or her life would be affected for a long time to come. Commitment to the state institution was often against the will of the person afflicted. Local services to see a mental illness specialist had a waiting list of up to six months, often resulting in the patient's deterioration and eventual commitment to the state facility.

The Martins took a local resident out of the state hospital to reside in their nursing home. Clara was deeply affected by this woman's loss of spirit and good nature after her stay at the hospital. Clara began a grassroots effort in the county with the help of some local clergy, and raised the need with the state legislature to bring services to local citizens. The initial services were offered out of the Chelsea health Center where Dr. Martin practiced.

Portrait of Clara, by Joan Feierabend—1980s.

Since 1966 the organization has grown from a one-person operation with an annual budget of $2,000 to a fully-operational, community-based system serving children and families in need of mental health and substance abuse care with an annual operating budget of $4 million.

The original name of the center was "Orange County Mental Health." The name change occurred on January 30, 1994. Clara Martin served on the board of directors of the Center until she became ill in the mid-'80s. Clara passed away on November 2, 1990. Brewster Martin then took a seat on the board of the Clara Martin Center to carry on her efforts; he still sits on the board today.

The Center has kept pace over the years, offering a full-range of mental health and additional services to the greater Orange County area. Currently, the organization consists of three sites. The main office is located in Randolph, Vermont. Due to the rural geographic nature of the county there is a satellite office located in Bradford, Vermont, and a third location in the town of Wilder, Vermont. This site serves children and adults in the area of substance abuse, offering both outpatient and intensive outpatient treatment services.

The '90s gave the Center new challenges and opportunities. With health care reform in full swing and changes in management, the Center faces the new millennium in full force. The creativity and grassroots efforts of the founder are alive and well in Orange County.

In January 1994 the leadership of the organization changed. Linda Chambers was appointed to the role of executive director. Under Ms. Chamber's leadership, a five-generation Vermonter, the agency assisted the town of Randolph in its development efforts.

In 1993, three fires in the downtown area devastated the town of Randolph. With a population of approximately 2,500 residents the town came together to rebuild its Main Street. The Clara Martin Center agreed to move to the center of town to help support the need to rebuild the "Winslow Block Building." This new building is the main building in the center of town. The move in March 1995 helped reduce the stigma regarding mental illness and has created an economic partnership with the town that is beneficial to all residents.

Clara Martin Center's philosophy is to serve the community to promote well-being for all. The commitment at a local level is valued and all objectives take into consideration the community as a whole, as well as the individuals and families.

Safe Haven, a homeless shelter for individuals suffering from mental illness, was implemented in February 1996. The Center donated one

Clara and Brewster at home between bridge hands.

of its buildings that was available due to the move downtown, to be used for those in need of housing in the area. The Clara Martin Center spearheaded development of this project by working with State Senator Patrick Leahy, the Vermont Historical Society and the Vermont Housing Conservation Board.

In collaboration with Vermont Psychiatric Survivors and local AMI of Orange County, the Clara Martin Center created a consumer-run Safe Haven. The Clara Martin Center provides management oversight to staff and services to residents as requested. The result is the first "safe haven" in the nation that is staffed and run by consumers.

Top row, left to right: Ken Libertoff, Mrs. Marcelle Leahy, Neal Husher; middle row, l-r: Boyd Tracy, Connie Morse, Senator Patrick Leahy; front row, l-r: June Phillips, Rod Copeland, Linda Chambers, Gus Seelig.

COMMUNICATION INDUSTRIES CORPORATION

When Scott Heller paused in 1995 to ask the strategic question, "What should this business look like 20 years from now?" the answer set the stage for profound and positive changes for Communication Industries Corporation (CIC). It brought the company to Vermont.

Communication Industries Corporation was started in 1976 in East Rutherford, New Jersey by Scott's father Joseph L. Heller, and a partner. But change was overtaking CIC, and long-range decisions needed to be made. Scott had gone off to the west coast to find success in large, international direct marketing advertising agencies, and then in consulting.

But the family business needed a fresh approach if it were to evolve from a "mom and pop" shop which served one limited market. CIC was selling audio-visual equipment, material and supplies by catalog to the education market. And the partners were still trying to do everything themselves—a classic case of entrepreneurs unable to let go of the day-to-day operations of a growing business.

Scott returned to CIC—which had evolved into a major client for

Scott Heller relocated CIC to the small town of Grafton in 1996, and it has been steadily demonstrating that a high tech company blends well with the rural Vermont work ethic and values.

Joseph L. Heller founded Communication Industries Corporation in 1976. The street on which CIC is located was named JLH Memorial Drive, in his honor.

his consulting services—and, with his father, bought out the partner. But instead of an orderly management transition, Joseph Heller died just as he and Scott were evaluating the future direction of the business. Decisive action was called for. The multi-million dollar company had outgrown its facility, its work force, and its methods of operation.

In May 1996, after a period of extensive preparations, CIC closed its doors, unplugged its telephones and computers, and turned out the lights in New Jersey. It re-opened the following Monday morning in a 53,000 square-foot building in the tiny southeastern Vermont town of Grafton, a community of about 600 people known for its cheddar cheese and picture postcard village. Of the 40 employees, 32 were new people from Vermont.

"I knew about the Vermont work ethic, and that was a big factor. For years I had been coming up in the winter to ski. Then I came up to compete in a triathlon and discovered summer in Vermont. It was even better than winter. When decision time came, all those factors

shaped the outcome. I was betting that a high-tech business could prosper in a rural, low-tech community."

Today CIC is running smoothly, growing at about 25 percent a year, and selling more than $12 million of audio-visual equipment annually to customers all over the world.

Says Heller, "We now sell to a broad range of market sectors that include government, business, industry, healthcare and education, anywhere people are engaged in teaching, training and presenting. Our product line includes everything from portable public address systems and overhead projectors to the latest computer presentation equipment. Our catalogs contain thousands of products. We are committed to supporting our customers and helping them get the most out of the products by offering free lifetime technical support—an industry first."

While the 1996 move to Vermont was swift, the preparations were elaborate and carefully orchestrated. "The new Vermont employees who would make up our sales team were at our New Jersey facility for four weeks before the move, with each week consisting of 40 hours of training."

Even before that a facility had to be located and fit up. In 1995, Heller began scouting for a location around the Interstate 91 exits in the Brattleboro area. But while working with the state's economic development staff he learned of a building that had been standing empty for seven years.

The 53,000 square-foot building was the only industrial/commercial facility in Grafton and had previously housed a printing company. Seven years of standing empty had taken a heavy toll on the building. The interior had to be stripped back to the shell and refitted. With help from Vermont's economic development staff, a loan from VEDA and financing through KeyBank, Scott turned it into an efficient headquarters and distribution center and a

A staunch believer in employee development and training, Heller has launched programs in team building and encouraged employees to use the company's vast line of presentation products to put together presentations on their jobs and their departments. "That was our solution to people knowing only what happens in their own departments but not understanding how all the parts of the company work together. People came up with everything from multimedia videos to elaborate flip chart presentations."

Training continues with a theme that Heller calls the key to CIC's success: underpromise, overdeliver. New employees in the growing company attend CIC's "Boot Camp" Training Program, which includes team building, problem solving skills, and training in how to "underpromise, yet always overdeliver." Some of the training is done with in-house resources, some involves presentations by suppliers on how to use products.

Each year an employee demonstrating outstanding personal qualities—and a sense of humor— receives the Joey Award, named in honor of CIC founder Joseph Heller. (from left, CIC president Scott Heller, Michelle McCormack (2000), Kevin Vancor (1997), CIC vice president Bob Singleton, Patti O'Brien (1999).

The small community of Grafton is not only a picture-postcard image of rural Vermont, it also embodies the Vermont work ethic that enables a technology company like CIC to provide excellent customer service.

pleasant place in which to work. The street on which it is located was named JLH Memorial Drive, in honor of the company's founder Joseph L. Heller.

"Once the move was completed," says Scott, "we set about creating a culture for a business that was more than 20 years old, but reborn in a new place with a new staff."

Each year one employee receives The Joey Award, also named for Joseph Heller. Among the criteria for the winning employee are tenacity, a thirst for learning, resourcefulness, a zest for life and a great sense of humor.

By 1997, Heller was ready to take the next step toward more employee involvement in the operation of the business. He set up a Supervisor Council with a mandate to take over day-to-day operation of the business. This has enabled him to accelerate the growth of the company to its fullest potential.

The catalog business, operated under the name National Audio-Visual Supply, has been completely refocused and the catalog, produced in-house, has gone to full color. The company's growing e-commerce business is located at www.nationalavsupply.com.

"From now on, my main priority is to focus on the future and what shape the company will take over the next 20 years." It's a bright future, because Heller's bet paid off. A high technology company will thrive in a rural area that shares its ethic of hard work and commitment to quality and service. CIC is the proof.

CHAMPLAIN COLLEGE

At a Rotary Club meeting held at the Hotel Vermont in 1956, Vermont's higher education arena would be changed forever. At that time, A. Gordon Tittemore was the head of the Burlington Business College. Over lunch he casually mentioned that he had taken ill and was putting the college up for sale. As the story goes, businessman C. Bader Brouilette, hearing of this opportunity for the very first time, looked the educator squarely in the eyes and said, "I'd like to have it!"

It's that kind of entrepreneurial spirit upon which Champlain College has moved forward through the years. Founded as the Burlington Commercial School in 1878 by G. W. Thompson, the private college was originally located in downtown Burlington. It evolved first into the Burlington Business College, later a junior college, and now an institution offering associate's and bachelor's degrees to residential students, commuters and online students.

When purchased by C. Bader Brouilette and Albert Jensen in the '50s, the school was renamed Champlain College and was moved

Founded in 1878, Champlain College has grown from humble beginnings in downtown Burlington (photo below circa 1905) to a handsome residential campus in the city's Hill Section.

to its first building in Burlington's historic Hill Section. Administrators purchased a former dormitory from the University of Vermont for $24,000 and called it Freeman Hall, named for Brouilette's wife, Marjorie Freeman Brouilette. The College quickly outgrew its single building, which had seemed like an abundant space when there were only 14 graduates.

Brouilette bought and refurbished older buildings because he liked the idea of keeping the College "invisible" by blending in closely with the style of homes in the Hill Section. Today, Champlain continues that legacy by maintaining historic buildings that make up a handsome campus. Only four of Champlain's 33 buildings have been newly built by the College. The state-of-the-art library, the Miller Information Commons, garnered architectural awards when it was built in 1998 in a style that complements its neighboring historic halls.

Today, Champlain students live in Victorian-era mansions that are wired for the Internet. They get hands-on experience in the latest technologies while enjoying an extraordinary campus with breathtaking views of Lake Champlain.

The College maintains its entrepreneurial outlook as it trains students for lifelong career success in

The Miller Information Commons (above) illustrates the College's commitment to state-of-the-art technology. Students enjoy the features of a traditional library with the added benefits of multimedia laboratories and electronic classrooms.

more than 25 fields. Champlain looks for innovative ways to keep itself on the cutting-edge of higher education. The College anticipates needs in the local and international marketplace and creates popular four- and two-year degree programs around these needs, with a particular emphasis in technology areas. New offerings in the 1990s included International Business, Computer Network & PC Support, Multimedia & Graphic Design, Web Site Development & Management, and e-Business & Commerce.

The College's reputable programs and job placement rate are in demand overseas, as well. Champlain offers its degrees at campuses in Israel, United Arab Emirates and Malaysia, for example. The College opened its doors to the world as it instituted one of the country's first online distance-learning programs and hosts many foreign students on its Burlington campus.

Champlain College graduates around Vermont and the world are testimony to the College's mission of empowering students with skills and professional experiences for lifelong career success.

COMMUNITY COLLEGE OF VERMONT

The Community College of Vermont is a two-year, open admissions institution, and the only community college in the state. A member of the Vermont State Colleges, CCV's mission is to focus on access and affordability. Special emphasis is placed on serving those Vermonters who would otherwise have limited access to higher education due to geographical isolation, lack of academic preparation, or other constraining factors.

CCV's roots can be traced to 1968, when Governor Philip Hoff appointed a task force to research higher education needs in Vermont. Two years later, Governor Deane Davis issued an executive order creating a Community College Commission to pilot a regionalized, non-campus institution. In October 1970, Peter Smith was hired as the college's first president. A few months later in December 1970, the college offered its first 10 courses in Washington County.

Community College of Vermont graduation— a statewide celebration.

Founding president Peter Smith.

In 1972 the CCV was approved for membership in the Vermont State Colleges, and the college awarded its first associate degree in 1973. Throughout the '70s CCV opened additional offices in the state's major population centers. Regional accreditation came in 1975. By 1980, enrollment reached 1,500.

In 1975, the college received its first accreditation from the New England Association of Schools and Colleges, CCV students became eligible for federal financial aid, and a grant from the Carnegie Foundation supported the college in designing academic programs. But 1979 was a difficult, near-fatal year for the college. Always a separate line item in the state budget, the college had a precarious financial future. A ground-swell of public support saved the college.

The 1980s were a period of rebuilding, especially in the area of academic reform. The college was granted the maximum 10-year accreditation in 1982 and continued to expand its sites, bringing the total to 12 and thereby serving virtually all areas of the state. Growth was dramatic, with enrollment reaching 2,639 in 1984, and climbing to 4,180 in 1990, representing an increase of more than 275 percent during the decade.

CCV will celebrate its 30th anniversary in 2000-2001. This is a time to look back over the college's history and to take pride in its accomplishments. CCV's Fall '99 enrollment was 4,723, making it the second largest of any Vermont college, second only to the University of Vermont. In the Fall '99 semester, 68 percent of the students were degree students, and 71 percent were women. Six hundred forty-one students were enrolled full-time. The median age was 30, and Vermonters comprised 98 percent of CCV's student body. The college employs over 500 part-time instructors each semester and a full-time administrative staff of 125.

On-line courses are now offered each semester, with an enrollment of over 400 students in the Fall '99 semester, and these offerings have proven to be a highly popular, academically challenging format for learning that provides access to more Vermonters. CCV continues to be a leader in innovative, creative higher education that meets the needs of students and communities.

EHV-WEIDMANN INDUSTRIES INC. AND WEIDMANN SYSTEMS INTERNATIONAL INC.

EHV Industries was incorporated in Vermont, in October 1969. Its founders were Gordon P. Mills and Robert C. Fuehrer, two young engineers with a dream to create a company that would become a new standard for the quality of its products and a caring place for its employees. After 27 years of service, both founders retired, in 1996. Sadly, Gordon P. Mills passed away in January 1997.

EHV Industries was founded as a producer of electrical grade, cellulose Transformerboard to be used as electrical insulation in liquid-filled transformers for the electric utility industry.

Construction of its first production facility began in Fall 1969 in St. Johnsbury, Vermont, also known as the Northeast Kingdom. A board machine and ancillary equipment for calendering, cutting and shipping were installed. Known as Boardmachine #1, this machine produces low-density pressboard called Hi-Val.

In 1971, EHV Industries drew the attention of 100-year old H. Weidmann, Ltd. of Rapperswil, Switzerland. H. Weidmann is the world's leading producer of transformer insulation systems. Weidmann had a history of providing technically-advanced

Founders Robert C. Fuehrer and Gordon P. Mills.

solutions to electrical transformer manufacturers in Europe and other continents. H. Weidmann and EHV Industries formed a partnership and changed the company's name to EHV-Weidmann Industries Inc. (EHV-Weidmann). H. Weidmann became the sole owner of EHV Industries in 1972.

The company's first expansion came in 1973. Its facility was doubled in size to accommodate additional manufacturing space needed to produce made-to-order fabricated parts for customers under license from H. Weidmann.

Two years later another expansion was implemented. This $7.5 million project increased the manufacturing area to allow for the addition of another board machine. Known as Boardmachine #2, this machine produces a high-density pressboard called T4. The material can be laminated into heavier load bearing insulating components and

is structurally stronger and dimensionally more stable than other grades of pressboard.

In 1976, EHV-Weidmann gave birth to a second company, System Sales Representatives, Inc. (now known as Weidmann Systems International Inc.), formerly a department within EHV-Weidmann. System Sales was established to serve the growing needs in the electrical equipment repair market for a single source supplier of materials. In 1989 SSRI moved to its own building in the Lyndonville Industrial Park. Knowledge of the marketplace and a close association with the industry's leading manufacturers of transformer insulation systems allowed SSRI to carve out its own niche as a "one-stop-shop" for a wide variety of products used in the domestic and international transformer and motor repair and manufacturing markets. In addition, SSRI's growing expertise in overseas countries has made it an ideal contract-sales arm for U.S. producers who were unable, or unwilling, to employ a full-time international sales force. Today WSI is a world leader in supplying materials and services to the transformer and utility industries, with sales offices in Vermont, Mexico and Brazil.

In the Fall of 1978 EHV-Weidmann supplied their first "package order" to the repair industry. The customer now had a source for made-to-order fabricated parts ready for installation upon receipt at their facility, greatly speeding up the repair process.

As the fabrication business continued to grow, more manufacturing space was needed. In 1980 they purchased and renovated a building that had been vacated by a company that had manufactured pre-fabricated homes, adding 45,000 square-feet of manufacturing space. This space was used for manufacturing parts mostly for large transformers. In 1995 this building was sold to a new company, Engineered Thermal Systems, making thermal

EHV-Weidmann Industries Inc.

insulation for the automotive industry. The early development of this product line had been done by EHV-Weidmann. Today this company is owned by Lydall Westex and is also in the process of expanding.

EHV-Weidmann continued its expansion in December 1981 with the purchase of a parts-making company in Burlington, Ontario, Canada. This company had been a subsidiary of B.S. and W. Whiteley of England, a maker of electrical papers and pressboard. With this acquisition, EHV-Weidmann established a presence in Canada and was now a company with international holdings. EHV-Weidmann Industries, Ltd. began making insulation components for the Canadian market, using the pressboard produced in St. Johnsbury.

In 1982 EHV-Weidmann entered into a partnership with the DuPont Corporation to produce pressboard made from Nomex®. Nomex® is a high-temperature, synthetic fiber known for its electrical insulating properties. Nomex® pressboard now compliments EHV-Weidmann's line of cellulose products.

By late 1982 business had grown from one company to three companies (EHV-Weidmann Industries, Inc., System Sales Representatives, Inc., and EHV-Weidmann Industries Ltd.). As a result, the decision was made to form a North American-based holding company, ELCON, Inc., under which H. Weidmann's North American companies would operate. In addition, a separate company, ELCON Management Services Corporation was formed to act as a management company for the ELCON holdings.

The company expanded again in St. Johnsbury in 1984, purchasing an existing 60,000 square foot building next door to its factory. After major structural renovations this building was equipped with several high tech CNC (Computer Numerical Controlled) machines to meet the growing demand for precision fabricated parts.

EHV-Weidmann became the sole producer of transformerboard in North America in 1987. Certain board producing assets of the former competitor Spaulding Fiber located in Rochester, NH were purchased by the holding company. Existing when EHV-Weidmann was started, Spaulding Fiber was the last competitor to exit the business as EHV-Weidmann continued to grow.

In order to provide better job training facilities and introduce new production methods, an Education and Training Center was established in 1990. It also allowed the company to prepare employees for statistical quality methods and to prepare them for the high customer expectations for quality products in today's world.

EHV-Weidmann continues to concentrate on quality. As part of its Quality Assurance system, they began the implementation of Standard Operating Procedures in 1992 for all office and production departments. By 1994 EHV-Weidmann had received ISO 9002 certification from QMI (a division of the Canadian Standards Association) and in 1995 EHV-Weidmann was awarded ISO-9001 certification.

In Spring 1997 EHV-Weidmann

Weidmann Systems International (formerly known as Systems Sales Representatives, Inc).

established its first off-site fabrication facility in the U.S. in Rockford, Tennessee. This facility produces fabricated parts used in distribution transformers—most of which are manufactured in the southern U.S. As part of this operation, they opened a remote site in a large customer's transformer manufacturing facility in 1998. They plan for and provide point-of-use stocking of all their insulation needs throughout the plant. Also in 1997 EHV-Weidmann established a fabrication facility in Saltillo, Mexico in order to produce timely and high-quality fabricated parts and packages for its Mexican customers.

EHV-Weidmann and Weidmann Systems International continue to look to the future to meet and exceed the expectations of their customers in the Americas. In its short history in Vermont EHV-Weidmann has become a major contributor to the quality of life of its employees and the economic well-being of the Northeast Kingdom. As an environmentally conscious company, EHV-Weidmann recently received the Governor's Award for Environmental Excellence in Pollution Prevention. At the same time Vermont, with its natural beauty and friendly people, has proven to be a wonderful place to live and work and is one of the key ingredients to EHV-Weidmann's success.

FREEMAN FRENCH FREEMAN, INC.

Freeman French Freeman, Architects was established in 1937, with the union of William and Ruth Freeman, (husband and wife), and John French. Originally located at 138 Church Street in Burlington, the small firm grew quickly. The company's early projects were primarily residences and local schools, where the architects demonstrated their understanding of and empathy towards Vermonters and their specific needs. These needs included designing buildings that could withstand the northern climate and accommodate the usually thrifty Vermont budget.

The architects established a rapport with the community by taking on all projects that were brought to them, whatever the size. "A small job, with a satisfied client," they wrote in 1949, "will lead to a larger project at some later date." By adhering to this philosophy and maintaining close, personal client relationships, larger projects followed.

"The Grill" at Middlebury College, Middlebury, Vermont.

The firm designed a new state office building in Montpelier in 1940, followed by a terminal at the Malone, New York airport. Other undertakings included the Thayer School in Burlington, the Chapel and Science buildings at Saint Michael's College and St. Marks Catholic Church, (which received national attention in articles in the *New York Times* and *Time* magazine).

By the mid-1950s the company had grown to 12 employees in addition to the three principals. It moved to 158 Bank Street when Bill Weise and Fred Senftleber joined the firm to become partners, in 1958 and 1967, respectively. It was in 1957 that they began a series of works for the University of Vermont, including the College of Medicine and the Gutterson Field House. The firm also designed the Rice Memorial High School.

The '60s proved to be an equally busy time as the company embarked on designing and building major additions to the Bennington Museum and the Essex Junction High School, and expansions to the Mary

Fletcher Hospital and Champlain College. In the late '60s they moved to the new Chittenden Bank Building where they would eventually employ more than 50 engineers and designers. "At one point," noted principal Fred Senftleber, "we were doing just about everything in Burlington and northern New England."

The early 1970s were a turning point for Freeman French Freeman. A plane crash claimed the lives of three senior associates and caused the firm to rethink its direction. The company decided to reduce its architect and engineer staff and become more focused on architectural design. They became immersed in being a planning architecture and interiors firm, designing colleges, universities, and medical and research facilities. A significant project in the late '70s through the early '80s was the Canal Plaza complex in Portland, Maine—a downtown revitalization plan where the architects contributed five office buildings that housed an IBM building, a six-screen movie theatre, a bank, and three levels of public parking.

Burlington International Airport, Burlington, Vermont.

In 1988 they brought on Jesse Beck, a Burlington native who was called in to fulfill a need to pass the company on to a new generation. Senftleber and Weise, who had both been with the firm for 45 years, were nearing retirement.

Presently, with Beck as president, David Ashley as senior vice-president, and Steve Mosman, vice-president, educational institutions remain an important focus. A recent endeavor, "The Grille" at McCullough for Middlebury College, won them an American Institute of Architects award. On this project they used a team of students and faculty to assist in planning, complying with Beck's idea that each job should be a team effort with the client having as much knowledge and involvement as possible.

Over the last five years, Freeman French Freeman has steadily increased its role in semi-conductor manufacturing projects supporting re-tooling of clean rooms and facilities expansion projects for IBM. The company is also currently designing a $30 million campus for IDX Systems Corporation, allowing the nationally-known medical soft-

ware firm to expand its home base and provide over 1,300 new jobs.

In 1998 the Burlington International Airport was completed, becoming the firm's largest civic transportation project. The design accomplished a new 1,100 car parking structure connected to a 43,000 square-foot expansion and remodel of the existing terminal via an enclosed sky-bridge crossing six lanes of vehicular traffic below. The

$17 million project achieved a new 21st century image for the gateway building to Vermont and received the AIA "Excellence in Architecture" Award.

Another recently completed project was Centennial Field, a classic 1921 baseball stadium for the Montreal Expos Farm Team at the University of Vermont. The restoration and expansion returned the park to its original 1920s charm, continuing Freeman French Freeman's 40-year service to the University and the historic character of Vermont.

For over 60 years Freeman French Freeman has honored its responsibility to the community by working hard to complete projects in a timely manner within budget.

Using the latest in computer technologies to advance its profession, Freeman French Freeman continues to diversify and specialize, responding to the changing needs of its clients and their working and living environments. Its efforts continue to establish and maintain satisfied clients through responsible leadership.

Canal Plaza complex, Portland, Maine.

DORE AND WHITTIER, INC.

Dore and Whittier, Inc. is a full-service architectural design and project management firm with headquarters in South Burlington, Vermont.

The present members of the firm and many of their consultants have been working together throughout New England and New York for over 25 years.

Originally formed as The Whittier Associates prior to 1975, the firm has grown through several name changes, including more than 15 years as the New England Branch office of Sargent-Webster-Crenshaw & Folley. The current firm name recognizes the two key individuals responsible for the success of the office over the last 25 years, with R. John Dore as principal in charge.

Dore and Whittier, Inc. established its reputation in architecture by providing extensive research, design and administrative services

A collage of projects which dot the Vermont countryside. From Top: The Green Mountain Power Corporate Headquarters, Williston Central School, Mt. Mansfield Union High School and St. Albans Town Educational Center.

The founders of Dore and Whittier, Inc. From left - Roland "Whit" Whittier and R. John Dore collaborate on a conceptual floor plan.

tailored to meet the individual needs and budgets of each client. They create and lead a project team of professional architects, engineers and planners carefully selected to best suit each project. The result of this approach is an excellent reputation for innovative and cost effective projects. Dore and Whittier's primary focus has always been educational architecture. Their educational facility design experience ranges from pre-kindergarten to collegiate work. Although educational design is a large part of the Dore and Whittier workload, they are very accomplished with architecture in other fields including commercial/industrial, religious, correctional, aquaculture, and municipal services.

Dore and Whittier, Inc. is committed to total client satisfaction. They approach each project individually, accommodating each unique site and responding to a projects' desired goals. Their designs do not take the "cookie cutter" approach, but rather evolve from the input of the users, community, and the site.

Vermont is home to Dore and Whittier's corporate headquarters. They have recently expanded in both Vermont and Massachusetts. A new satellite office is located near Boston to allow responsive service to their client base in that region.

The company logo, *"designing for the future,"* is a testament to the company's vision for innovation and their openness to new ideas. It is also representative of their commitment to the ever-changing world of technology and its beneficial uses to provide enhanced services to their clients.

Dore and Whittier, Inc. is proud to have had an opportunity to lend a guiding hand to the architectural diversity that makes Vermont unique. Their creative designs can be seen throughout the state, from schools and libraries to fish hatcheries, and from corporate headquarters to manufacturing facilities.

Dore and Whittier credits its success to the commitment, hard work and dedication of its staff. The company is excited for the future and the challenges that lie ahead in this new millennium.

GRANITE CITY TOOL COMPANY OF VERMONT

"Everything for Stoneworking," the motto of the Granite City Tool Co., has remained unchanged during its 115 years. Founded in 1885 as New England Tool Works by James Ahern, it was the first local tool manufacturer and supplier serving the stone industry, transforming Barre, Vermont from an agricultural village to "The Granite City." Stone-cutting tools of that time were mostly hand-held hammers and chisels that had changed little from millenniums earlier when the Pyramids were built in Egypt.

In 1892 the firm moved to its new woodframe plant on Blackwell Street, where it still remains. Soon, compressed-air powered machinery was introduced; from then on, stone cutting technology exploded. Unfortunately, failing health prevented Mr. Ahern, who had specialized in blacksmithing, from keeping pace with the changing market.

To fill the need, William G. Cumming, a highly-skilled young machinist, joined the firm in 1912. He was the son of a monumental letter and design carver of Scottish birth.

Will Cumming purchased the business in 1917 with his own savings and changed the name to Granite City Tool Co. Immediately, he drew up a plan of expansion to establish the company as a leader in serving the stone trades from quarry to cemetery, both locally and nationally. Assisting him were his brothers Harold and Francis on the sales staff and sisters Helen and Esther in the office.

In the early 1920s Will Cumming engineered vacuum dust collection systems for Central Vermont stone fabricators which proved so successful that the State made this type of dust removal mandatory by 1936. As a result the industry was purged of the dreaded occupational disease silicosis, caused by continual breathing of air-borne silica stone dust.

After years of experimentation, in 1936 Will Cumming patented and

began manufacture of an electrical grinding and polishing machine that processed granite from quarry slab to completed monument. Hundreds were installed in plants throughout the U.S. and abroad. During World War II Granite City Tool Co. produced chisels for the U.S. Navy.

William G. Cumming (1890-1947), business strategist and inventor, laid the foundation for the company's future.

Sheldon C. Allen (1900-1996), hard-working descendent of early Vermonters successfully led the company through much of the past half-century.

In 1947 Will Cumming died at the age of 57, and was interred in the granite family mausoleum he had built—one of the earliest in local cemeteries.

The task of continuing his work fell to Sheldon C. Allen, husband of Will's sister Helen, who had begun employment with the company in 1938. Scion of Vermont's early settlers, "Shel" led the company with hard work and determination from the age of wire sawing to the threshold of diamond technology, for a span of over 35 years. During this time he brought many new products to the industry. He was assisted by his two sons—William S. Allen (who died in 1998) and Donald G. Allen, along with Robert L. Eisenwinter, son of Will's sister Esther. He continued as counselor until his death in 1996 at age 95.

During the past decade, when Granite City Tool Co. has introduced computers to the monument industry, Donald G. Allen, son of Sheldon and nephew of Will Cumming, has been in charge.

GRACE COTTAGE HOSPITAL
IN THE OTIS HEALTH CARE CENTER

For a half century, Grace Cottage Hospital has provided excellent health care for residents, visitors and passers-by in the 26 communities of southern Vermont's West River Valley.

The state's smallest hospital, Grace Cottage has earned a widespread reputation for the skilled treatment of patients in need of acute, chronic, emergency or long-term care. The hospital is equally well-known for the compassionate manner in which patients and their families are treated—patients are treated as family and patients' families and friends are made to feel welcome. Hospital founder Dr. Carlos Otis set the tone when he said, "I want my hospital to be 'homey,' not hospitally."

Otis' vision made possible the creation of a local institution with a regional focus and, now, a national reputation. In 1949, using his considerable persuasive talents and perseverance, Otis secured the gift of a large house in Townshend for the hospital building. Later that year

The small hospital with the big heart.

The house that became a hospital in Townshend, Vermont was a gift to country doctor Carlos Otis (photo inset) in 1949. With foresight and perseverence, Otis created a critically-needed health care center. Grace Cottage is known for its tender, loving care of patients and their families.

Grace Cottage Hospital in 1985 (inset). "A model of integrated care" describes the new combined inpatient/skilled nursing home wing connected to the original hospital. The innovative design makes possible numerous efficiencies in use of common space, staffing and patient care.

when Otis' friend Dr. Abel Grout made a substantial cash gift (with the provision that the hospital be named for his wife, Grace), the Townshend physician had his much-needed facility. For the next 42 years Otis was Grace Cottage's administrator, CEO and board chairman. At his hospital, many of his neighbors were born and treated throughout their lifetimes. When

they became ill in their later lives, they returned to the hospital to spend their last days in familiar, friendly surroundings.

Despite the financial challenges common to all rural non-profit hospitals, Grace Cottage has added many of the health care services most needed by the community. Conforming to a comprehensive, long-range plan, an outpatient clinic was built in 1992. This clinic was financed by the contributions of supportive and generous community members who now receive these essential healthcare services without the added time and expense of traveling to more distant locations.

Thus, over the years, Grace Cottage had become the "crown jewel" of a small complex of healthcare buildings which included a 19-bed inpatient facility, an 18-bed skilled nursing home, a community care residence and an outpatient clinic. In 1992 all of these components were combined under the name "Otis Health Care Center," in memory of the founder. Since then, new departments and services under the corporate umbrella include a retail pharmacy, a new inpatient/skilled nursing home building mandated by the state, home oxygen services, and the Valley Health Council, providing homemaker and transportation services.

When asked how Grace Cottage has survived and even grown at a time of uncertainty in the nationwide health care community, current hospital CEO Al LaRochelle responded: "Our diversity is meeting the needs of our community. As we have done each year, we will continue to adapt to changing conditions. We make all possible cost containment measures without compromising our first responsibility—patient care."

LaRochelle added that Grace Cottage has reacted to the diminishing need for acute hospital care (a national trend) by providing more outreach programs. As examples he cited rural clinics, a strong rehabilitation program, and other outpatient specialties. The CEO also cited the important role that Grace Cottage's devoted volunteers have played over the years, in all departments of the facility. "And we have the only hospital with its own 24-hour ambulance service, staffed largely by volunteers," he noted.

With an annual operating budget of $7,500,000, the Otis Health Care Center has 162 employees, including three family practice physicians, a pediatrician, a midwife, a psychiatrist, and two podiatrists. To assure the long-term financial stability of the Otis Health Care Center and Grace

All the comforts of home are found in the Stratton House Nursing Home, including Rascal, a much-loved tabby cat. An adult care program, first in the state, offers special day or night care in Stratton House for non-residents and their spouses.

Cottage Hospital, the Grace Cottage Foundation was established in 1994. The Foundation's mission is to raise and manage funds for the Otis Center. By continuing to secure major gifts

Lifesaving is Grace Cottage's specialty. Trained volunteer EMT's and 24-hour ambulance and emergency room service protect the community.

and bequests, the Foundation will strengthen the endowment and help to offset the Otis Health Care Center's operating losses brought about by inadequate government reimbursement programs for rural hospitals. Otis Center trustees are encouraged by the increasing support given to the Foundation, realizing that the future of Grace Cottage is dependent on its success.

Working in close cooperation with neighboring hospitals and physicians, Grace Cottage has established a unique niche in Vermont healthcare. Combining the best from its tradition-rich past with the strategies of today's forward-thinking management team, Grace Cottage Hospital and its allied services face the future with confidence and optimism. Its credo that "patients always come first" remains in place, while its mission to provide the best possible health care at the lowest possible cost can only strengthen its partnership with friends and supporters.

Says Grace Cottage's Dr. Robert Backus, "This hospital, built on love and pennies, is a throwback to a kinder, gentler time."

THE INN AT SAWMILL FARM

Sawmill Farm is a place of firsts. On its site, William Gragg built a sawmill in 1796. On its site 171 years later, the Williams family began building a world class inn.

Though Gragg's enterprise missed by five years being the first sawmill in the area, it was the first building in a new village that would become West Dover. Its wheels powered by the North Branch of the Deerfield River, the mill led a long and prosperous life. Its ownership passed from Gragg through the hands of nine other owners to Ernest Burbee, who, in 1901, saw it destroyed by fire. Thirty-five years later, its older counterpart in East Dover would meet the same fate.

Early in the 1800s, Samuel Miller added a gristmill, fulling-mill (making felt), clothier's works, and potash factory at the site. Late in that century, John B. Davis and his son John A. made their mark manufacturing chair stock.

On the east bank of the river, the mill's dam created a lake along which ran the road. Farmers cleared land in the river's valley for crops. Of those farms that survived after the mill was destroyed, it was the

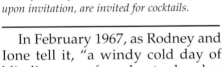

One of the two trout ponds at Sawmill, and the home of Rodney and Ione Williams where guests, upon invitation, are invited for cocktails.

Winston Farm, dating to 1880, that would become the base for the Inn at Sawmill Farm.

The Inn was an afterthought. Rodney and Ione Williams were an architect and interior designer, respectively, who lived in Atlantic City, New Jersey and had, for 15 years vacationed on the ski slopes near West Dover. The town is in the picturesque foothills of the Green Mountains and about three miles from Mount Snow, one of the foremost ski areas in New England.

In February 1967, as Rodney and Ione tell it, "a windy cold day of blinding snow forced us to abandon the ski trails. For diversion, we chose to bother a real estate firm. You cannot imagine the strange sensation we experienced when the realtor took us directly to a farm we had, in passing, greatly admired for years.

"We have never been quite sure who was more surprised that day when we purchased the lovely old Winston Farm—we or the realtor."

The farm had just gone on the market, and they made their decision, even though deep snow drifts kept them from seeing the inside of the little farmhouse and barn. Given their professions, Ione says, "We knew we'd change it, whatever shape it was in."

Change, it turned out, was in the cards for them as well as the farm. What they had originally planned to use as a vacation home became their permanent residence when they decided to leave a changing Atlantic City. However, there was little call for their professional skills in Vermont. They decided to open a ski

Walls of weathered barn boards compliment bright chintz sofas and copper tables in the living room where a fire blazes in the oversize brick hearth.

lodge, but one with much more style and grace than was normal for the area.

Rodney and Ione resurrected the old farm. "We discreetly claimed the existing hand-hewn posts and beams, the mellowed barn boards, the old bricks and field stones in the construction of a country inn," they note. Of their goal in a field so foreign to their professions, they say, "Many of our guidelines were our own responses to the many inns we had previously visited. We tried to capture and mold that which we most enjoyed from each of them."

This and their professional sensibilities led to a charmingly decorated four-star retreat on 20 acres, which has become an outstanding destination in all seasons of the year. In addition to downhill and cross-country skiing, and snowshoe hiking in the winter, it offers tennis, fishing in its trout ponds, and access to golf, antiquing, country auctions, theater and the Marlboro Music Festival during warmer weather.

The new innkeepers set out to retain the original flavor while creating a first-class lodge. One of the barn's red and white exterior walls became part of an interior hallway and the hay loft turned into a library, TV area and game room overlooking the living room as they opened their first nine guest rooms.

Over the years the family carefully expanded its facilities, retaining the intimate, small inn quality they cherished. Its 20 guest rooms are each unique and changing, as Ione ensures that their decor does not become "tired." The rooms include 10 "fireplace cottages," spacious rooms and suites with wood-burning fireplaces. Particularly noteworthy are the Cider House, the Woodshed (which overlooks a pond and private garden) and the Spring and Mill houses, originally built for Rodney and Ione's two children, Brill and Bobbie Dee, both of whom came to participate in operating the inn.

Brill, in particular, joined his

Plants, flowers and old-time farm implements adorn the soaring entryway to The Inn at Sawmill Farm.

parents as a partner after he finished college. He replaced Ione in the kitchen, developing his skills as a gourmet chef and wine expert. His menus contributed to The Inn at Sawmill Farm receiving the Dirona Award (Distinguished Restaurants of North America) and his skill at selecting wines led to *Wine Spectator* awarding the Inn its Grand Award and a place on its list of the 100 best wine cellars in the world. The Inn also captured a four-star rating from the Mobil Travel Guide.

Dining room specialties include an eclectic array of regional and international dishes, such as Peekytoe Maine crabmeat with roulades of mushroom duxelle; Vermont trout sauteed in white wine with lemon and capers; grilled

Chandeliers hung from rustic beams and candlelight cast a warm glow of romanticism in the dining room.

loin of venison in a green peppercorn sauce; Scotish smoked salmon; Osetra caviar; onion brioche and quail eggs; and Indonesian curried chicken breasts with caramelized bananas, toasted coconut and chutney.

Thus, what began as a mom-and-pop operation a third of a century ago continued to amass firsts. Its owners envisioned it as a romantic inn before the term was known, and pioneered rustic elegance. Its style is considered refined and posh, no telephones or televisions in the rooms, excellent service, and fine chocolates at bedside.

All of this led to The Inn at Sawmill Farm being one of the first properties in America invited to join Relais & Chateaux, the high-end hotel directory and guide published in France. European hotels still predominate the publication, which focuses on "Five C's" in selecting entries: Calm, Courtesy, Cuisine, Character and Charm.

These qualities, and the warmth of the Williams family, have made the Inn at Sawmill Farm itself, first.

HAZELETT STRIP-CASTING CORPORATION

The origin of Hazelett Strip-Casting Corporation dates back to 1919, when Clarence W. Hazelett, a physicist, writer, and inventor, founded the Hazelett Storage Battery Company in Cleveland, Ohio. Rather than individually cast lead plates for automotive batteries, Hazelett developed a method of continuously casting the molten lead into the shaped plates. This pioneering effort initiated a distinguished endeavor into the field of continuous metal casting that has now spanned three generations of the Hazelett family.

In the 1930s Clarence developed and sold various casters for aluminum, brass, copper, and even steel, some of which were for Europe and Japan. Later he worked in his shops in Greenwich, Connecticut with his sons Bill and Richard, gradually developing the "twin-belt" concept, the basis of the company's work today. At that time, Bill was living in Burlington, Vermont, and commuting to Greenwich.

When his father died in 1956, Bill formed Hazelett Strip-Casting Corporation. Starting with only his brother and a handful of employees, the company has grown to over 130 employees, with annual sales of $20 million. It remains in the Hazelett family today, undergoing a gradual change in leadership from Bill, now 81, to his son David, and his daughter Ann Cordner.

A 48" wide Hazelett copper strip caster is the heart of a new copper strip casting and rolling plant in Europe.

Hazelett offices and plant on Malletts Bay on Lake Champlain, north of Burlington.

The company remains focused, yielding neither to the pressures by overseas customers to have equipment made abroad, nor to the temptation to expand into related equipment that could be tied-in with the proprietary casting machines. Hazelett continues to be the world's only commercial supplier of twin-belt continuous-casting machines, despite numerous failed attempts in other countries to copy the design, for which the basic patents have long expired. Experience and know-how are the keys. Bill Hazelett delights in telling visitors that the strength of his group lies not in knowing what works, but what does not.

Continuous casting offers a method of metals fabrication requiring a fraction of the capital, operating, and energy costs of the conventional ingot casting and rolling process.

Despite its tranquil manufacturing site on the shores of Malletts Bay, the company's activities are quite far reaching; engineers constantly travel the globe. The casters, which can take up to 18 months to manufacture at costs of up to $10 million, are the critical component of dedicated metal melting, casting, and rolling facilities often representing an investment of $50+ million.

Many plants run 24-hours a day. If the Hazelett caster goes down, lost production costs accumulate quickly.

Therefore, Hazelett is extremely customer-driven and thrives as such. Spare parts and service supplied (sometimes overnight) to customers in 28 countries account for over half of the company's total sales. As Hazelett does not cast metal in its own plant, new inventions are constantly being tested by Hazelett engineers in customer plants.

In many ways, the company is a throwback to a by-gone era, maintaining costly machine shops to provide fast response to customer needs as well as to be in a position to try out a new idea immediately.

All this originates from Vermont because that is where Bill Hazelett came to ski and sail 55 years ago. The values of Vermont continue to serve Hazelett well. With most customers coming from heavily industrialized areas, Vermont is a revelation, serving as a positive reinforcement to the value and quality of the American innovation and craftsmanship that prevails within the company.

KARL SUSS AMERICA, INC.

The employees of Karl Suss America are highly-skilled technicians who can manipulate objects as small as one-fiftieth the size of a human hair. In the making of microcircuits, time and temperature, size of objects, rate of spin, and volume of metals are only some of the variables that must be exactly controlled. Timing and precision are essential in the manufacture of a product range that includes the world's fastest production mask aligners, spin coater products for high-end application markets, bonders and test equipment for semiconductor manufacturing.

The executives of the SUSS Group showed the same careful attention to detail in 1980 when the German-based company decided to locate its U.S. headquarters in Waterbury Center. A stable and highly-qualified labor force, existing electronic precision industries in northern New England, and proximity to Europe were practical considerations for choosing Vermont. But the employees at the 25-acre center like to believe it was the rolling countryside, so like the mountain meadows near Munich, that really brought the international company to central Vermont.

ACS 200 Spin Coater Module.

View of the production facility.

Twenty years later, the North American headquarters has grown from five employees in 1980 to approximately 130 people in Waterbury and 30 sales and service representatives in San Jose and Phoenix. Peter Szafir, president of Karl Suss America, notes that the company is entering a rapid growth period. "We expect to increase revenues by 20 percent per year," he reports.

The expansion of the research and development arm of Karl Suss America has played an important role in the development of new products. Szafir is especially proud of the ACS200 Coating Cluster, an automated coating system designed and developed at Waterbury from 1995 to 1998.

The ACS 200 is used as a key toolset for many of the latest semi-conductor labs and foundries as they work to package the chips in the smallest possible footprint.

The international consortium of Karl Suss also marked a major shift in May 1999, when the family-owned company went public on the Frankfurt Stock Exchange. The publicly-owned company, which also celebrated its 50th anniversary in 1999, is now targeting its revenues toward the development of new product and product technology in the fast-paced semiconductor manufacturing and testing industry.

Herr Karl Suss founded the German company in 1949, in a bombed-out basement with three workers who sold precision optics. In the early 1960s, the company shifted from sales to producing equipment for the fledgling semi-conductor industry. "Karl understood the need for a particular type of machine, and in typical entrepreneurial fashion, he and his two sons Ekkehard and Winfried, designed and built the first mask aligners," says Szafir.

As the company grew throughout the 1970s and '80s, Karl Suss developed its reputation for excellence through exceptional engineering and customer service. According to Dr. Franz Richter, president and chief executive officer, "We are now strong in the world markets because we have been able to fuse together the German characteristics of quality and precision, the American strength of total customer orientation, and the Asian service concept into a single corporate philosophy.

KENCO, INC.

K.D. Distributors was established in 1971 by Ken Griggs and his wife Jean. With Ken's 18 years experience in sales and several in the custodial/janitorial field, their dream was to establish a company based on the philosophy of distributing quality, environmentally-safe custodial supplies through an establishment based on Christian principles of truth and moral integrity. These products would be user-friendly, performing in such a way that the customer would see quality results from their labors. It would provide training and advice in the best, most efficient way, to care for schools, industry, hospitals, nursing homes, etc., where sanitation and attractive professional appearance are to be desired. Important decisions were to be taken to the Lord in prayer, a practice that continues today.

The business started in a one-car garage in Barre but due to growth it became necessary to rent a vacant restaurant on North Main Street. The next move was to 3,000 square-feet of space on South Main Street with provision for a small office and storage, all on one level. With no loading dock, 55-gallon drums were rolled off trailers onto rubber tires, righted and stored! Until now Ken had been the salesman, delivery person and warehouse manager with one part-time employee. Reg,

Seated is Ken Griggs, president and standing is Reg Griggs, vice-president and marketing manager.

oldest son and student at the University of Vermont, did the books when on school breaks. This business now covers all of Vermont and New Hampshire with special accounts in New York and Gordon College in Massachusetts, and employs about 24 people!

In 1973 Reg Griggs, upon his graduation from UVM with a degree in business, became a partner. They decided to incorporate under the name, Kenco, Inc. An excellent chemical company, Buckeye International, with many of the same principles of honesty as Kenco and

with trustworthy products and chemists, was chosen to provide the products distributed, along with other reliable manufacturers. Growth necessitated the purchase of the "Skyline Ski Lodge" on Railroad Street Extension, where an addition provided for further storage, loading docks, provision for trucks and office space.

The staff grew, and in 1974 daughter Patsy Knapp came on board and remains as office/purchasing manager. Daughter Lori Beede was next to join and continues as assistant office and customer service manager. Daughter Donna Gallagher was part of Kenco for several years in many capacities, as billing clerk, receptionist and general secretary; she has since moved on to work for "Wheels Transportation Company" where she is ride match manager. Son Scott Griggs joined the company as credit manager upon his graduation from Barrington College with degrees in business and Bible. He has since

Grand opening preparations in 1985.

gone into the teaching profession as instructor of computer networking at Barre Technical Center. Sons-in-law on staff include Harry Gallagher, sales staff for over 20 years; Luke Knapp, Jr., warehouse manager; and Leon Beede, driver/service employee. Luke Knapp, Sr. is valued as he cleans, paints and runs errands as a part-time employee. Long-time employees include salesman, Ken Pratt; Wayne Holt, in deliveries; and Don Leno, machines serviceman who also cares for company vehicles and equipment. Wayne's brother, Dennis Holt, worked in repairs for many years until his tragic death from leukemia in August 1999. All employees are valued and considered a part of the "Kenco family."

In October 1983 ground was broken on Route 302 in Barre Town for the present Kenco, Inc. facility. Constructed of steel, it was designed by Ken and Reg with guidance from their architect. Construction was done in the early stages with Ken acting as general contractor, assisted by an experienced construction man. December found Ken, Reg and others 35 feet off the ground, straddling rafters to get the building enclosed before winter hit. It was finally completed with the help of family and employees for the grand opening on July 5, 1985.

Life has been busy. Ken joined The Gideons International, an association of Christian Business and Professional men placing God's Word in 1971; Jean also became a part of the Gideon Auxiliary. Ken's active roll in this ministry led to his election in 1983 to the International Gideon Cabinet as Zone 8 trustee, overseeing the ministry in New England and New York. After six years he was appointed to Area 3 Representative, requiring his travel to oversee Gideons in 13 countries in South America and the Islands. He traveled there several times each year for two to six weeks at a time. God provided, and family members took over while he was away, making

necessary decisions and handling emergencies, freeing him to do the Lord's work. Without their assistance and commitment he could not have served in this way. Often he could not be reached for days, and the family and employees carried on.

Community activity has included donations to the Food Shelf, Websterville Christian School and other local groups. Ken, Jean and three of their children live in Orange, where Ken has been a lister and cemetery commissioner and Jean has served on the school board. As members of the Orange Alliance Church, Ken has been elder and trustee and Jean, clerk and deaconess. They now have 11 grandchildren and three great-grandchildren.

Kenco constructed a new building in 1985 to meet its ever-expanding needs.

Kenco staff in 1998.

As company president at 68, Ken is still very much in charge and active in all phases of the business. He may be found at any time repairing machines, working with Patsy in ordering, teaching how to clean and coat a floor, leading a sales meeting, plowing the yard, behind his desk, or, at his favorite pastime, on the road, selling! The "work ethic" Ken and Jean grew up with and tried to instill in their children keeps Ken humble. He doesn't see retiring any time soon. They say the future is in the hands of God as it has been from the beginning as they pray for His guidance. They would say, "We don't know what the future holds, but we know Who holds the future."

MACINTYRE FUELS, INC.

MacIntyre Fuels, Inc. entered the fuel oil business on January 1, 1943 as a distributor of home heat products throughout Addison County. Henry MacIntyre started the business out of his home—literally from the kitchen table—branded as a Mobil Oil dealer. He began to peddle fuel from house to house, gradually gathering new customers along the way. It was his commitment to quality products and outstanding service that allowed him to grow and gain new customers and accounts. As the home heat business grew, Henry was able to acquire a service station in the center of Middlebury (also branded Mobil) to serve the needs of motorists as the town continued to grow. In 1954, Henry's health began to deteriorate. Without help, Henry

One of the MacIntyre Fuels, Inc. fleet of railroad cars.

had no choice but to sell off the home heating portion of the business. As times became tougher, Henry ended up selling the service station in 1961. Henry's son Roch had just graduated high school and was willing to help make a second attempt at the home heating business with his father. With Henry's knowledge and Roch's physical ability, the timing was right.

This time around there were more competitors with the same outlook as MacIntyre Fuels, Inc. Once again, MacIntyre's commitment to quality and service paved the way, as they were able to regain some of the accounts they had sold off, and more to boot. The business did well, and things were on a roll. Then, in April 1968, Roch was called to serve his country in the Vietnam War. This again left Henry stranded, but he was able to pull through until Roch returned in the fall of 1969.

That same year they were given the opportunity to buy out a local fuel oil retailer. They did what had to be done and discovered they had acquired a great deal of new business. As the business continued to grow they brought new employees on board.

With growth the headquarters moved from Seymour Street to Route Seven, north of Middlebury. This location served as home base for quite some time, until it too, became restrictive. The home heat business needed more space for trucks. The services available by being close to the rail line would allow larger volumes by rail cars. In 1988 another local fuel oil company became available, and MacIntyre Fuels, Inc. purchased the business, continuing their growth in the petroleum business.

Now at a central location in Addison County, the groundwork

Motor transport fleet.

was laid to further build the oil business, which Roch did. As time went on and Roch's knowledge of the oil business grew, he saw fit to buy out another company in 1990—a local plumbing and heating company which would compliment the home heat business. Now when customers came to buy their fuel, they could also get their furnace cleaned and checked out for the winter. In addition, MacIntyre Plumbing and Heating could work off of the established customer base to do plumbing and other service work. A year later, MacIntyre Fuels, Inc. bought out a petroleum equipment company. This new addition was able to provide larger scale of fuel oil work such as bulk oil storage facilities, reconditioning gas stations, and removal, disposal, and replacement of aboveground and underground fuel oil tanks.

MacIntyre Fuels, Inc. had aligned itself for the future in the oil industry—not only to compete, but to stay. MacIntyre Fuels, Inc. has

progressed to yet *another* level, by becoming the only fuel dealer in Vermont to operate four bulk oil terminals distributing petroleum products throughout Vermont, New Hampshire, northern New York and northern Massachusetts, as well as by owning bulk petroleum transport vehicles and railroad cars for distribution.

MacIntyre Fuels, Inc. has come a long way since 1943, and intends to continue the quality products and profound service that originally gave them their start.

Rutland, Vermont terminal.

LOVEJOY TOOL COMPANY, INC.

The Lovejoy Tool Company was founded on the strength of one patent and a promise.

The patent was awarded on September 5, 1916 to Frederick P. Lovejoy, then serving as chief designer for Jones & Lamson, for an inserted blade boring bar.

The promise, made in Lovejoy Tool Company's first catalog in 1917, stated simply, "We are entering the metal cutting tool business to stay and our aim is to give service."

James Hartness, Lovejoy's boss at Jones & Lamson, described the device in the founding prospectus as a "turning tool, such as may be used in engine lathes... It consists of a shank and cutter with a novel means of affixing the cutter to the shank." He added that "this company seems to start with a favorable prospect, with an invention of promise, and with men of the right character and experience."

The first building Lovejoy Tool Company occupied was directly next to Jones & Lamson, which had helped Lovejoy get started. Eventually, Lovejoy took over the Jones & Lamson building, filled the lot between the two structures with manufacturing space, and in 1975 replaced the old wooden structure with one made of brick.

Frederick P. Lovejoy, founder.

Jones & Lamson is credited with creating "Precision Valley" in Springfield by encouraging young inventors and helping set them up in business. The Fellows Gear Shaper Company and the Bryant Chucking Grinder Company had already started when Hartness brought Lovejoy together with

Charles N. Safford to form Lovejoy Tool.

The firm began operations in a Jones & Lamson shop opposite the U.S. Post Office on Main Street, in what is now its business office. Lovejoy prospered and by 1942, it employed approximately 30 people. In 1943, the Lovejoy sales department expanded to distribute its products nationally; today the company has nearly 50 U.S. representatives, as well as salespeople in Canada, Mexico, Asia and Europe.

In 1944, Lovejoy earned the Defense Department "E" Award and required additional manufacturing space. The firm bought the three-story brick Jones & Lamson building next to its factory in 1947. In 1952, an area in the basement was leveled off and a concrete floor was poured for the steel room and carpenters' shop.

Douglas Priestley, president of Lovejoy, explains that prior to 1935 the company grossed less than $50,000 per year manufacturing regrindable cutting tools. Sales increased during World War II and surpassed the million-dollar mark during the Korean War. In the early 1960s the firm developed an indexable milling cutter with disposable blades—a great convenience for customers—and started a boom that pushed annual sales over four million dollars by 1970.

Additional manufacturing and office facilities were constructed to increase sales during the next decade. Later, a computer-aided design and manufacturing (CAD-CAM) center was installed to develop the sophisticated milling cutter designs and the computer-generated machine tools programs for the manufacturing of these cutters.

During the 1990s, many multiple axis computer controlled machines were acquired to increase productivity and the doubling of Lovejoy Tool's sales once again.

McCARTY LAW OFFICES, P.C.

McCarty Law Offices, P.C. is typical Vermont—strong, singular, independent, and free of obligation to any third person.

The firm has prided itself on its independence and separation from all forms of business ties which would in any way fetter its client representation. It has been termed the most aggressive and successful law firm (aggressive in the positive sense, on behalf of its clients) in the recent history of Southern Vermont.

It has prided itself on independence and dedication to clients and their cause. This attitude as a professional advocate has never been compromised or intimidated by any adversary, whether government or individual.

McCarty Law Offices, P.C. was originally founded by William M. McCarty in 1971, after a successful career with an insurance defense firm in Brattleboro.

The firm has excelled in areas that many other firms avoid, especially in the area of recreational and ski litigation.

William M. McCarty, the principal shareholder and officer of the corporation, was born in Trenton, NJ in 1938, and was admitted to the Bar in 1967. This was after four years in the United States Marine

Offices of William M. McCarty, P.C.

William M. McCarty.

Corps at the Ceremonial Guard Company in Washington, D.C. at Marine Barracks (thereafter working his way through college at American University in Washington, D.C. and at Dickinson College in Carlisle, Pennsylvania). He attended the Dickinson School of Law and graduated in 1967 in the top 10 percent of his class.

He has been listed in "Who's Who in American Law," 1983; "Who's Who in the World," 1991; "Who's Who in Finance & Industry," 2000; and "Who's Who in Executives and Professionals," 1994. He is a speaker and lecturer with the Vermont Bar Association, the Vermont Trial Lawyers Association, and National Education Network on subjects involving litigation, advocacy, ski liability, automobile and personal injury, and family law, discovery,

and the arts of cross examination.

Mr. McCarty has been involved in the Vermont Bar and local activities including as Brattleboro representative to the Windham Regional Planning and Development Commission; clerk of the Brattleboro Zoning Board of Adjustment; member of the Board of Governors and president of the Brattleboro Winter Carnival (1968-1972); president of Vermont Legal Aid (1970-1980); a member of the Board of Managers of the Brattleboro Chamber of Commerce (1971-1972); president, Windham County Bar Association, 1992-1993; chairman of the Windham County Bench Bar Liaison Committee from 1989-1997; and chairman, American Bar Association Standing Committee on Membership, 1970-1976. He is the representative of the United States Supreme Court Historical Society 1999-2000, a member of the Bar Associations of the National Council of School Attorneys; American Judicature Society; Vermont Trial Lawyers Association recipient, Outstanding Litigation Achievement award for 1994; Association of Trail Lawyers of America; Vermont Criminal Defense Attorneys; and an advocate with the American Board of Trial Advocates (by recommendation and reference only). He is also formerly a Master of the Vermont Inns of Court.

McCarty Law Offices has understood that enhancing the quality of life for all Vermonters involves more than the mere legal representation of individuals—it leads to the ultimate representation of all involved. The firm has dedicated itself to creating quality community organizations such as Brattleboro Child Development, a day care center, (in 1970 before it became a publicized or popular issue) and the continued representation of individuals, in their cause against unjust and abusive treatment by the government, corporations, or other individuals.

MED ASSOCIATES, INC.

MED Associates is the leading manufacturer, software developer and supplier of products for behavioral psychology, pharmacology, neuroscience and related research and teaching areas. MED Associates was founded by Karl R. Zurn in Allentown, Pennsylvania, in 1970. The business was incorporated in 1972 and moved to East Fairfield, Vermont in 1973. It now employs over 50 people and manufactures over 400 products. The main manufacturing and R&D facility is located in St. Albans, Vermont; with a satellite sales office in Lafayette, Indiana and several dealers and distributors throughout the world.

In May 1993, MED Associates consolidated its operations and relocated from East Fairfield to the Georgia Regional Industrial Park in Georgia, Vermont. This facility provided 7,000 square feet of new office and assembly space, plus 2,900 square feet of storage space to house staff and product line. This new facility allowed for growth to a staff of 40 employees and the addi-

The Zurn family clockwise from left: Mary Dove, J. Brooks, Karl and Jane, Bridget.

tion of new instrumentation and software for research product lines. By 1996 however, increasing demand for MED Associates' hardware and software mandated another expansion for the facility.

In August 1997, a 12,000 square foot addition was constructed to meet growing customer needs. This addition houses the machine shop; cabinet making shop and closed raw stock; finished product storage;

shipping and receiving and finally, assembly and test operations. By May 1998, more space was required to keep up with demand, and a 4,000 square foot mezzanine was added in December 1998, for a total of 26,000 square feet of space. In 2000 a new, expanded sales office opened in Lafayette, Indiana and a 5,000 square foot manufacturing and storage facility in St. Albans was utilized.

Drawing upon Karl Zurn's background in electrical engineering, behavioral psychology, and cardiology research, the company's initial product line was in the EEG field with the design and development of an EEG frequency analyzer for the Maryland Psychiatric Institute. In early years, MED also performed hospital safety inspections and sold test equipment as a representative of Bio-Tek Instruments, Inc. This work was augmented with the design of custom instrumentation systems and the production of an inexpensive high performance general-purpose amplifier module that was based upon a modification of a NASA design. Under contract with NASA Ames Research Center, MED Associates developed a four-channel, battery-powered EEG amplifier for use in centrifuges. Independently, MED developed a standard product line of modular physiological instrumentation for research use that has evolved into the current main-stay product line.

The majority of MED Associates' sales at this time include instrumentation and software for research to pharmaceutical companies, government-sponsored laboratories and university teaching and research centers. Expanding markets and increased market share resulted in an increase of 280 percent in sales over the years from 1995 to 1999. With most markets expanding, the university teaching and research market began to shrink. Conversely, reflecting society's concern with the drug issue, government-supported research laboratories dealing with

The new plant constructed in 1993 in The Georgia Regional Industrial Park provided approximately 10,000 square feet of assembly, storage and office space for a staff of 40.

Representatives of Engleberth Construction, Inc. at ground-breaking in winter 1993, including from MED: Karl R. Zurn, president (to left of sign); J. P. Aja, executive vice president (4th from right); Jane T. Zurn, corporate secretary (3rd from right); Marilyn Partridge, valued employee (front row-far left) and (front row: right to left) future corporate officers J. Brooks, Mary Dove, and Bridget Zurn.

the problem of drug addiction began receiving additional funds yearly, a trend that is expected to continue. The sale of behavior testing instrumentation to pharmaceutical companies has provided a consistent growth market with continued profitability for MED Associates. Pharmaceutical companies have shown new interest in Central Nervous System compounds. CNS compounds deal with such diseases as AIDS and Alzheimer's. Behavioral testing of cognitive enhancing compounds shows promise in this area. Revived interest by the EPA and toxicology laboratories in the use of behavioral testing methods are expected to provide additional market growth for the future.

Disposable electrode collars and electrodes constitute another segment of MED Associates' annual sales. These are sold direct and through dealers for physiological and biofeedback applications.

Because of growing concern about cross contamination from Hepatitis B and HIV, and the 1992 voluntary recall of a major disinfectant, hospitals became increasingly interested in replacing reusable electrodes with disposables.

From its beginning, MED Associates was built upon the president and founder's background and strong commitment to both institutional safety and research and development, and has expanded its product line to support these market areas. MED's market base has grown from hospitals and research centers in the United States to an international clientele.

Among those using MED Associates' designed and manufactured behavioral testing instrumentation in the United States and abroad are Johns Hopkins University and

Medical School; Harvard College and Medical School; National Institutes of Health's Addiction Research Center; Wake Forest School of Medicine; Wyeth Ayers Research Center; Eli Lilly; Pfizer Pharmaceuticals; American Home Products; Abbot Laboratories; Pharmacia & Upjohn; Rohrer, Paris; The University of Auckland, New Zealand; Danish drug maker Nova Nordisk AS and the Netherlands' TNO Health Research Department of Neuro-toxicology. Canadian users include McGill University and Montreal General Hospital, as well as the universities of Laval, Toronto, Alberta and British Columbia. Beijing Everbest Co. in Beijing and Hunan Medical University are among China's users, while numerous universities and companies in such varied places as Mexico, Japan, Israel, Hungary, Italy, Brazil, Sweden, Argentina and Australia also dignify MED's users list.

Most recently MED began a complete redesign line of physiological software, amplifiers and signal conditioners. Completion is expected in the near future.

As the product line has expanded, MED has hired individuals who share a common strong commitment to research and development. MED Associates, Inc. expects to continue this strong commitment to excellence and continues its dedication itself to this end.

In August 1997 a 12,000 square foot addition plus a 4,000 square foot mezzanine brought on site operations to 26,000 square feet.

MERRIAM-GRAVES

When Henry K. Wakeman, Jr. began buying compressed gas distributorships more than 30 years ago, there was no way he could envision the array of markets that would proliferate as a result of new technologies, customer needs, demographics, and changing cultural environments. One thing he did know with certainty, however was that no customer is too small to ignore. He learned that philosophy in the propane business he shared with his father-in-law before venturing into the welding, medical and specialty gas markets.

Born in 1927 on a farm in Fairfield, Connecticut, Wakeman had an upbringing modest in material terms, but one that he remembers as happy and, in particular, honest. Like many, his father was hit hard by the Depression, and as a result Wakeman held jobs from paper routes and collecting bottles at the Fairfield beach to stocking shelves at the local grocery store. From nine years of age, Henry held a variety of continuous jobs until the close of his senior year in high school, at which point he enlisted in the Army. Wakeman served for three years with the infantry in Europe in the immediate aftermath of the Second World War.

Following his military service Henry Wakeman completed his Bachelor of Science at the University of Connecticut. He then moved

Left to right: Scott Wakeman, president; Henry K. Wakeman, Jr., chairman and CEO; Henry Wakeman III, executive vice president.

to Northampton, Massachusetts where he started a small propane gas business. For his first business address, he could afford nothing better than a former chicken coop. Though he scrubbed it down repeatedly, the building never altogether surrendered its former identity. On rainy days in particular, the air bore the suggestion—faint but undeniable—of chicken dressing.

After three years of operating the propane business, Wakeman realized his growth was limited by both business knowledge and access to capital. He then made the decision to sell the business and utilize the cash from the sale to fund his MBA, which he received from Harvard in 1956. It just so happened that the purchaser, George Hammond of Westfield, Massachusetts, had a daughter, who became Henry's wife

shortly after his graduation from Harvard.

Upon completion of his MBA, Wakeman took a position as vice president at his father-in-law's propane business, Rural Gas. This position lasted eight years, at which point Rural Gas was acquired by Phillips Petroleum. Henry was given an opportunity to run Phillips' overseas propane operation, which he declined. Henry Wakeman was once again at a turning point in his life. He had no desire to play "corporate politics" and very much wanted to be his "own man," answering only to the customer—a classic entrepreneurial spirit.

Built on Wakeman's homespun philosophy, $2,300 of his own money and a loan from Union Carbide enabled the 1966 acquisition of R. S. Graves, which also included three stores under the G. L. Merriam name, thus Merriam-Graves. The original two stores in Springfield and Greenfield, Massachusetts were the beginning of what is now the largest privately-held distributorship of industrial, welding, medical and specialty gas and supplies in the Northeast with 34 retail locations and close to 300 employees.

One of the many MG trucks seen on the roads of New England.

Computerized cylinder-filling equipment.

Subsequently, in 1968, Grady's Welding in Vermont was purchased and merged with the initial acquisitions. Most of the expansion that followed, however, has been through start-up branches that were located in areas where Henry Wakeman identified customers that needed his type of value-added expertise. Vermont locations include Winooski, Barre, White River Junction, St. Johnsbury, Rutland, Bennington and South Burlington.

Throughout all of its 34 satellite locations, the company's philosophy has always been to serve the small markets that abound in Vermont, New Hampshire, Maine, and Massachusetts, as well as those in Connecticut and New York.

Merriam-Graves distributes its inventory from a 22,000 square foot facility adjacent to the 35,000 square foot computerized gas cylinder filling plant in Charlestown, NH. At this main location, they take pride in the fact that customer orders are filled accurately and promptly. Their well stocked showrooms are replenished weekly through a responsive, industry-tested inventory management system.

The product lines Merriam-Graves carries lend themselves to the welding trade, carrying everything anyone in their territory could want. Maintenance and repair

operations represent a very large segment of the business, and that alone requires a diversity of products, services, and capabilities.

With the growth of medical gases, Merriam-Graves has evolved into two distinct divisions: Merriam-Graves Industrial and Merriam-Graves Medical.

Merriam-Graves has been serving the medical gas and equipment needs of medical professionals since the business began. As this market has grown, it has expanded to meet the needs of any medical application. Whether the customer is a hospital, nursing home, dentist, doctor or veterinarian's office, rescue squad or an individual in need of home care, the customer comes first. Merriam-Graves understands the urgency of this market and treats all of their medical customers as if they were family members.

The industrial gas division handles all of the specialty gases sold to laboratories, universities, food processors, chemical plants, and environmental agencies. Over the years, the company went from purchasing and selling packaged gases to filling their own cylinders. Here the computer-driven filling and mixing equipment assures accuracy of mixtures, purity of products, and lot number control, guaranteeing customers the highest

quality products in the industry.

Quality is of primary importance to the specialty gas market. Merriam-Graves provides a comprehensive line of both the highest purity gases and multi component mixtures, and works closely with customers to meet their specific needs. The laboratory and manufacturing facility can create custom blends in answer to customer needs and specification, with purity certified by state-of-the-art testing equipment.

While the company has grown considerably over the years, it prides itself on maintaining a "family" environment throughout, and believes this carries forward to its customers with friendly, caring, personalized service that exceeds the attempts of other establishments

Henry's sons, Scott and Kit manage the day-to-day functions of the business. They both received Bachelors of Science degrees from the University of Vermont (1979 and 1984 respectively).

Scott and Kit continue their father's attributes of hard work and integrity. They believe that a company is only as good as its employees and maintain an appreciation of *all* customers, small and large.

MOBILE MEDICAL INTERNATIONAL CORPORATION

Mobile Medical International Corporation of St. Johnsbury, Vermont has developed the world's first Mobile Surgery Units™ and advanced telemedicine Mobile Diagnostic Units. These units have changed the paradigm of health care services while utilizing technology to provide high quality, cost-effective health care across the country and throughout the world.

The project was designed to provide a U.S. health care code compliant facility that could be deployed within 60 minutes. Today MMIC has the only state-licensed and

Mobile Surgery Unit™ Operating Room.

Medicare-approved mobile surgery units in the country.

Initially Rick Cochran conceived the mobile concept while he was consulting with physicians in the development of their own permanent-based surgery centers during the early 1980s. According to the article entitled *Ambulatory Surgery Centers, The Future for Expansion and Survival for Some Ophthalmologists* in the Spring 1992 issue of *Administrative Ophthalmology*, "The formative years of ambulatory development primarily consisted of entrepreneurial physicians" and only a limited number of projects are being developed across the country. Today there are over 2,400 permanent-based ambulatory surgery centers.

For approximately 14 years Rick worked on the development of the mobile concept. By September 1995 the project had the necessary development funds to begin and on March 16, 1996 the world's first Mobile Surgery Unit™ debuted in St. Johnsbury, Vermont. By April 1996 clinical trials began with the U.S. military at Wilford Hall Medical Center at Lackland Air Force Base, and the first surgeon to utilize the unit was Major General Paul K. Carlton, Jr., M.D., who was installed as the Air Force Surgeon General in November 1999.

General Carlton commented about the first week of surgery during a televised interview in Washington, D.C.:

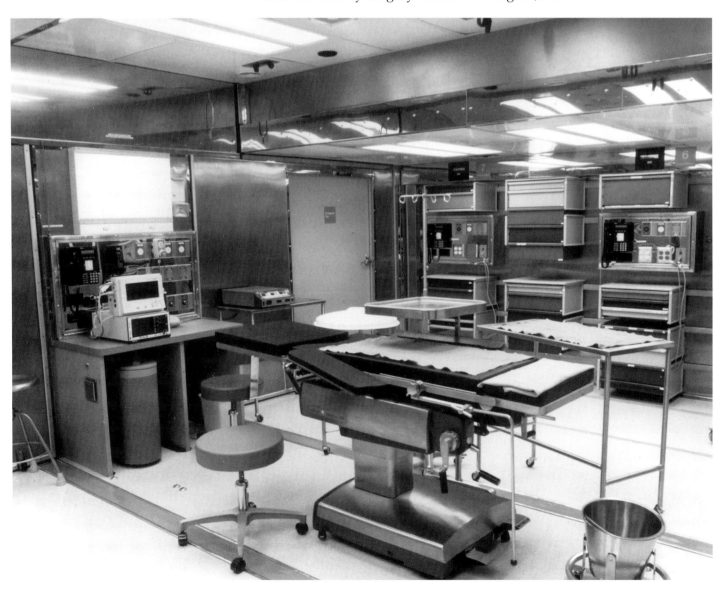

"The potential for this unit in our readiness mission—our wartime mission—is very, very significant in terms of having an immediate U.S. Standards health care facility on the ground in the first hour that we can land an airplane someplace. It is a quantum leap over what we have now—we took out colons, we did hand cases, we did eye cases, we took out tonsils and adenoids—we did the whole spectrum of surgical procedures, and it was invisible. It was exactly the same as operating in my fixed facility."

Rick's concept was to take high quality health care to a variety of markets including private physicians, hospital renovations, military, prisons, international, organ procurement organizations and disaster health services.

Vermont is home to Rick, where he distinctly and proudly proclaims that he is a "real" Vermonter of five generations. His goals in moving back to Vermont were to allow his

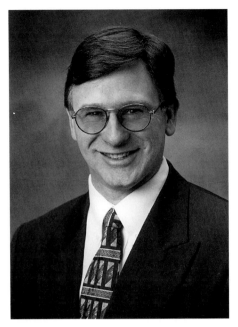

Above
Rick Cochran, president and CEO.

Below
World's first licensed mobile surgery unit™.

children to have the "Grammy and Grandpa" experience. Rick feels Vermont has a great work ethic, but he acknowledges that the economics of having a clean manufacturing facility in the Northeast Kingdom also made good business sense. As a strong community supporter and school board member, Rick has supported educational programs and reached out to youth in the area to encourage them to follow their dreams and to become entrepreneurial.

Today, MMIC is an innovative health care company that is changing the paradigm of health care delivery and supporting the economic base of Vermont. Many of Mobile Medical's customers enjoy viewing current developments on their website at mobile-medical.com. MMIC's mission is to deliver the highest quality health care in the most cost-effective manner to as many people as possible throughout the world.

MILLER, EGGLESTON & CRAMER, LTD.

In 1983 Jon Eggleston and Marty Miller created a firm to provide distinctive legal services in the manner of the sophisticated law practiced in small, specialized firms in metropolitan areas.

Drawing on his experience as an early participant in Act 250 proceedings, as lead trial counsel for the State of Vermont in its epic lawsuit with the State of New York and International Paper Company over pollution in Lake Champlain, and as chairman of the Public Service Board and the Vermont Nursing Home Rate Setting Committee, Marty Miller predicted that state regulation would increase significantly in the next quarter century. His prediction proved accurate, and Miller, Eggleston & Cramer, Ltd. has played an active role in the state regulatory arena.

Since the late 1970s the influx of foreign-based businesses, particularly from Canada and Europe, has been a major commercial influence in northern Vermont. Jon Eggleston, with his specialties in corporate law and taxation, has developed successful relationships with foreign businesses, assisting them in evaluating and obtaining the benefits of a United States presence. Today he represents U.S. and foreign businesses in mergers and acquisitions, reorganizations and related financial transactions.

Anne Cramer, who joined the firm in 1985 from a major Midwest law firm, became one of the first women to achieve seniority in a Vermont corporate law firm. While she has broad experience in antitrust and employer/employee relations work, today Anne is recognized statewide as a preeminent practitioner in health care law.

The three principals have been recognized individually by fellow lawyers for expertise in their specialized fields by inclusion in *The Best Lawyers in America*. In addition, based on its reputation and active representation in public sector legal issues, the firm was chosen to be the sole Vermont member of the State Capital Law Firm Group, a group of independent law firms from each of the 50 states. State Capital Law Firm Group members include many former governors, attorneys general, and other state officials. The member firms of the SCLFG practice independently and not in a relationship for the joint practice of law.

The firm has expanded its practice to include other specialized legal services including immigration, intellectual property, anti-trust and trade regulation, and public and private security offerings, in addition to banking, commercial litigation and corporate advice. The experience its lawyers have brought from nationally-recognized firms, combined with the firm's commitment to deliver first class legal services, has enabled it to provide the quality and sophistication of advice associated with boutique firms in more urban areas.

Miller, Eggleston & Cramer believes that a law firm is far more than a collection of individuals who provide services to clients. It must also demonstrate a deep and ongoing commitment to its community. Lawyers of the firm have helped found the local Ronald McDonald House, headed a United Way campaign, and served as elected officials at the state and local levels and as president of the Vermont Bar Association. The firm is an active participant in the Vermont Business Roundtable and its attorneys contribute to the many community organizations that make up the fabric of northwestern and central Vermont.

Of all the matters in which the firm has been involved, the Rosalyn L. Hunneman Hydroelectric Station, pictured here, may best illustrate the firm's core values and expertise. Completed in 1993, the hydro project represented the culmination of eight years of extensive legal work requiring deployment of expertise in environmental, public utility, banking and construction law as well as administrative and federal court litigation. In addition to providing a benign source of electricity in the middle of Winooski, the project has also resulted in the restoration of a public park and the renewal of a historic fish migration route from Lake Champlain.

Firm members believe that "honesty, integrity, creativity and excellent work accomplished in a timely manner are a lawyer's stock in trade," according to Marty Miller. "If any one of those ingredients is missing, an attorney cannot deliver the service a client expects and deserves. It is our aim to provide this level of service on a consistent and continuous basis."

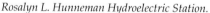

Rosalyn L. Hunneman Hydroelectric Station.

NATIONAL LIFE OF VERMONT

A Vermont country doctor is credited with the vision and energy to have founded, in 1850, National Life Insurance Company.

Julius Y. Dewey had become increasingly appalled at the hardships imposed by the death of the family "breadwinner" in the America of 1850, years before the emergence of modern social legislation.

And when, in 1848, the State of Vermont approved a charter for a "national" life insurance company, Dr. Dewey became an enthusiastic supporter as well as the company's first medical officer.

Early organizers bought newspaper ads praising life insurance and the proposed company, and promoting the sale of stock. Two such circulars announced the 12 incorporators had been "constituted as the first Board of Visitors and Honorary Members for Life."

The Vermonters named directors of National Life were—as was to be expected—strong-minded and somewhat independent. They were not convinced that "honorary members" from places such as Kentucky or New York City, no matter how famous were needed to run a Vermont enterprise. Given the roads of the day, long-distance travel was impractical anyway.

William C. Kittredge, speaker of the house in the Vermont Legislature, served as president of the firm during its year of formation and first business year. After he resigned, Dr. Dewey was named its second president. When he died at age 76, he had been the firm's president for 26 years and was succeeded by his

son Charles, who remained president for another 26 years.

The first policy was issued to Daniel Baldwin, founder of The Vermont Mutual Fire Insurance Company (1828) and a member of the first board of directors of National Life, on January 17, 1850. His annual premium on a $1,000 policy was $62.70.

An extra premium of three and a half percent was attached to policies covering the California Gold Rush, providing policyholders took specific routes as outlined by the company. The 467 Gold Rush policies proved unprofitable due to high mortality. In fact, the first death benefit went to the survivors of Rowland Allen, a Vermonter who died aboard ship in San Diego Harbor on May 17, 1850.

At the close of its first business year, National Life reported 381 policies worth $479,950 of insurance in force. In December 1853 the company reached its first $1 million of insurance in force. In 1949, on the 99th anniversary of that first policy, the firm reached $1 billion of insurance in force. The $2 billion mark occurred 10 years later, doubled again by 1966, and exceeded $10 billion by 1980. National Life shot past the $35 billion mark in 1999 with record sales and profits.

The firm expanded steadily over its history, outgrew six home offices, and moved to its present building in 1960 when Deane C. Davis was president. (Davis later resigned and went on to serve two terms as Vermont's governor in 1968.) The home office now has 1,000 employees and is represented by over 3,000 career and independent agents nationwide. In 1996, National Life acquired a majority interest in Life Insurance Company of the Southwest (LSW), a Dallas, Texas-based financial services company. In July

Dr. Julius Y. Dewey, founder of The National Life Insurance Company, served as its president during its formative years.

1999 National Life purchased the remaining outstanding shares of LSW.

In 1998, National Life's board of directors unanimously approved and adopted a plan of reorganization to a mutual holding company structure. The Board's action reflected its assessment of competitive conditions in the life insurance and financial services industries by submitting an application to reorganize. The plan was approved by the Vermont Department of Banking, Insurance, Securities and Health Care Administration and at a special policyholder meeting held on November 30, 1998.

The current board chairman and chief executive officer of National Life is Patrick E. Welch.

With over 300,000 policyowners, National Life is known for its steady growth. The company prides itself in the quality of its products and services and the integrity of its people.

National Life of Vermont moved to its hillside location overlooking Montpelier, Vermont's capital city, in 1960. By 1983 over 1,000 people were working there.

OKEMO MOUNTAIN RESORT

In March 1955 a group of Ludlow, Vermont businessmen considered developing a ski area on the big mountain just outside the town. Statistics showed that the mountain's location in the heart of the state's "snowbelt" and its accessibility from metropolitan areas would make the project feasible. On January 30, 1956, with four inches of snow on the ground, Okemo Mountain Ski Area opened with two trails and two poma lifts in operation. A small log cabin served as a base lodge; under the ownership of a few local businessmen, the mountain was run by a staff of eight people. The resort grew gradually until 1971 and began a downhill spiral due to its antiquated lift system and lack of snowmaking capabilities and on-mountain services and amenities. The name "Okemo" came from an Indian word meaning "All Come Home," and established a tradition for friendliness that would flourish under the leadership of the Muellers.

On August 2, 1982, Tim and Diane Mueller secured controlling interest in Okemo Mountain Ski Area, which had seen little or no improvements in over 10 years. In an industry driven by cutting-edge technology, Okemo Mountain Ski Area needed to be modernized if it

Okemo Mountain Resort.

Top-ranked snow conditions is what Okemo is renown for.

was to survive even one more season.

In their first year of ownership, Tim and Diane invested $2 million in reviving the resort, building a new triple chairlift, adding trails, and expanding snowmaking coverage. In the following years, Okemo Mountain's base area was completely reconstructed and now features a 76-unit condominium hotel, restaurant, welcome center, and a 50-foot signature Clock Tower. Other base area enhancements included new administration offices, expanded parking, expansion of the ski shops, rental and repair shop, daycare, children's ski

center, three cafeterias, an on-mountain full-service restaurant, lounge and maintenance garage. Slopeside enhancements included the addition of 13 new lifts (including three highspeed detachable quads) and over 50 new trails and glades. A state-of-the-art snowboard park, two halfpipes, two alpine terrain parks and a quarter pipe, complete with a riders-only surface lift were added to appeal to snowboarders. An aggressive snowmaking system was developed and now covers 95 percent of the mountain's vast terrain—the most snowmaking coverage of any resort in Vermont. The improved quality of skiing at Okemo drew more skiers, thus increasing the demand for slopeside lodging. In response, the Muellers developed a variety of additional ski-in/ski-out condominium units to provide the ultimate in convenience, comfort and affordability that provide all of the amenities of home within the deluxe slopeside accommodations.

Snowmaking capabilities are of paramount importance to provide the finest snow conditions possible. The Muellers built an eight-acre, 73-million gallon water storage pond to provide an unlimited resource of water to make snow. While some ski areas battled with environmental groups like the Agency of Natural Resources and the Conservation

Law Foundation, Tim and Diane Mueller sought them as allies. The pond cost $1.5 million to build and was completed in the summer of 1994. The addition of the snowmaking pond further reinforced Okemo's position as a snowmaking leader and an industry leader. The Mueller's interest in preserving the environment has been a strong factor throughout the resort's growth.

Since 1982, Tim and Diane Mueller have reinvested over $100 million into the resort's infrastructure. Today, Okemo Mountain Resort is not only an incredible success story, it is just one of a handful of ski areas in the country that is still family-owned and operated. Under the Muellers' guidance and hands-on ownership, skier visits

Tim and Diane Mueller, owners of Okemo Mountain Resort have invested more than $100,000,000 in improvements since they purchased Okemo in 1982.

members and employee students to pursue their education. They also instituted a partnership program with local schools which funds and encourages interaction between Okemo Mountain employees and the educators and students of the surrounding area. An Annual Ski

Okemo's snowboard zone is ideal for riders who are looking for big hits, tabletops, rails and big air.

soared from 80,000 visits in 1981 to over 555,000 visits in 1999. Okemo Mountain Resort has expanded its terrain from 32 trails (in 1982) to 98 trails (1999) and has seen extensive capital improvements each season.

While cultivating one of the finest ski and snowboard resorts in the country, Tim and Diane haven't neglected the needs of their employees and local community. In 1987 they implemented the Okemo Mountain Employee Scholarship Awards and give a total of nine scholarships per year in the amount of $500 each to encourage staff

Ball fundraiser raises over $75,000 each year to benefit educational and charitable endeavors within the local community, while over $500,000 has been raised for local charities since 1983.

Plans are being finalized and, pending permit approval, construction will begin in Spring 2000 in the North Village area, called Jackson Gore. Jackson Gore is located below the popular Solitude Peak area on an impressive tract of land that encompasses 546 acres. The expansion will include a new base area facility complete with its own access road off Route 103 and near Route 100, 16 new trails and four new lifts, a

base facility with a condominium hotel, restaurants, shops and additional winter sports amenities with ice skating and tubing. This expansion will not only increase the overall skiable terrain of the resort by 30 percent, but the addition of golf and other summer activities will help to create a four-season recreational facility that will promote economic growth and vitality in a manner that supports sound environmental protection.

The purchase of Okemo Valley Golf Club & Nordic Center in 1997 enables Okemo Mountain to operate a cross-country and snowshoe center in the winter and offer 18-holes of championship golf during the summer months.

On April 1, 1998, Tim and Diane put in a bid to the State of New Hampshire to lease Mt. Sunapee Ski Area, located in southern New Hampshire. The Muellers were chosen to lease Mt. Sunapee from a select group of resort operators. On July 1, 1998, Tim and Diane Mueller took over the lease and operation of Mount Sunapee Resort. Given Okemo's tremendous transformation over the past 18 years from a once failing ski area to one of the most successful, independently owned resorts in the country, Tim and Diane are confident that they will bring balanced economic prosperity to the Mount Sunapee community and region through continued reinvestment into the mountain. The Muellers' philosophy is one of thoughtful progression—the kind of prosperity that enhances, not changes.

The family appeals of Okemo Mountain Resort offer some of the finest values in New England.

OMEGA OPTICAL, INC.

Omega Optical's founder and President Robert Johnson, grew up in Brattleboro, Vermont on his family farm and graduated from Brattleboro High School in 1963. After working for five years in Boston for an optical filter manufacturer, Bob decided to return to southern Vermont in 1968 to start his own company. To equip the business he scoured the scientific salvage yards of the growing high-tech community in Boston with $10,000 in his pocket, gathering bits and pieces of obsolete vacuum and electronic equipment.

Like many start-up companies, Omega Optical began in a garage. The facility was a 400 square-foot shop on the Johnson family homestead that could not be labeled a business because of zoning regulations, but was permitted as a "hobby shop." Using basic hand tools, the pieces of high-tech scrap collected in Boston were reassembled into four high-vacuum reactors capable of manufacturing interference filters. A Vermont corporation, Omega Optical, Inc. was formed January 1, 1969, the name chosen for its symbolic meaning of resistance, relating to an alternative approach to business.

Whereas many companies are formed from the belief that a core product has value in the marketplace, Omega Optical was created to pursue research and development. Out of research efforts it was hoped that products would eventually develop. Although product application could be varied, the focus of research would be optical thin-films, a branch of the science of photonics involving the study of light. Thin-films are used to control the flow of light and are produced by condensing the vapors of elements and compounds on ordinary glass. The most common product is the interference filter.

Omega began making filters for researchers almost from its first day of operation. But early in the company history the mission to pursue

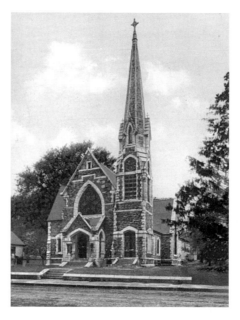

Unitarian Church, Main Street, Brattleboro. Built in 1875 this historic stone church became Omega Optical's first major facility in 1975.

research and development also led down a variety of other paths. An interest in alternative energy stimulated research into thin-films manufactured from semiconductor materials that would produce electricity from the sun. Manufacturing equipment was developed and the goal of cheap "photo-electronic conversion" plastic sheets that could be installed on buildings was nearly realized. But the return of cheap fossil fuels put the project on hold.

A parallel project involving a solar-powered, urban transport vehicle moved ahead through several road-worthy prototypes. This vehicle named Mho, the inverse of Ohm or "resistance," could travel up to 50 miles with nearly 10 miles of the trip powered by the thin-film photovoltaics covering its body. The vehicle was acclaimed at the "Towards 2000" Futures Fair for its forward-looking use of low weight materials and advanced electronic designs. However, as with the photocell project, a change in the political and cultural climate made commercialization difficult.

While these efforts didn't lead to commercial success, others did. The

science of using light as an analytical tool was relatively new and the company directed its research toward the creation of filters for analytical instrument makers. Early applications were in the biomedical and agricultural sciences with universities and researchers the primary customers.

As the manufacturing portion of Omega blossomed, the company outgrew its small "hobby shop" and moved onto Brattleboro's Main Street in 1975. The new home was the former Unitarian Church, an historic stone structure built in 1875. While the basement was renovated to create a manufacturing area, the main floor was retrofitted into offices preserving the interior and exterior façades of this historic building—the stenciled ceiling and walls, the Tiffany stained-glass windows, and the organ pipes were left untouched.

Research and development projects continued in the "garage," while the Brattleboro facility took on the business of producing filters for the growing analytical instrument markets. At the same time, the company saw a possible future in a

Modern CNC (computer numeric controlled) glass patterning and scribing equipment for fabricating interference filters, 1993. Photo by Robert McClintock.

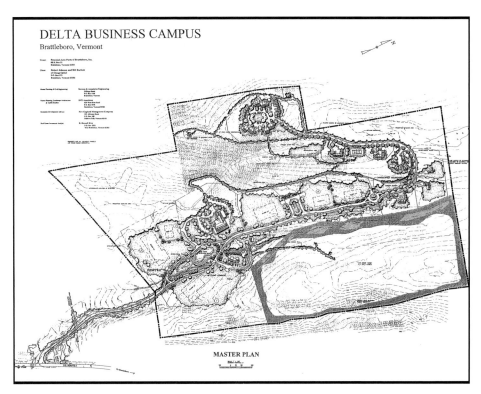

DELTA BUSINESS CAMPUS
Brattleboro, Vermont

MASTER PLAN

more subtle analytical tool, the detection of fluorescence, a technique which was first being discussed in the scientific literature.

Meanwhile, Omega also began research and development of protective goggles for laser applications. Omicron Eye Safety Corporation was formed and in 1985 the growing work force moved into a second Brattleboro facility—the American Building on lower Main Street—where work continued for several years. As with the alternative energy development projects, the market didn't develop as expected, but the extra space was quickly absorbed by the growing demands of the biomedical filter manufacturing business.

During the 1980s Omega spunoff several businesses and institutions, effecting the commercial and cultural landscape of the Brattleboro area. Friends of the Sun was organized as a retail and service provider for alternative energy products that Omega planned to manufacture. Solar Hill was established as an alternative energy educational institution. Today Friends of the Sun remains an alternative energy store, while Solar Hill–located at the former site of Mark Hopkins College and the Governor Gibson Mansion—evolved into a center for alternative health care practitioners and a private primary school, the Neighborhood Schoolhouse.

By the mid-1980s Omega's development work in fluorescence paid off commercially. The sciences of fluorescence microscopy and flow cytometry, which allow for the visualization of cellular structures and the sorting and analysis of cells, were made possible by design and manufacturing developments invented at Omega. These advances set the state-of-the-art and allowed Omega to define the science, and for many years capture the entire market worldwide.

The 1980s also saw the beginnings of Omega's work in the field of astronomy. One of the first projects was manufacturing filters for the analysis of Halley's comet. With success, a number of high-profile observational astronomy projects followed. The 1990s saw the challenge of creating filters for the Hubble Space Telescope's Widefield Planetary Camera and for NASA's Martian Lander.

At the turn of the century Omega occupies three buildings in downtown Brattleboro including the Unitarian Church, the American Building, and a recent expansion into the Paramount Theater Building. The company has enjoyed its downtown presence, but is planning to consolidate the entire operation in a new facility—the Delta Business Campus located on the Brattleboro-Guilford border. The plan for this

Solar Hill, Brattleboro. Former site of Mark Hopkins College and before that the Governor Gibson Mansion. Omega Optical established an alternative energy education facility on the site in the 1980s.

Delta Business Campus, Master Plan. This planned "industrial campus" includes seven "high-information technology" businesses, an educational institution, and residential units. It is located on the Brattleboro-Guilford town line, with construction scheduled to begin in 2001.

"industrial campus" includes six other "high-information technology" businesses and an educational institution, as well as residential units. The campus will have walkways, bike paths, and ponds in a secluded, natural setting. Construction is scheduled to begin in 2001.

Omega Optical has grown steadily over its three-decade history. What began as a "one-man" operation in a garage is now a $10 million company with over 125 employees and 33 international distributors. The company, its founder, and an assortment of collaborators hold a variety of patents. Omega's filters are used in instruments that have led to scientific advancements in the life sciences, clinical medicine, and astronomy. They have helped unlock the mysteries of the human gene sequence and probe the depths of the universe. While the late 20th century has been called the digital age, it's been said that the next scientific revolution will be in the science of photonics. Wherever that revolution leads, Omega Optical will be there—where there's no end in light.

NEW ENGLAND CULINARY INSTITUTE (NECI)

New England Culinary Institute (NECI) was founded in 1980. Combining clinical experience, progressive educational tradition and the European apprenticeship system, the Institute's educational programs feature "learn-by-doing in real life" situations, with no more than seven students to each chef/instructor in production kitchens. The Institute has grown from seven to 700 students with two campuses—in Montpelier and Essex (near Burlington), and is recognized the world over for producing sought-after chefs and other culinary professionals.

Also known for fine dining and catering, New England Culinary Institute operates 12 diverse food service outlets and restaurants including La Brioche, Chef's Table, Main Street Grill & Bar, Butler's at The Inn At Essex, and the popular NECI Commons in Burlington, where students learn their craft. Over a half million meals are served each year in these facilities.

An accredited, degree-granting post secondary institution, New England Culinary Institute offers an Associate of Occupational Studies degree in Culinary Arts, a Bachelor of Arts degree in Food and Beverage Management, a Certificate in Basic Cooking, and a host of Continuing Education and non-professional cooking programs including *Whisk Away Weekends*.

In the Associate's Degree Program and the Certificate Program, students benefit from a personalized education, working in small groups of seven students under the watchful eye of a master chef, in production kitchens that serve discriminating customers. Each year students spend six months on-campus and then work for six months on paid internships throughout the United States and other countries. As one graduate says, "At most schools you watch the chefs do the cooking. At NECI the chefs watch you do the cooking. It's real life. On Saturday night in the fish station at the Main

Street Grill, it is your responsibility to feed 120 hungry people. You're a student, but that's what it's all about—seven stations on the line and seven students; feeding the public is what you are doing while you learn." Upon graduation from the Associate's Program, students will have spent 3,000 hours hands-on cooking in real food service operations and served 10,000 meals. A culinary degree moves a career along faster than merely getting a job. Two years of good education can cover what may take many years of work experience to learn.

The Bachelor's Degree Program is an upper-division program that also utilizes small classes, hands-on training and paid internships. This one and a half year program is

designed to give students the knowledge and skills necessary to succeed in a variety of management positions in the hospitality industry. With culinary training as a prerequisite for admission, students have characterized the program as an applied MBA that includes a final project which, in many cases, is a plan to open one's own business. NECI graduates have been employed by resorts, hospitals, colleges, and international food service companies; a number have started their own businesses.

Dining in Vermont has changed dramatically since the school opened. Graduates who have enjoyed the beauty of the state and the lifestyle of the region have stayed to work in many wonderful Vermont eateries. Visitors will find many excellent places to eat, especially near-by the school's two campuses. Nothing delights guests more, however, than a visit to one of the school's fine restaurants, not only enjoy an excellent meal, but to chat with the students who serve them.

A.M. PEISCH & COMPANY

Born on a farm in Chippewa County, Wisconsin on January 27, 1894, Archibald M. Peisch began his education in 1899 at the local country school where one teacher taught eight grades. In 1915 he graduated from the University of Wisconsin, majoring in economics and immediately accepted a teaching position at the University of South Dakota. There he met Josephine, (his wife of almost 70 years) who was also teaching there.

Volunteering for the U.S. Army Field Artillery in June 1916 to participate in the military expedition into Mexico to capture Poncho Villa, he soon returned to the University of South Dakota for one semester in 1917, until accepting a teaching position in public finance and history at Iowa State College. He re-enlisted in the Army later that year, and upon his discharge on Armistice Day 1918, he joined his brother Herman in the practice of public accounting in Minneapolis.

September 1920 came and he accepted his next challenge at Dartmouth College, teaching taxation and accounting at the Amos Tuck School of Administration and Finance, continuing there until 1930.

At this time housing was virtually nonexistent in Hanover, New Hampshire, so he and Josephine rented a home across the Connecticut River in Norwich, Vermont. It was there on October 1, 1920 that he established the firm of Archibald M. Peisch & Company for the practice of public accounting.

Over the next 50 years, A. M. Peisch associated with numerous partners who practiced with him and then went on to join or create other firms, or enter industry. In 1975 the practice was sold to Richard E. Belisle and Alan L. Brock. Richard E. Belisle became the second managing partner of the firm. During his tenure the firm grew considerably, and is now composed of five Vermont offices employing approximately 50 people.

A. M. Peisch

Archibald Peisch retired from the firm in March 1976 and the firm was renamed A.M. Peisch & Company. Mr. Peisch died in 1984 at age 90. Dick Belisle retired from the partnership July 1, 1996. In the same year, Alan Brock became disabled and now works for the firm part-time.

On April 1, 1995, David M. Wood was elected the third managing partner of the firm. Dave graduated from the University of Vermont in 1972 and joined the firm that year as a staff accountant. He was promoted to partner in 1978 and has served as partner in charge of the Burlington office since that date.

Since its inception, the firm of A.M. Peisch & Company has been known as auditors of clients in the banking industry and governmental organizations. Today, A.M. Peisch & Company offers a wide range of accounting, tax, and business consulting services. These services are offered to clients in a wide range of industries, including banks, credit unions, automobile dealers, small businesses, non-profit and governmental organizations, individuals, and others.

The current active partners also include Glen Bolster (Burlington), Kevin Manahan (St. Albans), Anne Smith (St. Johnsbury), Norman Ladabouche and George Means (Rutland) and Aaron MacAskill and Edward York (White River Junction). Each heads a staff of area residents who are familiar with their respective communities. Additionally, the firm's staff is constantly trained in recent developments through professional education courses. Its objective is to provide professional service of the highest quality, and help its clients to prosper.

To assist in meeting the evolving needs of its clients A.M. Peisch & Company has formed an investment services company, employed technology experts, and obtained specialized training for all team members. The firm joined Polaris International, a worldwide association of CPA firms based in Atlanta, Georgia in 1987. This association expands the firm's resources to include over 100 sister firms in the US and around the world. It regards clients' individualized financial needs as of the foremost importance, and in keeping with the tradition that began 80 years ago, A.M. Peisch & Company treasures the fact that its clients have come to rely on its professionalism.

Find more about their global presence at www.polarisna.org, and about them locally at www.ampeisch.com.

Richard E. Belisle.

RAY'S SEAFOOD MARKET

Just because Vermont is the sole state in New England without a seacoast, doesn't mean you can't get quality fresh seafood there. Indeed, the pride of the Dunkling Family has guaranteed the availability of the finest fish and shellfish in Vermont for half a century.

The business began in 1949 with one truck, lots of ice, and lobsters. At the time, Ray Dunkling and his family—wife Mae, son Reginald and daughter Jane—lived in Wiscasset, Maine, near the Atlantic coast. When they had moved there from Plainfield, Vermont Ray bought the truck and began bringing lobsters to Burlington. A year later, the family moved back to Vermont and set about building a permanent business there. By then, Ray and Reg were hauling all kinds of fish and seafood, supplying stores and restaurants in the area.

In 1951, Ray's Seafood opened the doors of a retail outlet at North and Drew streets to supplement wholesale deliveries being made in Maine, New Hampshire and Northern Vermont. Two years later it leased space at North and Park to accommodate growing sales. In 1959 Ray and Mae moved back to Wiscasset

Victor Raymond and customer at fish market in Burlington, 1954.

to open a restaurant, leaving the Vermont operations in the hands of Reg and his wife, Hazel who bought a building at 74 North Street in 1962. There, they built a walk-in cooler and freezer as well as a large refrigerated lobster tank room to supplement their retail space. The lobster room still includes the original wooden tanks Ray had when he started the business, with water circulating through them constantly to keep the tasty crustaceans fresh and alive.

In the years that followed, the wholesale business grew steadily, while retail sales ran into pressure as competition from supermarkets and independents increased. To meet this challenge, in 1988 Ray's

purchased a building at the corner of North and Front and relocated the retail space there. The more accessible location was bright and modern, and had plenty of parking.

In 1992 Ray's added a small retail outlet in Essex Junction, managed by Hilda Clark. Two years later, this outlet moved to a new, leased building on Pinecrest Drive. Ray's opened a restaurant and a creemee stand adjoining the retail fish market, still under her guiding eye today.

This proved to be an excellent move. The restaurant started with seating for 21 and doubled its capacity by the start of the new century. As the *Free Press* reviewer described it, before supermarket shaved-ice fish palaces; way before fish was not only healthy, but cool, good old Ray's Seafood Market hauled cod and scallops, haddock and lobster from Boston, New Bedford and Maine.

"Some things in the food business never change... Fresh fish needs little more than simple frying or broiling and a lemon squeeze... Maine-style, (the cook) calls it. Seafood in the rough, where you gather up the kids after shopping, sit on stackable chairs placed around vinyl-covered tables in a homey dining room with picture windows, douse your catch with tartar sauce and grab a creemee (even in December).

"Underneath the fish-'n-chips exterior lurks a Lazy Man Lobster Casserole containing 8-plus ounces of lobster meat baked in butter and wine. When sole looks decent, they do a Florentine (and crabmeat cakes are made with real Maine crabmeat, not the phony stuff.)"

The down-home quality helps keep the cost of eating reasonable.

The basis of Ray's quality—wholesale, retail and prepared—has always been its fleet of trucks. They bring fresh seafood in from Maine and Massachusetts every day except Sunday. In the old days, the fish was covered with ice to keep it fresh.

Joe Yantz at the 74 North Street wholesale location.

Essex Junction store.

Robbie Dunkling learning the family business at the Burlington wholesale location in 1990.

This led to spoilage concerns, and slightly warmer seafood, on particularly hot days. Today, with modern refrigeration units, everything stays properly chilled.

In addition to lobster and a full range of other ocean fish, Ray's brings in fresh-water fish from Lake Champlain. Most of these are sold through wholesale channels. All (except for frozen offerings such as shrimp and lobster tail) are on the road to their final destinations within 24 hours of leaving the water.

Shipping logistics can be complex. Trucks destined for locations outside of Burlington are ready to go by 7:00 am, six days a week. Trucks delivering locally are on the road by 8:00 am. Trucks may be dispatched to Boston or Portland to fill holes in orders, or routed so they complete their deliveries near these ports and can pick up the next catch. Burlington to Boston to Maine and back is another common route. All this brings fresh seafood to Burlington daily.

"Hauling is a lot of hard work," says Hazel, "but it guarantees our quality."

At the heart of everything is the family. Reg and Hazel had five children: Janice, Deborah, Karen, Mary and Paul. All worked in the business growing up and four are still employed at Ray's, making it what it is today. Even Karen, who with her husband owns and operates a farm in Alburg, still likes to help out when she comes to visit.

Paul handles lobsters, lake fish and trucking; Janice and Debbie wholesale, retail and the restaurant; and Mary manages the retail market in Burlington along with Norene Dickinson, a 13-year veteran of Ray's. Janice's husband Morris, works in wholesale and trucking, and several grandchildren join trusted long-time employees throughout the company.

Indeed, the generations of the Dunkling clan involved in the business extend from Hazel's Uncle Ed to members of a fifth generation who already like to help out. Ed worked for many years hauling lobster and seafood from Maine, Boston and Montreal before retiring in 1974. He moved to Florida, but after several years there, came back to Vermont. At age 90, he continues to do the banking and run other errands.

Such is the call of Ray's Seafood.

Some of the 4th and 5th generation members of the Dunkling family.

SAINT MICHAEL'S (VT) COLLEGE

"The stone which the builders rejected, in the France of that time, has indeed become a cornerstone in the spiritual and cultural life of Vermont."— *Bishop Robert F. Joyce*

Joyce wrote these words in 1954, on the 50th anniversary of Saint Michael's College, but they could just as easily introduce the Catholic liberal arts college as it marks its centennial in 2004.

A visitor to the college's Colchester campus walks across tree-shaded greens that stretch between modern classroom buildings, red brick dormitories, a renowned theater, a sprawling sports complex and a chapel set against the mural of Vermont's highest mountains. In addition to educating about 1,850 undergraduates each year, the college also offers graduate degrees and an English language school that draws students from across the globe.

Its graduates include Robert White '52, former ambassador to El Salvador; Edmundite Father Moses Anderson '54, auxilliary bishop of Detroit; Patrick Leahy '61, U.S. senator from Vermont; Tom Freston '67, MTV whiz; Michael Koziol '73, Rhodes Scholar; Jeffrey Good '81, Pulitzer Prize winner; and Loung Ung '93, a leader in the campaign to ban landmines and author of the critically acclaimed book, *First They Killed My Father: A Daughter of Cambodia Remembers.*

Saint Michael's College opened in 1904 with 34 students.

The college was founded in 1904 by the Society of St. Edmund, a small order of Catholic priests who had fled their native France rather than accept harsh government restrictions on religious orders. The priests had to learn English quickly, but that was not their only challenge. Previous attempts to found a Catholic college in Vermont had fallen short, sometimes in spectacular fashion.

In 1826, for instance, Bishop Benedict J. Fenwick of Boston explored opening a Catholic college atop Mount Ascutney, a site recommended by the local faithful. According to one history, the bishop climbed to the top "amid many hardships and copious perspiration."

Once there, he decreed that the idea be put in an early grave, "where no mention of it more should be made."

The Edmundites had better luck (though no less perspiration). They scraped together $5,000—much of it borrowed—and bought an 18-acre farm atop a hill near the bustling lakefront city of Burlington. They added a four-story wooden college hall to the farmhouse and welcomed their first 34 students.

In addition to imparting lessons in life and Latin, the Edmundites worked the farm. "The founders could cultivate more than the minds of their young pupils. Their farm would help feed them and the students and keep expenses down. Even today, a sizeable farm and a herd of 75 cows serve the same purpose," said an article published in a 1954 edition of *Vermont Life.*

In its first four decades the college grew slowly, with the full-time enrollment never reaching 250. Then Japan bombed Pearl Harbor, and World War II left the college forever changed. One of Saint Michael's own, Joseph Napoleon

Saint Michael's Playhouse opened in 1947, bringing professional theater to Vermont.

Cabana '33, died at Pearl Harbor. On campus, the students found themselves torn from a life that had been relatively free of care.

"The school with air raid wardens and all the fixings took part in a blackout which was held just before the Easter vacation and figuratively jumbled into the same coal hole as millions of other Americans," Thomas J. McNeil, '44, wrote in a 1942 issue of *The Lance*, a student publication. "A motion picture and lecture by the local fire chief helped the lads to learn what to do if they suddenly found themselves in bed with an incendiary bomb. And all during the last quarter here at school fellows were receiving letters from our boys at camp and in combat."

When the allies prevailed, thousands of soldiers returned to America eager to make a life for themselves. With the help of the G.I. Bill families that had been unable to afford college tuition sent their sons to Saint Michael's, and the college's student body boomed over the 1,000 mark.

Many of the veterans brought not just eager minds, but also wives and children. The once-quiet little campus echoed with the sounds of trucks and hammers, as barracks from nearby Fort Ethan Allen were transplanted and turned into a family housing complex dubbed "Miketown."

In 1947, the Saint Michael's Playhouse raised its curtain for the first time, bringing professional summer theater to Vermont and providing students with an opportunity to learn from the best. Theophilus Lewis, drama critic for *America* wrote: "The Playhouse is one of the unique theaters of the nation. It presents an annual selection of plays that are mature without being highbrow, edifying without being stuffy."

The fifties brought rapid change: the beginning of the School of International Studies in 1954, the arrival of Hungarian freedom fighters in 1957, and a hard-won second place

The College sits on a hilltop between Lake Champlain and the Green Mountains of Vermont.

finish by the "Iron Knights" basketball team in the 1958 NCAA championships.

The turbulence of the 1960s had its impact at Saint Michael's. Colonel Donald Cook '54 died a hero as he sacrificed to save fellow American prisoners of war in Vietnam. Edmundite Father Maurice Oullet became the first white man to publicly support black voter registration efforts in Selma, Alabama. Students

Saint Michael's students come from across the nation and around the world.

protested American involvement in Southeast Asia. And in 1969, the college named its first lay president, Bernard L. Boutin '45.

The first full-time female students arrived in 1970, and the final decades of the century saw them along with female professors become leaders in learning, sports and the arts. Take for instance, Karen Smith, class of 2000.

In 1997, Smith started the "Adopt-a-Family" program, pairing members of the college community with needy Burlington-area families. Each of the families receives a full Christmas holiday package including such items as clothing, toys and grocery store gift certificates. "It's the whole spirit of Christmas," Smith says. "It really is better to give than to receive."

Smith embodies the qualities Saint Michael's hopes to nurture in young men and women as they become the leaders of a new century. They are men and women whose learning comes not just from books, but from an education formed—as the college's mission statement makes clear—"in the light of the Catholic faith."

SMUGGLERS' NOTCH RESORT

Nestled in a remarkably beautiful setting amidst the folds of the Green Mountains in the northern tier of Vermont, Smugglers' Notch Resort stands out in this tourist-oriented state as a well-known family resort. The award-winning programs offer visitors of all ages the perfect spot to enjoy a variety of snow sports in winter, waters and mountains in summer, and spectacular foliage in autumn.

Smugglers' Notch Pass, from which the resort derives its name, is itself a geographic wedge between rugged Mt. Mansfield, at 4,393 feet the highest peak in Vermont, and Sterling Mountain, an only slightly less imposing brother. The cluster of condominiums that form the lodging core of the Resort are located in the wide meadows below the shadow of the Notch which today offer skiing and snowboarding on the three inter-connected surrounding mountains of Sterling, Madonna and Morse.

Imposing in its magnificence and scope, the Notch is extremely steep on the south side where it originates in Stowe, climbing by a switchback road that zigzags around boulders as big as houses, then flattening out at the top before gradually descending towards the north. Due to its

The first trail map of Smugglers' Notch Ski-Ways showing the original six trails which included two connecting the area to its neighbor, Stowe. All trails are still in use.

The Poma Lift on Sterling Mountain, 1956.

inaccessibility to snow plows and its delicate ecology, this road is closed during the winter months, but the resort remains accessible via route 15 from the north. Given this remarkable geography, the Notch has a history as colorful and fascinating as its name implies.

While yet a footpath, the pass through the Notch first developed into a smuggling route when President Thomas Jefferson sponsored the Embargo Acts of 1807 and 1808, forbidding export trade with Britain. Settlers in the Green Mountain State protested loudly, since there was

considerable movement of goods such as food stuffs, clothing and potash at this time to and from Montreal through the Champlain Valley. The remoteness, encircling forests, large caves and caverns, as well as the seeming impassability of the Notch trail, gave it ideal cover for illicit trade.

More than one hundred years later, the footpath now a roadway called Route 108, the Notch pass was again used for smuggling when the U.S. Congress passed a law prohibiting the sale of alcohol in the U.S. The ever-versatile caves this time provided room temperature storage for liquor smuggled the 45 miles south from the Canadian border, and a hiding spot from the revenue agents.

The uniqueness of this area was not lost on the local business people of the Town of Cambridge, who in 1956, headed by the local physician, Dr. Roger W. Mann, opened the Smugglers' Notch Ski-Ways. At that time the ski facility consisted of two Poma Lifts on Sterling Mountain. For 10 years the folks of Cambridge ran the ski area primarily for their residents, until one of the most successful entrepreneurs in the world acted on the potential he saw in this undiscovered "diamond in the rough."

Tom Watson, Jr., visionary and primary thrust behind the success of IBM, wanted to duplicate in the East the type of European-like ski villages he had experienced at Zermatt in Switzerland and Vail in Colorado. Mr. Watson, along with his brother Arthur, bought the Smugglers' Notch Ski-Ways, Inc. in 1960. They began aggressively expanding both the skiing terrain and uphill lift capacity while simultaneously developing a ski-from-your-doorstep Village.

In 1963 the Madonna I chairlift was installed to the summit of Madonna Mountain, which at that time made it the longest bottom drive double chairlift in the United States, and the resort was renamed

Madonna Mountain. Mr. Watson replaced the two Poma lifts on Sterling with a double chairlift in 1964. When the third double chairlift was fixed on Morse Mountain in 1967, the trail network connecting the three mountains was completed and the Village concept could be inaugurated. Mr. Watson was realizing his dream.

Since Tom Watson, Jr. wanted to focus his energy and attention on mountain development during these early days, he asked Stanley Snider, a successful developer of resort property from Massachusetts, to plan and build the adjacent Village complex. In 1967, Mr. Snider began the first condominiums and over the next 20 years saw that even more of the dream envisioned by Watson came true. Snider bought the entire resort in 1973 and expanded the concepts first embraced by Watson. He renamed the resort The Village at Smugglers' Notch.

The responsibility for nurturing the Resort's legacy was passed to William Stritzler who bought the property in 1996, making Smugglers' Notch Resort, or Smuggs, as it is affectionately known by locals,

Smugglers' Notch Resort Village in summer mode today with the ski trail networks visible on Morse, Madonna, and Sterling mountains in the background.

one of only a few private, independently-owned ski areas in Vermont. Under Stritzler's guidance, the Resort has continued its 40-plus year commitment to families—building on its reputation as a world-class resort with families at its center. Today the resort operates nine lifts servicing 67 trails, and offers its guests a "home away from home" in nearly 450 condominiums.

The depth of this commitment is readily apparent in the Resort's extensive award-winning programs developed specifically for children and families and the honors Smugglers' has earned over the years. Among the awards are: #1 Family Resort in Northeast (*Family Fun* a Disney publication); #1 Family Resort in North America (*Skiing Magazine*, Editors' Choice); #1 Family

Ski Resort (*FamilyFun* – a Disney publication); #1 for Children's Programs in North America (*Mountain Sports & Living*); Favorite Family Resorts (*Better Homes and Gardens*) and many others.

Smugglers' objective is to design programs and activities, with an emphasis on family, that are offered in surroundings which promote a true sense of belonging, sharing and caring about others. So confident is Smugglers' in its ability to ensure a family-friendly environment, that it is the only resort in North America to guarantee family fun year round.

At the same time, the Resort takes its responsibility as a community citizen seriously. Over the years Smugglers' has been recognized by Lamoille County and state organizations for its recycling and composting efforts and was cited as the Outstanding Business of the Year by the Vermont Chamber of Commerce for its dedication to its employees and the community. Says Mr. Stritzler, "I really believe that a business like ours needs to look at the community as a place that we have a responsibility to serve. It's in our culture and it's in our mission statement. From a business point of view, it's a smart thing to do, but it's also something that is the right thing to do."

Families enjoy the beauty and splendor of Vermont throughout all its magnificent seasons. This was the reason for the founding of Smugglers' Notch Resort over four decades ago; that inspiration and vision still flourish today, as the very essence of what makes Smugglers' so special.

Mogul Mouse, the area's mascot, embraces the new owner of Smugglers' Notch Resort, William Stritzler, at a press conference announcing the purchase, November 5, 1996.

SOUTHWESTERN VERMONT HEALTH CARE

Southwestern Vermont Heath Care provides services to over 53,000 people in southwestern Vermont and neighboring Massachusetts and New York. Southwestern Vermont Health Care (SVHC) providers include: Southwestern Vermont Medical Center, Southwestern Vermont Regional Cancer Center, Bennington Area Home Health, Centers for Living and Rehabilitation, Deerfield Valley Health Center, Northshire Medical Center, Southwestern Vermont Health Care Auxiliary, Bennington Allergy Practice, and Southwestern Vermont Associates in Psychiatry and Psychotherapy.

SVHC's vision is to make the communities it serves the healthiest in the nation. Through its state-of-the-art medical facilities, its highly-trained and skilled staff, and community outreach through Healthier Community Partnerships, SVHC has grown from a small town hospital to the third largest medical facility in Vermont. But through all of its change and growth, its commitment to patients has not changed since its first admission over 80 years ago.

The story of SVHC's founder and major benefactor, Henry W. Putnam, is not an uncommon one. Putnam, an ambitious young man, headed west in the 1840s and built a successful business selling bottled drinking water to the thirsty prospectors of the California Gold Rush. Henry W. Putnam embodied the 19th century ideal of an Horatio Alger story. Hard work and self-reliance reaped their rewards, and when Putnam moved to Bennington in 1864, he had developed several successful businesses and was an affluent young man.

Upon settling in Bennington, Putnam became involved in several enterprises, among them the creation of a clean water system for the town. After a series of successful business ventures in Bennington, Putnam retired to the West Coast in 1912. Before he left, he made one last gift to his adopted hometown—he donated his water company to the village of Bennington, with the caveat that the profits be dedicated to building, maintaining, and operating a hospital. In 1912, the Vermont State Legislature authorized the creation of Putnam Memorial Hospital Corporation to oversee the development of a hospital for Bennington.

In 1915, Henry W. Putnam, Sr. died in San Diego. His son Henry W. Putnam, Jr. donated $90,000 for the construction of the hospital and asked that the facility be named after his late father. Putnam Memorial Hospital opened on June 10, 1918. The hospital had 30 rooms whose rates ranged from $12 per week for a ward to $35 per week for a private room with a bath.

Echoing the national prosperity of the 1920s, Putnam Memorial Hospital, through the continuing support of Putnam, Jr., added two wings with x-ray and physical therapy departments, and built the Lodge to house laundry and housekeeping. In sharp contrast to the previous decade, the Depression of the 1930s caused hard times for Putnam Memorial Hospital, —30.5 percent of the hospital budget supported charity care and the hospital could only charge patients $6.39, plus 46¢ per day for food. In 1938, Henry W. Putnam, Jr., who had underwritten all the costs of construction and the annual deficits of the hospital, died and bequeathed $3 million to the hospital for an endowment. Putnam Memorial Hospital expanded the medical staff to include a full-time pathologist, radiologist, and anesthesiologist. In 1948, the Vermont State Legislature approved the creation of the Putnam Memorial Hospital School of Nursing.

In 1950 the first class of hospital volunteers, "the gray ladies" went to work. In 1955, through community efforts, $976,128 was raised for a new East Wing. In 1962 psychiatry became a recognized component of the health care services. In 1965 a gift of $650,000 from the Irene Heinz Given and John LaPorte Given Foundation provided support for the additional expansion of patient services and an extension of the North Wing. In the mid-1960s a new kitchen and boiler plant were added and the North Wing extension housed the hospital's first Intensive Care Unit. In 1968, the coronary program was developed and a third floor was added, bringing the total bed count up to 166.

In 1971, aided by $1.65 million in community support, the West Wing was added and a department of respiratory therapy was started. The new West Wing added a new entrance and waiting room, coffee and gift shops, an emergency department, offices, patient rooms, and operating rooms. In 1975 the entire hospital was equipped with air conditioning, and in 1977, due to the growth of medical practices in town, the Medical Office Building was built, doubling in size 10 years later.

In the early 1980s, the hospital corporation decided to expand its services beyond the hospital and build a long-term care facility, Weston Hadden Convalescent Center (presently Centers for Living and Rehabilitation). With the Medical Office Building and Weston Hadden on campus, it was clear that the hospital had become sufficiently diverse to require reorganization. The corporation restructured under the umbrella of Putnam Memorial Health Corporation (presently Southwestern Vermont Health Care), and the hospital was renamed Southwestern Vermont Medical Center. Other subsidiaries were renamed or created; they included Putnam Healthcare Auxiliary (presently SVHC Auxiliary), Mt. Anthony Housing Corporation to oversee management of Weston Hadden; and the Putnam Building Management Corporation to manage the

medical office building and other facilities. In 1985 Weston Hadden Convalescent Center opened, offering long-term residential care services. In 1983 the West Wing was expanded to include a new ICU, respiratory care, laundry and meeting rooms.

The 1990s were a time of great expansion of services and the merging with other health care providers throughout the service area. In 1991 Northshire Medical Center in Manchester became an affiliate followed by Deerfield Valley Health Center in Wilmington in 1996, and Bennington Area Home Health in 1997. Weston Hadden also expanded its services in 1995 by adding a new wing for short-term, subacute care and rehabilitation. In 1995, the Southwestern Vermont Regional Cancer Center opened, and added radiation therapy to its other oncology services. At the same

time, SVMC undertook another major building project to update the departments of surgery, ambulatory care, maternal-child health, and central sterile supply.

SVHC took a new direction in the 1990s and developed an innovative approach to health care, based on its new vision "to make the communities we serve the healthiest in the nation." To achieve this vision, the trustees and administration committed resources for a community outreach program—Healthier Community Partnerships, whose goal was to "partner" with a variety of community groups to improve the health and well-being of the community. Alongside the traditional role as health care providers, SVHC began to actively encourage prevention and to support healthier lifestyle choices through a variety of programs offered by the Wellness Connection and through the

Southwestern Vermont Medical Center, part of Southwestern Vermont Health Care, Bennington, Vermont.

Healthier Community Partnerships.

As the new millennium begins SVHC announced a new name for its growing health care system. On February 1, 2000 Southwestern Vermont Health Care became the name of the parent corporation and replaced PMHC. Weston Hadden Convalescent Center was renamed Centers for Living and Rehabilitation to reflect the changes in resident care that encourage as active and independent a lifestyle as possible.

Entering its second century SVHC will continue to respond to the health care needs of its community by expanding and improving services, facilities, and technology, while keeping its patients at the center of all its efforts.

263

SPRINGFIELD HOSPITAL

At Springfield Hospital, the continuing ability to provide the highest quality service in a cost-effective manner depends on three essential ingredients: a caring and highly-skilled staff, advanced technology, and modern facilities.

Springfield Hospital is a full-service, not-for-profit hospital serving 16 area communities in southeastern Vermont and southwestern New Hampshire. The medical staff of over 60 physicians offers primary care and specialty services including cardiology, neurology, dermatology and oncology.

Since its founding in 1913, Springfield Hospital has continued to grow to meet the changing needs of the communities it serves. The hospital facility itself has also seen many changes.

It all started in 1913 when the Men's Brotherhood Bible Class of the Methodist Church, believing Springfield had grown enough to support a hospital, researched the need for such a facility. The group incorporated August 4, 1913, and as a result of their survey the first Springfield Hospital opened in 1914 in a three-story, 10-room house on Mt. Vernon Street. A board of trustees was elected with George F. Leland becoming the first president of the board. The original site of Springfield Hospital was purchased for $3,000 and had accommodations for 13 patients.

Four years later the Hospital Aides Association, forerunner of the Springfield Hospital Auxiliary and Volunteer Services, was formed and commenced its invaluable service to patients and administration. Their donations of time and fund-raising activities support programs like the Auxiliary Scholarships, Patient and Visitor Greeter, Patient Escort Service, and the Springfield Hospital. In 1999 alone, Auxiliary Volunteers donated nearly 4,000 hours of service to Springfield Hospital.

In 1922, Henry Whitcomb donated six acres of land on Ridgewood Road for a new hospital, and the following year the new facility opened with the capability of caring for 44 patients. The next big change was in 1942 when a new maternity wing opened.

An important and long-standing tradition began in 1957 when the auxiliary sponsored the first Apple Blossom Ball. This cotillion, featuring seniors from area high schools, is still held every spring. It has become an important annual fund-raising event for the hospital and one of the community's premiere social events.

The cornerstone was laid for a modern addition which opened and was dedicated in 1959, as the first

Original home of Springfield Hospital on Mount Vernon Street, circa 1913.

Springfield Hospital today.

special care unit in the State of Vermont. The $1.2 million expansion and alteration established a Pediatrics Department; semi-private rooms to replace wards; enlarged Laboratory, X-ray and Emergency Departments; a new surgical suite; and a four-bed recovery room and a central sterile supply room.

The hospital continued to grow with its expanded services more in demand each year, and new outpatient psychiatric services were inaugurated in 1964. Today, The Windham Center for Psychiatric Care is a 20-bed in-patient adult psychiatric center located at the Health Center at Bellows Falls. The Windham Center also offers a Partial Hospitalization Program as a day-treatment alternative to inpatient hospitalization or a transition from the hospital before reentering the community.

In 1978 the fourth stage of expansion was initiated with a groundbreaking ceremony for a $1.6 million expansion and renovation. The new construction included an expanded Emergency Room and Outpatient Department with a new lobby, administrative offices and a new

maternity area. Renovation included in the project involved laboratory expansion, physical therapy, radiology and pharmacy. Construction of a professional office building adjacent to the hospital was also begun.

In 1987 another extensive renovation project resulted in a new entrance and expanded registration and information systems.

In 1991, upon the closure of Rockingham Memorial Hospital in Bellows Falls, Vermont, Springfield Hospital began offering services at The Health Center at Bellows Falls. The Health Center (the former Rockingham Hospital) houses many of Springfield Hospital's Services, including: three physician offices (family medicine, internal medicine and a pediatrician); an Urgent Care Center, physical therapy, radiology services and the Windham Center for Psychiatric Care. Health Care and Rehabilitation Services of Southeastern Vermont and the Visiting Nurse Alliance of VT and NH also provide services at The Heath Center, which is owned and managed as a facility by the Greater Rockingham Area Services, a successor to the Rockingham

Memorial Hospital organization.

One of the more recent changes to Springfield Hospital is the development of the ChildBirth Center. The Center offers mothers and fathers a birth experience in a home-like setting with labor-deliver-recovery rooms. A variety of prenatal, parenting and lactation consulting services are available. The Emergency Department was also renovated in 1997 to streamline patient care and increase patient privacy and comfort.

In 1998 a renovation of the Ambulatory Care Unit was completed. The new Ambulatory Care Unit (formerly One Day Surgery) is designed to improve privacy, enhance patient care services and allow a smoother transition from surgery to home. Also recently built is a non-denominational chapel, allowing visitors and patients a quiet place to reflect.

Improvements in diagnostic equipment & treatment services have been numerous. The Radiology Department now has a Spiral CT Scanner, allowing physicians to more accurately and efficiently diagnose disease at an early stage. A new mammography imager has improved technique and comfort for patients. Springfield Hospital also offers MRI (Magnetic Resonance Imaging). Bone Densitometry, designed to measure bone loss over time, is now also available at Springfield Hospital.

The most recent program to be offered at Springfield Hospital is an Alternative Therapy Center. Massage Therapy and Acupuncture are now offered on site.

Springfield Hospital will continue its tradition of providing high-quality, convenient health care to you, your family, and friends. As the health care needs in the area change, Springfield Hospital will change to meet them. It is the Hospital's mission to provide high-quality, accessible, cost-competitive primary and secondary care to the residents of its service area.

RUTLAND REGIONAL MEDICAL CENTER

Rutland Regional Medical Center was, from the start, a collaboration between hospital staff and the community.

In 1892 community leaders, seeing the need for a local hospital, incorporated as Rutland Hospital and pledged to create such a facility. By 1896 a wood-frame residence on Nichols Street had been bought and converted to a 10-bed facility.

The demands on the community hospital grew and between 1909 and 1911 two wood-frame wings were added to the original structure, expanding its capacity to 70 beds. In 1930 those wood-frame wings were razed and a fireproof "addition" of brick put up, bringing its capacity to 140 beds.

In its first six months the hospital served 34 patients. By 1947, when 5,478 patients were admitted, the hospital board voted to start a $450,000 building fund campaign in 1948. However, in 1949 the hospital had developed a deficit that threatened to close its doors, and the idea of a new building was suddenly deferred while hospital personnel and the community raised $100,000 within a month's time, to keep the hospital solvent.

When the dream of a building program was revived, Albert Cree

When the Rutland Hospital was founded in 1896, it occupied the Victorian house to the left and by 1909 required the wood-frame addition that extends off to the right.

The new Rutland Hospital opened in 1958 and within six years a fifth floor had to be added. In 1973 two new wings were constructed to expand the radiology and emergency devices.

persuaded the board to build an entirely new complex on land his critics claimed was, " way out in the country." In 1951 the hospital bought 60 acres of land, the former Newman Chaffee farm. This time, the community raised over $1.1 million. In 1958 a new 155-bed facility on the Allen Street property opened.

Within six years a fifth floor was constructed on top of the entire building, adding 57 beds. This time the hospital did not have to go to the community for financial help.

Albert Cree again headed a $2-million-plus building fund drive to expand the hospital's radiology and emergency services and in 1973 the hospital grew to 301 beds. In 1975 a 13-bed psychiatric unit opened as a result of cooperation between the Rutland Hospital and Rutland Mental Health.

Although Vermont's regulatory agencies deemed a CAT scanner unnecessary, the people of the community determined that the hospital needed one, raised the money, reversed the state's decision, and installed the scanner in 1980. An outpatient surgery facility was added in 1983.

That same year the board of directors voted to change the hospital's name to Rutland Regional Medical Center to reflect a broader scope in area and service as a sophisticated and innovative health center.

In 1989 a 93,000 square-foot expansion, Rutland East, was added to expand outpatient services and to house a linear accelerator for cancer treatments.

In 1999, the hospital employed over 1,100 people and had a medical staff of more than 125 physicians in 35 medical specialty areas.

STERLING COLLEGE

Located in the Northeast Kingdom, where people still live close to the resource base, Sterling was founded in 1958 as a boys' preparatory school. It was named after Margaret Sterling, the wife of Douglas Field, one of the founders. Its educational philosophy soon became rooted in the precepts developed by the founder of Outward Bound, Kurt Hahn. His compelling educational pillars included combining academics, physical challenge, craftsmanship, and service to others. In the early 60s, these found solid footing in Craftsbury Common under the leadership of a new headmaster, W.E. "Ted" Bermingham. In late November 1964, the first Winter Expedition bivouacked at the base of West Mountain near the Canadian border. Winter Expedition is still the culmination of each fall semester.

When the "alternative" preparatory school market waned in the early 1970s, Sterling was well positioned to respond creatively. First came the Academic Short Course in Outdoor Leadership—a 21-day program for students 13 to 16 years old. It brought hundreds of

Another expedition crosses Craftsbury's common.

young people to Sterling for an intense learning experience with one of the most effective teachers— the Vermont winter. The Short Course also solidified women's presence on campus to share equally the benefits of a Sterling education. An extension of this idea became the year-long "Grassroots Project." Designed by a core of dedicated faculty—Dave Brown, Ned Houston, Ann Ingerson, and Bill Manning, as well as veterans from the boys school, Dave Linck and Steve Wright—it was an immediate success. Manning became president in 1977. He and this team, with Diane and Ross Morgan, shepherded Sterling into the world of higher education. The first Associate of Arts degree was awarded in 1982. Full accreditation by the New England Association of Schools and Colleges was granted to Sterling College in 1987.

Carrying forward with these traditions, Jed Williamson—a former Outward Bound School director and University of New Hampshire faculty member, where he designed a graduate program in experiential education—took over as president in 1996. Under his tenure, re-accreditation in 1997 included a newly-designed baccalaureate program.

Facilities on the 100 plus acre campus include 12 residential, administrative, and classroom buildings, a wood shop, and library. Outdoor teaching facilities include a managed woodlot, a challenge course, an organic garden, and a

Sterling students, alumni, faculty, and staff join forces for the new McCarthy barn raising.

working livestock farm with two barns. What is grown and raised is consumed in the dining hall.

On-campus programs are augmented by off-campus internships which allow students to gain valuable work experiences and provide service to others while earning college credits. Being a member of the national Work Colleges Consortium means that every student engages in chores and work for all aspects of campus life.

Sterling attracts faculty dedicated to undergraduate teaching, interdisciplinary curriculum and diverse learning modes. They have forged lasting and mutually beneficial ties with the local community. The mottoes of the school—*Fovete Stirpes* (Nourish the Roots)—and the college—*Working Hands, Working Minds*—epitomize this unique, dynamic, forward-looking educational setting.

A graduation ceremony on the Brown Library lawn. Mt. Mansfield is on the far horizon.

SUPERIOR TECHNICAL CERAMICS CORPORATION

Like many teens his age, Theodore Church spent his youthful summers working for his father at the office and doing menial tasks at company headquarters. Years later, in 1949, after completing his tour with the Army, he joined the company, and since 1964 has led Superior Technical Ceramics Corporation into the 21st century as president.

Lured by Vermont's industrial development programs, Superior Technical Ceramics Corporation re-located to St. Albans in 1975. The important availability of natural gas, that runs to this area through a pipeline from Canada, was a significant attraction because it's natural gas that runs the kilns.

The kilns fire the products for which Superior Technical Ceramics Corporation has become famous. The process involves using powders such as talc, clay and aluminum oxide, and by various mixing methods creating a dough, or a "slurry." A slurry is shot up into the air under high heat for drying, and becomes a powder, similar to the way powdered instant coffee is produced. The powder is pressed, or extruded, into initial shapes and then machined into more specific shapes.

Moritz Kirchberger, founder of the company.

The machined product is fired at temperatures of 2,500°-3,000°F in special kilns to produce the finished ceramic product. During this process the material shrinks 20 percent and becomes very hard. If closer tolerances are required than possible through firing, the product is polished/ground with diamond wheels to as close as one-half of 1/1000 of an inch.

This highly-technical process is the end result of the work that

Mortiz Kirchberger began in 1898, and shows how dramatically the company has grown and adopted new technologies through the years.

Leaving his homeland in the area of Koblenz, Germany, M. Kirchberger emigrated to the United States and founded M. Kirchberger & Company in Manhattan, New York. He began importing gas lighting fixtures and lamps through connections he had to this industry in Czechoslovakia, which was at the time part of the Austro-Hungarian Empire.

At the turn of the 19th century the United States was struggling with the question of powering the wheels of progress with gas or electricity. Acetylene, a gas derived from burning coal, was made all over the country and piped into houses where it burned through a ceramic tip. Many old brownstone houses in Boston and New York still bear evidence of this lighting system. It was M. Kirchberger's imports that fit these types of applications, as well as the popular tiffany-style lamps and chandeliers. He also sold chimney mantels wholesale for $1.00-$2.00 per dozen which today retail at $3.00-$4.00 each.

In 1910 M. Kirchberger & Company began manufacturing acetylene burners for lighting fixtures and burner tips for producing carbon black used in ink and tires. A European procedure was mimicked, using block talc as the main ingredient. This raw material, a natural stone grade I lava, was imported from Italy, the best known source at the time.

Ten years later M. Kirchberger recognized the country's move towards electricity as its main power source and saw the potential for electrical insulators and other related products. He relocated his business to Brooklyn, New York, adding insulators as a new product line, and manufacturing them from the same raw materials. The insulators were used for toasters and other home appliances including lighting

Employees from the early 1900s manufacturing parts.

Superior Technical Ceramics Corporation after two additions to the building, as it stands today.

fixtures, radio tubes, and dozens of other applications. The number of employees swelled to 75, a new high.

As the great market crash of 1929 hit, Rudolf Church succeeded his Uncle Moritz as president. The recession forced the company to contract its operations and manufacturing.

At this time radio insulators became critical and the standard Italian materials had been cut off and materials from India were used as a replacement. M. Kirchberger & Company became a key supplier to companies such as RCA, Westinghouse, and Raytheon, who began manufacturing radio tubes and radar equipment for the government.

Additional ceramic technologies attracted the company's attention in 1945, and Rudolph Church founded the Superior Steatite and Ceramics Corporation as an affiliate of M. Kirchberger & Company. Steatite is Greek for talc, a substance comprising 85 percent of a ceramic body. Combining steatite with clay, the new corporation manufactured wire wound resistors and electrical insulators for appliances and a variety of other purposes.

Aluminum oxide precipitated the next innovation. The addition of this substance allowed for production of a harder body which could withstand greater temperatures and was 10 times as strong. This material was primarily used for radio tube insulators, textile guides and welding products, and represented a major advance in the company's technology. To accommodate this advance, the affiliates relocated to Englewood, New Jersey in 1953 under the name of Superior Steatite and Ceramic Corporation. During the Korean Conflict the company once again became a major producer of electrical and electronic insulators for the military.

The last move for the company was to St. Albans in the northern

Ceramic components made by Superior Technical Ceramics.

tier of Vermont. Vermont business and winter recreation attracted Theodore's family. They decided to settle and bring their business into the region. Here they have had a positive impact on the community, creating approximately 100 jobs. They are actively involved in state party politics and have helped to fund a local technical school. The Corporation is a participant in the Franklin County Workforce Investment Board, National Association of Manufacturers, the Associated Industries of Vermont and Human Resources Roundtable, as well as in local high school career days, senior programs, and career fairs.

Always looking to expand and improve, they purchased Wagner Ceramics of Texas in 1990 and moved all of the equipment to St. Albans to be housed in their 85,000 square-foot building.

"Manufacturing is growing in this country, but the landscape has changed," says Theodore Church. "We are going to continue to grow in volume and people, but especially technical people, because that is what will allow us to improve quality and productivity."

Theodore Church's ability to guide the specialized company can be measured by the changes in Superior Technical Ceramics Corporation over the years. Their highly-technical ceramic products range in size from the head of a needle to objects 12 inches in diameter. Their use has expanded from the early days of simple burners for lighting fixtures to the white ceramic body used on spark plugs for aircraft engines and D-8 diesel tractors, ion-implant parts for computer chips, plasma cutting torches and other technical instruments.

Their operating philosophy to offer the best possible service to customers, and to incorporate the latest technology into their processes, has allowed Superior Technical Ceramics Corporation to rise to the top of its industry and will continue to keep it competitive in the future.

TIVOLY, INC.

Along the boundary line that runs east and west nearly 4,000 miles between the United States and Canada, you will occasionally see a house, a store, or a farm which straddles the border. However, in Derby Line, Vermont you will find a huge factory that is partly in the U.S. and partly in Canada. Here is the home of Tivoly, Inc., an American cutting tool manufacturer.

It all began 120 years ago, when Lewis Young, an enterprising young resident of Rock Island, Quebec designed a wagon axle cutter that would restore worn axles so that the wheel would fit as tightly as when the vehicle was new. The demands for his product were so great it necessitated the formation of a partnership with F.D. Butterfield.

This was the start of Butterfield's line of cutting tools, and by 1887 its

product line was large enough to justify a catalog and the construction of new buildings at the factory's present site. The buildings erected in both Rock Island and Derby Line

One of the major industries at the Boundary is the Butterfield Division of the Union Twist Drill Co. Above photo shows the original Butterfield plant, now replaced by a large modern establishment. Photo courtesy J.J. Parker, Derby Line.

ITM flute grinder.

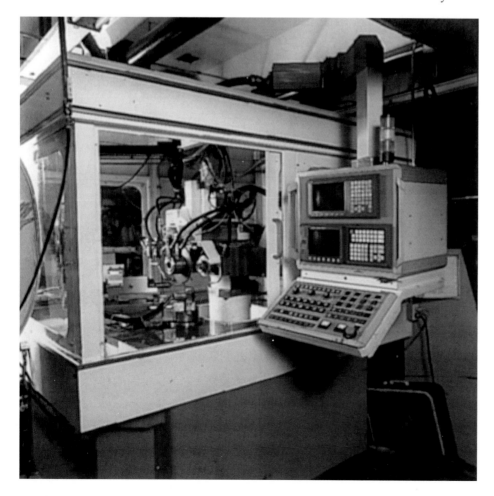

were so close that they actually straddled the Tomifobia River and the Canada-U.S. Border. Even now, visitors entering the Tivoly factory will notice a red line on the staircase wall that determines the U.S. and Canadian sides.

In 1897, F.G. Butterfield joined his older brother, F.D., and the partnership was incorporated as Butterfield and Company.

The Butterfields were native Vermonters and their ancestral home was in Saxtons River, Vermont. Colonel F.D. Butterfield was a Captain in the 8th Regiment, Vermont Volunteers during the Civil War. General F.G. Butterfield was Brigadier General of the 6th Vermont Regiment and was awarded the Congressional Medal of Honor for gallantry in May 1863 at Salem Heights, Virginia.

In 1913, the success and reputation of Butterfield & Company attracted the attention of an American cutting tool company. This company was looking for an opportunity to manufacture twist drills, milling cutters and gear hobs in Canada. Butterfield & Co. was then sold to the Union Twist Drill Company, becoming Butterfield Division, Union Twist Drill Company.

By 1918, Butterfield Division was manufacturing and shipping additional tools in good quantities to both Canadian and United States outlets, as well as building a sizable export business.

By 1925 Butterfield marketed its first high-speed ground thread taps. The company continued to expand and prosper and was able to weather the severe depression of the early '30s.

In 1964, the directors of the corporation changed its name from Union Twist Drill Company to UTD Corporation. In 1968, UTD Corporation was merged with Litton Industries, and in 1972 a consolidation took place which resulted in the establishment of Union/Butterfield Division of Litton Industrial Products. The drill, cutter, and end mill manufacturing facility was consolidated in Athol, Massachusetts, while the tap, die and reamer facility was consolidated in Derby Line, Vermont.

In 1988, after more than a century of continuous operation, the Derby Line operation became part of Groupe Tivoly, a leading European cutting tool manufacturer with several manufacturing facilities in France and Spain.

Since the early days, design, manufacturing and sales of taps have been a priority. Tivoly, Inc. was one of the first high-speed steel cutting tool manufacturers to become ISO 9002 registered.

Its dedication to uncompromising quality is recognized with a Q-1 rating by large end users such as Ford Motor Company, and by Caterpillar with a "Certified Supplier" award.

Tivoly's slogan, "Quality First," expresses its ultimate goal to exceed its customers' expectations of reliability, competitiveness, performance and response.

Its unique location in the "North-

Tivoly, Inc., Derby Line, Vermont. Photo by Ace Aero Services.

east Kingdom" of Vermont, the Green Mountain State, led the company to implement an environmentally-friendly process and to be the first Vermont company to be ISO 14001 registered—and the first cut-

Cutting tools.

ting tool manufacturer in North America to receive ISO 14001 certification.

Tivoly, Inc., with 160 full-time employees in Derby Line, Vermont, was recognized with a Governor's Award for Environmental Achievement in Pollution Prevention in 1997. The company's environmental slogan, "A Crystal Clear Policy: PosiTIVOLY Committed to Environmental Excellence," helped build employee support for the belief that environmental protection is everybody's responsibility.

Just as the modern Tivoly, Inc. factory in Derby Line, Vermont, presents a marked contrast to the original Butterfield plant of 1880, so too does the Tivoly production of today represent an aggressive progress in the manufacturing of fine cutting tools. The Research and Development Department is constantly being carried forward toward the development of new and superior cutting tools for its market and continually improves on existing products. As the world moves into the new millennium, Tivoly, Inc., with its pioneer background in the cutting tool field, moves with it.

UNION MUTUAL OF VERMONT

The Vermont Legislature granted Union Mutual Fire Insurance Company its charter in 1874, primarily through the efforts of a local lawyer named Samuel Wells. At the time, Sam Wells was the president of another insurance company, the Farmers Mutual Insurance Company of Montpelier. Wells' basic view was to provide mutual insurance protection for Vermont property owners and Vermont companies which could not be insured in the Farmer's Mutual, since it only served the agricultural community. With the establishment of the Union Mutual, it was decided to discontinue the Farmers Mutual. As a result, Vermont's second oldest mutual fire insurance company was off and running, ready to serve customer needs throughout the state of Vermont.

Union Mutual's first president was E.B. Campbell and its first policy was issued on July 28, 1875 to Marcus D. Gilman (who also happened to be the Union Mutual's vice president) on his home located at 1 Baldwin Street in Montpelier. This home is now used as office space by the Legislative Joint Fiscal Office, next door to the State Capital.

During its first year of business, the Union Mutual wrote 547 policies, insuring $640,447 in value, and received cash premiums of $4,093.33. It paid expenses of $1,140.38, policyholder losses of $1,128.91 and ended the year with a working balance of $1,823.94. These results reflected the Union Mutual's immediate financial success as a result of its frugality of business practice, despite a raging fire in Montpelier in 1874 that caused some $200,000 worth of damage in the city. The Union Mutual Fire Insurance Company was definitely off and running.

Union Mutual began its operations in rural, agrarian Vermont and the assessment plan of insurance was the accepted manner of doing business. This plan involved taking back a premium note and establish-

John F. McLaughlin, president and chief executive officer.

ing a contingent liability. By World War I, industrialization and the advent of the automobile had taken hold in the Green Mountain State. The wheels of industry brought new corporations, progress and change.

In 1917, the first dividend policy was issued. This new form of policy eliminated the premium note and provided for dividends to policyholders based upon the Company's

Douglas J. Wacek, executive vice-president and chief operating officer.

financial success. Through the 1920s Union Mutual was strictly a fire insurance company. Over the next two decades, additional types of protection were added and finally combined with a homeowner's package policy in 1950. By its 50th anniversary in 1925, the Union Mutual had accumulated assets of $220,143 and had premium revenues of $379,820 and surplus of $78,142.

Union Mutual began its operations in the former offices of the Farmers Mutual in the Reed Block in Montpelier. Eventually, the Company needed additional space and moved first to the Union Block and subsequently to the Post Office Block. However, by 1900 it had outgrown its offices and moved into a new, "permanent" home on the second floor of a building located at the corner of State and Main streets in downtown Montpelier, the current home of the Howard Bank. The Company purchased this building in 1925 and remained there until it constructed its current location at 139 State Street in 1958. These facilities were subsequently expanded and remodeled in 1990 with a four-story addition.

For most of its years in business, Union Mutual operated only in the State of Vermont. In 1954 and 1955 the Company commenced writing insurance in the adjoining states of Maine and New Hampshire. In 1959 operations began for developing business through general agents in the states of Florida and Texas. The Texas business developed at a much faster rate of growth than it was believed advisable for Union Mutual. As a result, the operations in Texas were subsequently discontinued in 1964. Concerns about exposure to catastrophic windstorms and hurricanes in the State of Florida led the Company to discontinue business there in 1968.

In 1962 Union Mutual acquired the State Mutual Insurance Company. This company was originally chartered in Rutland in 1898 and in

1901 had acquired the stock of another company known as the New England Fire Insurance Company of Rutland, Vermont. The Union Mutual changed the name of the State Mutual to "New England Guaranty Insurance Company, Inc.," so that together with the Union Mutual Fire Insurance Company, the two entities formed the Union Mutual of Vermont Companies. In 1979 Union Mutual began writing insurance policies in the State of Massachusetts, followed by Connecticut in 1986 and Rhode Island in 1987. Also in 1987, the Company participated in a joint venture to satisfy the automobile markets by creating the Champlain Casualty Company. In 1991, the Company obtained its license to write business in the State of New York.

Although it was no longer strictly a fire insurance company, in 1967 Union Mutual adopted as its emblem an antique torchbearer's lamp, once used to light the way of volunteer fire brigades. This logo represents the continued program of the companies for leadership in protection and service.

Today the Union Mutual of Vermont Companies is a regional property and casualty insurance

Corporate office—139 State Street, Montpelier.

carrier with a broad product base, serving families and small businesses throughout New England. Its primary market emphasis is on personal lines of insurance, where it provides an array of policies and coverages that protect an individual's home, automobile, and personal property. It also provides broad-based property and liability protection to a variety of small commercial and industrial enterprises.

The Union Mutual provides its products through approximately 400 professional Independent Insurance Agencies located throughout New England. Working with its agency partners, the Company strives to provide the best possible level of protection to its policyholders with a level of service that is "Second to None" in the industry. The Company enjoys a very strong relationship with its agencies, many of which are family enterprises that have represented the Company for generations. It is through these strong professional relationships and top quality service that the Union Mutual continues to be successful in coping with the many changes in the insurance marketplace.

Members of Union Mutual's management and board of directors, both past and present, demonstrate a deep commitment to service. No fewer than five former governors of Vermont have been (or are) directors of the Company. These include Franklin S. Billings, Charles M. Smith, Deane C. Davis, F. Ray Keyser, Jr. and Thomas P. Salmon.

Salmon is still currently on the board of directors, along with

eight other prominent members of the local community: John F. McLaughlin, Lawrence H. Reilly, Frederic H. Bertrand, David R. Coates, Allen Martin, John E. Corning, James A. McDonald, and S. John Osha. Union Mutual's current officers are: president and CEO, John F. McLaughlin; executive vice president & COO, Douglas J. Wacek; senior vice president, John E. Corning; vice presidents, John R. Walker, Ian B. Chisholm, Bradley S. Keysar and Harold Robinson; treasurer, William B. Robie; and corporate secretary, Eileen M. Corti.

Through its commitment to quality and service, the Union Mutual of Vermont continues its long tradition of solid growth and financial strength and stability. 1999 marked the Union Mutual's 125th anniversary; it now has over 112,000 policyholders, total assets of $85 million, premium revenues of $52 million, and Policyholder Surplus of $32 million.

With nearly 100 employees, the Union Mutual is a substantial employer in central Vermont. It strives to be a good corporate citizen that appreciates its employees, supports the local community, treats people with courtesy and respect and conducts its affairs with the utmost level of integrity. Adherence to these basic principles has served the Company well over the past 125 years and should continue to serve the Union Mutual of Vermont as it begins a new century of service.

John E. Corning, senior vice-president.

VERMONT ACADEMY

Nestled in the charming village of Saxtons River in the Southern Connecticut River Valley, Vermont Academy was founded in 1876 as a "first-class Literary and Scientific Institute for the education of our youth of both sexes." The Academy's first headmaster, Dr. Horace Mann Willard, was an energetic and visionary educator who insisted on a course of study unique for its time—a broad curriculum which challenged students to think independently. This characteristic of the Academy remains today, as does Dr. Willard's dedication to developing the "whole student."

The Academy flourished until the Depression, and was in receivership when Laurence G. Leavitt became headmaster in 1934. During his 25 year tenure Mr. Leavitt revitalized the Academy. The energy, inspira-

The chemistry between students and teachers is enhanced because of small class size. With the majority of teachers living on campus, students are able to get extra help during the day, evenings and on weekends.

All-school photo taken in 1925 includes students, faculty and staff.

tion and legacy he and his wife engendered gave rise to four decades of remarkable progress under the leadership of six subsequent headmasters.

Notable alumni and faculty from the early years include: Dr. Florence Sabin, 1889, the first woman to be accepted into the Johns Hopkins Medical School, who later did extensive research on the lymphatic system; civic leader Paul Harris, 1888, founder of Rotary International; Russell Porter, 1891, noted inventor and arctic explorer who helped design the Palomar telescope in California; associate principal James Taylor, father of the Long Trail, organizer of the first school Winter Carnival at Vermont Academy in 1909; Warren Chivers, former Olympian and faculty member, who developed and coordinated one of the most competitive school ski programs from the '40s, through the '80s.

Vermont Acad-

emy was, and still is a student-centered school dedicated to developing responsible and self-disciplined, college-bound students. The curriculum has evolved over the years to challenge students who have the potential and are willing to do the demanding work necessary to become confident and independent learners. The Academy's philosophy is based on the belief that learning takes place in a small, supportive environment dedicated to personal attention. Its close community, centered around honesty, integrity and mutual respect, depends upon open communication, trust, vigilance, and a shared commitment to its purpose and core beliefs.

Today, Vermont Academy remains a small, independent secondary school, primarily boarding, focused on preparing students for entrance into and success at college or university. The bustling campus is host to 256 students hailing from 25 states and 10 countries. It is situated on 500 acres, and still utilizes many of the original buildings. The average class size is 11 and there is a 7:1 student to faculty ratio. The school is non-denominational and is accredited by the New England Association of Schools and Colleges.

The school's academic philosophy embraces oral and written expression, critical thinking and analysis

Girl's varsity soccer is just one of many sports available to women.

and the cultivation of good instincts—intellectual, creative, athletic and social. Vermont Academy helps students discover their individual talents and develop the character, strength and skills necessary to effectively handle the challenges of college and beyond. Courses are offered in English, science, foreign languages, history, computer, math, visual and performing arts. Beginning in the sophomore year, an honors curriculum is offered to challenge highly- motivated students. A dedicated faculty and staff are involved with students outside of the classroom as coaches, dorm parents, advisors, and extracurricular activities and programs directors.

The Academy believes that athletic participation contributes to developing the whole student. Focus is on teamwork, sportsmanship, and self-discipline, an appreciation for being fit and having fun. Nineteen interscholastic sports are offered, including cross country running, equestrian, field hockey, football and soccer in the fall. Winter sports include ice hockey, dance, basketball, skiing (cross country, alpine, jumping), snowboarding and wrestling. Baseball, golf, lacrosse, softball, tennis and track and field are offered in the spring. During one season, students may choose to participate in an afternoon activity including community service, drama, outdoor education, photography, recreational skiing or snowboarding, rather than a competitive sport.

Students meet twice a week with their advisors who assist with academic planning and personal development. Parent profiles, acquired during the application process, allow advisors and teachers to identify strengths and weaknesses a student may demonstrate in academic disciplines and permit evaluations of progress. A learning skills program is available to students who need to improve study skills and compensatory techniques, and college counseling begins in the sophomore year.

A variety of activities, concerts and guest speakers take place after classes and on weekends. On weekends students may find themselves hiking, fishing, canoeing, skiing or snowboarding, as well as going to museums or cultural events in Hanover, Boston or New York.

All of these factors contribute to the success of Vermont Academy— its location, faculty and staff, student-centered philosophy and its appreciation and development of individual talents—all making for a winning combination.

The Outing Club gives students an opportunity to experience the natural beauty of Vermont. Here, students hiking on the Long Trail take a lunch break near Stratton Pond, spring 1950.

VERMONT GAS SYSTEMS, INC.

On February 16, 1966, Vermont became the 49th state to use natural gas.

In the late 1950s a group of businessmen (who would later form Vermont Gas Systems, Inc.) began to look at introducing natural gas into Vermont from Canada. That undertaking would require laying 45 miles of pipeline through rugged terrain from the Quebec border to the city of Burlington, Vermont's most densely populated municipality.

Because of the size of the project, the state studied the costs and impacts for six years before giving the go-ahead. Then, in 1965, Vermont Gas Systems was founded. That same year, the company signed a contract with Trans-Canada Pipelines, Ltd. of Toronto to begin flowing natural gas into Vermont.

Vermont Gas sponsors many community events like this parade on the Church Street Markeplace.

One year later, Vermont Gas had made natural gas available to 6,400 customers throughout parts of Chittenden and Franklin counties. Clean-burning natural gas was quickly becoming recognized as a high-value source of energy.

Today Vermont Gas is an integral part of these Vermont communities. The company serves over 32,000 customers through a network of more than 450 miles of underground pipes. Over 3,500 of the state's trademark small businesses rely on natural gas for their energy needs, as do most of Chittenden and Franklin counties' largest commercial and industrial establishments.

To keep pace with the growing demand for natural gas, in 1987 Vermont Gas moved its headquarters from 31 Swift Street in South Burlington (where it had been since 1965) to its current 25,000-square-foot building at 85 Swift Street. The company now employs over 100 people—about twice the number Vermont Gas began with in 1966.

Growth of natural gas use in Vermont should not be surprising. Not only is natural gas a sound economic value, it is also the cleanest-burning energy. Its use in the community can actually improve air quality because it does not emit the pollutant levels typical of fuel oil or coal. Further, in addition to space heating, water heaters and clothes dryers energized by natural gas achieve savings and efficiencies of operation. And most professional chefs prefer to cook with natural gas.

These benefits of natural gas have helped Vermont Gas convert over 2,500 customers from fuel oil to natural gas during the 1990s. As a result of these conversions, environmentally-friendly natural gas displaced nearly three million gallons of fuel oil in Vermont during that decade.

Vermont Gas offers services that enhance the natural benefits of gas as an energy source. A centerpiece of the company's value delivered to its customers is long-term price stability. Through the company's active management, natural gas has not observed the price spikes characteristic of other fuels.

Vermont Gas nurtures proactive relationships with residential, commercial and industrial customers alike. Contributions of time, money and talent strengthen the economy and quality of life of the areas served by Vermont Gas through diverse cultural, social service, community service and educational programs. Vermont Gas makes it a priority to be responsive to customer expectations and needs.

Since 1992 Vermont Gas has also offered valuable energy efficiency programs known as ENERGY EXTENDERS. Over 5,000 residences and businesses have taken advantage of these programs and have saved an estimated $1.5 million in annual energy costs as a result. Among these programs, the com-

Vermont Gas moved into its new corporate offices in 1987.

pany sponsors energy audits for qualifying customers, and provides financial incentives in many cases to help customers install efficiency measures. The company also works with property developers to encourage the most energy-efficient designs for new construction projects.

Vermont Gas also works closely with commercial and industrial customers to identify cost-effective uses of emerging gas technologies. Examples of successful projects include gas-fired refrigeration, air conditioning, site-specific electricity generation, and even a natural gas-powered Zamboni.

While improving the value of natural gas for its customers, Vermont Gas has also been responsive to its shareholders by delivering consistent growth and competitive returns since its inception. At the same time, Vermont Gas has been a leader in investing in the communities of Chittenden and Franklin counties.

Vermont Gas strives to be a responsible citizen to the community in which it operates. Working with the Champlain Valley Weatherization Service the company contributes time, money and expertise to help retrofit low-income housing

with energy-efficient equipment and insulation. In addition, the United Way annually recognizes Vermont Gas as one of the top companies for participation and giving.

Significant to Vermont Gas' role in the community is the company's emphasis on safety. Through intensive training and relationships with key safety officials, Vermont Gas has maintained an excellent safety record. In recognition of these efforts, Vermont Gas has received numerous regional and national safety awards, including the 1996 National Safety Council Award of Commendation, and the 1998 American Gas Association's Leader in Accident Prevention Award.

All of Vermont Gas' success is tied to its commitment to the continuous improvement of its employees. The company prides itself on being a respectful and rewarding place of employment. Vermont Gas provides growth and development opportunities to enable employees to perform to their full potential, with emphasis on teamwork, continuous learning and trust-building.

The company's employees are also encouraged to build strong ties with the communities in which they live and work. Many Vermont Gas employees serve important community roles, lead volunteer efforts, donate time to community pro-

grams such as youth sports and Girl Scouts, and hold public offices.

Since 1965, Vermont Gas has been Vermont's only natural gas supplier. Through three-and-a-half decades of strong growth, the company has remained committed to the changing needs of its customers, shareholders, employees and the community-at-large. This commitment is woven deep into the fabric of the entire organization, and provides the foundation from which Vermont Gas can be expected to continue its positive presence in Vermont.

Vermont Gas installs new 16" transmission line in Northern Franklin County.

VERMONT HEATING & VENTILATING COMPANY

It was the year Harry Truman promised to give Americans a "Fair Deal." It was 1949, and Nathan Brown started his business with the same goal in mind for his customers. In a small garage in Burlington, he started Vermont Heating & Ventilating Company (VHV). Over the next 50 years, VHV evolved into one of the premier mechanical contracting companies in New England.

Born in Quincy, Massachusetts in 1907, Nathan Brown moved to Vermont in 1944 to simplify his life and live off the land in the noble pursuit of farming. Realizing farming was not going to adequately support his wife and five children, Nathan fell back on the skills he had developed building heating and ventilating systems in Liberty Ships for the war effort. He got a job with a local mechanical contracting company making the handsome sum of $1.00 per hour.

After only a few years Nathan got the itch to start his own business. By cashing in his life insurance policy and treasury bonds, and getting a $500 loan from his sister, he and his friend Jack O'Brien started their own heating and ventilating business. They purchased the least expensive fabrication equipment they could

Vintage Vermont Heating vehicle.

Founder Nathan Brown and wife Miriam on vacation in Arizona.

find and housed it in a rented garage for the outrageous fee of $15 per month. They were on their way.

Although differing business philosophies caused Nathan to buy Jack out only seven months after they began, their lasting friendship survived. Jack went on to become a prominent Vermont State Senator.

In the 1950s, Nathan branched out from residential into commercial and industrial markets. Since

money was tight, Nathan used his charm and salesmanship to convince his first few customers to provide him some financing to complete their projects. Although reluctant, they obliged him and were very happy they did.

During the 1950s and '60s many members of Nathan's family joined the business. By 1963, his four sons Gerald, Kenneth, David, and Peter, one son-in-law Charlie Spence, and a family friend Robert Miller had all become Nathan's new partners. It had truly become a family affair.

The 1960s and '70s were substantial growth periods. In 1957 IBM located one of the largest manufacturing facilities of semiconductors in the world in Essex Junction, Vermont. This provided a substantial boom for VHV during the growth stages of this facility. During this period, VHV also expanded geographically by pursuing projects from Caribou, Maine to Dover, Delaware.

Upon Nathan's retirement in 1970 his eldest son Jerry took over as president of VHV. Jerry's tenure was marked primarily by his strong commitment to education and training both for VHV and the State of Vermont. His leadership was critical to the development of statewide apprentice programs for the sheetmetal trade. In 1992, Jerry's efforts culminated in VHV receiving the national LIFT (Labor Investing For Tomorrow) America Award for excellence in employee education and training, putting VHV's name alongside nationally-recognized leaders such as Ford Motor Company, AT&T, and Polaroid Corporation.

In 1980 VHV leveraged its experience building clean rooms for IBM by establishing a new division of the corporation, Quality Air Control. This division has blossomed into a full-service provider of design and construction services to the semiconductor, biomedical, and pharmaceutical industries for the purpose of building clean rooms

Jerry Brown accepting LIFT America Award from Elizabeth Dole.

and other specialty applications.

In 1987, VHV sold the manufacturing arm of the business to a newly-established company named Fab-Tech, Inc. Due to high capital costs in the manufacturing business and the cyclical nature of the construction industry, the idea was to diversify the manufacturing business by developing and selling multiple product lines. Again, from the many years of experience at IBM, Fab-Tech, Inc. developed a very successful product called Perma Shield Pipe (PSP®). This product is a teflon-coated stainless steel pipe designed for highly corrosive exhaust environments. Through the leadership of its president John Moore (son-in-law of Jerry Brown), Fab-Tech now sells PSP® throughout the United States and internationally, including in Taiwan, Singapore, Korea, Israel, Ireland and others. In 1997 Fab-Tech was the second fastest-growing business in Vermont over the prior five-year period (VHV was third). Fab-Tech was also the recipient of the 1999 Vermont Exporter of the Year award by the Vermont Chamber of Commerce .

The success of VHV and Fab-Tech reflects the unparalleled hard work and loyalty of the many individuals who have contributed, past and present. The two companies currently employ over 300 dedicated people. Many of the original employees from the 1950s and '60s have descendents who currently contribute to the businesses. Colorful stories of the many families and individuals who have contributed to the business over the past 50 years are often remembered.

Today VHV is a full-service, mechanical contractor serving customers all over New England. In 1998 VHV responded to customer requests by developing a plumbing and mechanical piping crew to augment their highly-skilled sheetmetal and service personnel. This addition fills out VHV's field capabilities by providing the customers with what they desire— a one-stop shop for mechanical services. The highly-skilled field crews, coupled with the experienced engineering and management staff provide VHV an unmatched combination in their industry.

In addition to providing their customers a "Fair Deal," VHV's mission for the new millennium is simple: to be their customers' preferred provider, and to be the employer of choice in their industry. The third generation of leadership will accomplish this by continuing the traditions of the first two generations. These include completing jobs on time and within budget, delivering a superior product, and providing a safe, fun and rewarding environment for employees to grow and learn. VHV is proud of its first 50 years and with the help of a dedicated workforce plans to successfully carry its vision into the 21st century.

Computer-aided design enables VHV to produce professional design documents.

VERMONT SOAPSTONE

Featured in home interior and decorating magazines, products from Vermont Soapstone in Perkinsville grace the countertops and kitchens of some of the finest homes in the United States. Architects and designers looking for natural stone with a flat finish turn to Vermont Soapstone for sinks, fireplace surrounds, countertops and finishings for other interior details. But the current trend toward the use of soapstone is nothing new; soapstone has been quarried in Vermont since the late 18th century. Centuries before that, indigenous people fashioned bowls out of the highly-malleable material.

Soapstone, or silicate of magnesium with water, is a form of talc with enough iron impurities running through it to bind it together. Rated number one on the scale of hardness (as soft as possible), the fireproof material can be easily worked, sawed, sanded and fashioned into

Perkinsville quarry, 1880s.

sinks, stoves, countertops, fireplace surrounds, stove linings and other items for indoor and outdoor use. In the 19th century, soapstone was also a popular material for hitching posts, window and door caps, griddles, flameless cookers, boot-driers and bed-warmers. The company now known as Vermont Soapstone on Stoughton Pond Road in Perkinsville, has been manufac-

turing soapstone sinks, stoves and architectural fixtures since 1850.

According to local accounts, the first soapstone quarry was found in Francestown between 1790 and 1808 when farmer Daniel Fuller dropped his axe which "cut the rock like old cheese." Another early discovery was made in 1850 by farmer J.M. Billings as he plowed the side of Hawks Mountain in Perkinsville, according to Henry Hicks. Three generations of the Hicks family—grandfather Hiland, father John, and son Henry—worked in the Vermont soapstone industry from approximately 1883 until 1962.

The Geology of Vermont, published in 1861, describes the quarry in Perkinsville. "In the town of Weathersfield—one mile from Perkinsville, near the line of Baltimore—is located the quarry now owned and worked by the 'Windham County Mining Company...About 10 rods east of the quarry a steam mill is erected, in which there is an engine of 12 horse power for carrying the saws and machinery used in sawing posts, window and door caps, slabs for export, and those used for manufacturing register frames, stove linings, cake griddles which are manufactured to order at this establishment. It is estimated that there were raised

Fred Barton at "new" Perkinsville Mill, 1960.

"Old" Perkinsville Mill, 1880s.

from the quarry last season (1859) about 800 tons of stone, of which about 300 tons where sent off to the markets of Boston, Providence and New York."

The next 50 years of the soapstone industry in Vermont shows a complicated chronology of ownership, with established companies buying newly-discovered soapstone fields. J.M. Billings, Asa Wentworth, L.B. Darling, Hyren Henry, Oren Taylor, Porter Dodge and James Flagg were all active in the early soapstone industry in Perkinsville. By 1884 Charles Williams, whom Henry Hicks described as the first person who was able to make any money quarrying soapstone, had control of nearly everything related to soapstone in Weathersfield except the lower ledge of the quarry, which was owned by the Union Soapstone Company. Union Soapstone also owned the quarry in Chester, which is still mined for soapstone today by Vermont Soapstone.

In 1884, Hiland Hicks became superintendent of Williams and Company, with quarries in Grafton and a mill in Cambridgeport as well as the Perkinsville operations. Around that time, the quarries

employed 25 men and the mills employed 25 men. From 1885 until 1900 have been described as the peak years of the soapstone industry. Soapstone was mined by hand in blocks about six feet square. Derricks at the quarry lifted the blocks of soapstone and loaded them on quarry wagons for transport to the mill. Hiland Hicks introduced the use of black powder to mine soapstone.

John Hicks joined the industry in the 1890s when he began operating a quarry leased by Charles Williams in Ludlow. In 1904, John bought the soapstone interests of Charles Williams' estate and formed the Vermont Soapstone Company, Miners and Manufacturers. After a flood in 1908 wiped out the mill, John Hicks built a new mill on the site of the old Call Cotton Mill on the east side of the Black River. Although the mill was ready for operation by 1910, by then the soapstone quarry on Hawks Mountain had run out. Vermont Soapstone acquired material from old quarries and also imported soapstone from Virginia until 1936, when John Hicks bought the Chester quarry after Ira Holden died.

Along with operating the soapstone business, John Hicks founded the Perkinsville electric company,

and was actively involved in the telephone industry and real estate. The North Springfield dam, built in the 1950s, wiped out lower Perkinsville and the mill that John Hicks built in 1910. In 1962, Henry Hicks sold Vermont Soapstone Company and the Chester quarry to Clyde and Judy Barton, who manufactured stoves as their primary product until federal emissions requirements made it prohibitively expensive about 1980. When the Bartons retired in 1987, Glenn Bowman acquired Vermont Soapstone Company.

Under Bowman's ownership, the company offers three soapstone sinks: the Williams sink designed in Boston in 1835; the Windsor sink from Philadelphia in 1885; and the Wright sink from Chicago, circa 1907. Employees travel throughout the eastern United States to install sinks, countertops, fireplace surrounds and other soapstone products, including custom-made bath and spa tubs.

"Each piece of stone has its own personality," says Bowman. "Soapstone doesn't require regular stoneworking tools, but it takes a skilled worker who knows when to push and when not to. Every so often, one of the guys in the mill will tell me it didn't quite come out the way they wanted it to."

Vermont Soapstone now employs a dozen workers, and imports much of its stone from South America, although some stone is still mined from the Chester quarry. The company mines and manufactures products from approximately 8,000 to 10,000 square feet of soapstone per year. Vermont Soapstone products are featured in kitchen and bath showrooms throughout the United States. Pennsylvania is the biggest purchaser, with Texas and California following close behind. With typical Vermont ingenuity, Bowman beats the high cost of transporting soapstone from South America by offering the soapstone as ballast in the ship's hold.

WORLD LEARNING

World Learning is set high atop a hill overlooking the Connecticut River Valley at Brattleboro.

One of the first international educational exchange organizations in the United States, World Learning, formerly known as The Experiment in International Living, was founded in 1932 by Donald and Leslie Watt. They believed that the most effective way to achieve international and intercultural understanding is through citizen exchange programs, primarily through homestay experiences. Although the Experiment's first home was in Syracuse, New York, it moved to Putney, Vermont in 1937, and relocated to its present site in 1962.

Most of the 233 acres which World Learning and its School for International Training call home were originally a dairy farm and apple orchard owned in the late 18th century by the Bliss family. Taking advantage of the magnificent view southward past a new settlement (later known as Brattleboro) to the river beyond, the family built their farmhouse in 1775 and cultivated the land for several generations. Bliss Cottage was built in 1892 on the slope where World Learning's international circle of flags now stands. In 1892-93, British author Rudyard Kipling and his bride

SIT graduation.

Caroline, of the prominent Balestier family of Brattleboro, rented the cottage while their home "Naulakha" was being built nearby. It was here that Kipling wrote many of the *Jungle Book* stories and his novel, *Captains Courageous.*

Later in the1890s the Dickinsons purchased the property from the Bliss family. Mrs. Dickinson was a niece of the 19th century railroad "robber baron" Jay Gould, who died

in 1892. It is thought that her inheritance from him may have been used to develop the property. Ownership passed to the Bibby family in 1936.

In 1961 President John F. Kennedy asked his brother-in-law, Sargent Shriver, to launch the Peace Corps. Shriver, who had participated in several Experiment exchange programs during the 1930s and had kept in touch with the organization, turned to the Experiment to train Peace Corps volunteers. In 1962 the Experiment, needing space for this Peace Corps training, acquired all of the land and buildings for $75,000.

Today World Learning offers a broad spectrum of educational and training programs with a presence in over 100 countries. Its participants— individuals and institutions—are able develop the leadership capabilities and cross-cultural competence required to advance international understanding, work effectively in multicultural environments and achieve sustainable development at the community level and on a national scale.

The School for International Training (SIT) was established in 1964, an outgrowth of the wide-ranging intercultural expertise developed by The Experiment. SIT's language and intercultural management training credentials are rooted in The Experiment's history as the charter training institution for Peace Corps volunteers.

Today this fully-accredited institution of higher education awards master's degrees in Teaching, International Education, Sustainable Development, Intercultural Relations, Organizational Management, and International and Intercultural Service. A center of knowledge, SIT conducts research in teaching and learning, and provides training programs in languages and language teaching, conflict transformation, intercultural communication, and management for individuals, governmental and non-governmental organizations and corporations. Nobel Peace Prize-winner Jody Williams is a prominent example of social activism found among SIT's 4,000 graduates.

A founding member of the Global Partnership for NGO (non-governmental organization) Studies, Education, and Training, SIT operates the Center for Social Policy and Institutional Development and the Center for Teacher Education, Training, and Research. SIT's new Extension program provides continuing education opportunities for educators, taught by its faculty online or on campus.

A national leader in academic study abroad, with 57 programs in more than 40 countries, the School has awarded undergraduate credits to over 20,000 student participants from over 200 colleges and universities in the United States. Students in these programs engage in the study of world issues, cultural diversity and the impact of globalization on topics as diverse as arts and social change, peace and conflict studies, natural and human environment, ecology and intensive language studies. A hallmark of SIT's summer abroad program is its presence in non-traditional sites in Africa, the Americas, Asia, Oceania, Europe and the Middle East.

The Experiment in International Living is World Learning's first program, and heir to the organization's original name. It carries on the tradition of the international student exchange program begun by Donald and Leslie Watt. Today The Experiment's summer abroad youth programs offer talented and deserving high school students (many with scholarship support) opportunities for international service/learning through experiential education and, of course, the family homestay. These students represent diverse economic, ethnic and cultural groups from throughout the United States. They have the opportunity to attend any of 41 programs in 23 countries, including the Navajo nation in the United States. As we enter a new century, over 50,000 participants have benefited from a life-changing Experiment experience.

World Learning also provides language and intercultural training to meet the needs of global organizations such as Exxon Company, International, Procter & Gamble and J.P. Morgan. Customized training in all languages is provided at World Learning sites in Vermont and California or at clients' sites anywhere in the world, through individual or group classes and guided self-instruction. Executive communication coaching and orien-

World Learning Program in Ghana.

tation programs are available to assist those preparing for international negotiations, meetings or assignments. In addition, U.S. educational study tours of two to six weeks' duration are custom-designed for each client's needs.

The Projects in International Development and Training division, based in Washington, D.C., is a leading private voluntary organization which administers social and economic projects worldwide under U.S. government and international contracts and grants. Involved primarily in the world's developing countries, this division designs projects to foster public involvement in basic education and to improve skills that enable individuals to address development challenges in their own communities. Other projects are aimed at increasing the effectiveness of non-government organizations and other community groups through specialized management training and grants programs, and strengthening the ability of individuals and civic groups to contribute to civil society and govern themselves effectively.

In the words of World Learning president James A. Cramer, "As we go forward in this new decade of a new century, World Learning will draw upon its rich history of building lasting relationships between people, communities and nations. Through our programs in languages, intercultural communications, study abroad and international development, we will continue to work worldwide for healthy and sustainable communities, celebrating the richness in diversity of culture and people, where social justice is no longer a dream, but a reality."

Buddhist Monks in Nepal.

WAITSFIELD AND CHAMPLAIN VALLEY TELECOM

Only a few years after Alexander Graham Bell invented the telephone in 1876, telephone poles and telephone wires appeared in Vermont. In 1880, a line was run from Montpelier to Warren by the New England Telephone & Telegraph Company, paid for mostly by popular subscription. The only telephone in Waitsfield was in Jacob Boyce's general store; anyone communicating by telephone did so at the store.

In 1900 a local telephone exchange was started, and it grew quickly. The benefits of 'telephony,' as this new technological miracle was called, were clear, and in 1904 Ziba McAllister and Walter Jones, two prominent telephone subscribers, purchased from New England Telephone & Telegraph "all lines of telephone poles together with the wires thereon" in both Waitsfield and Fayston. They, and 20 other Waitsfield businessmen, then petitioned the legislature to incorporate The Waitsfield & Fayston Telephone Company, and the incorporation became effective on November 30, 1904.

Alton E. Farr, previously of New England Telephone & Telegraph, became manager of the new company, which had "the purpose and right of acquiring, building, maintaining, and operating telephone lines." This Farr did—with zeal. He purchased more pole lines from the Roxbury Telephone Company that ran into Moretown. He also maintained and repaired the lines, traveling about the township by horse and buggy and later by Model T or on his familiar motorcycle.

By 1908 the company had grown. Rates were $1.50 per month, and phone bills were sometimes paid with farm produce–eggs, hay, vegetables, firewood, and even ashes. The central office moved from building to building in the early years, depending on the location of the manager's residence at the time, and service was available only during the working day. One housewife attended the switchboard, doing her

Alton Farr, manager of Waitsfield-Fayston Telephone Company, was a familiar sight as he made line repairs on his motorcycle in the 1920s.

housework between calls. Twenty-four hour service started when the firm rented separate quarters—an apartment for the two "central girls." The weekly salary was $15.00.

In 1924 Alton Farr married Eunice Buzzell, who became the company's bookkeeper and secretary. Together they coped with the damage caused by the flood of 1927, which felled poles all over the system and disrupted telephone service for an entire week.

When Alton died in 1940, Eunice Farr began operating the phone company herself, not only keeping the books, managing the office, and installing phones, but sometimes going out with her long pole during a windstorm to poke apart lines that had crossed and short-circuited. One of the few female utility managers in the country, she ran Waitsfield-Fayston Telephone for the next 21 years.

In 1942 a fire completely destroyed the switchboard office. Seconds before fleeing the burning building, the operator called New England Telephone & Telegraph, and within 24 hours an antique switchboard was set up in an old building nearby. This disaster was followed in 1946 by a second fire that gutted the workshop and destroyed most of the telephone

equipment stored at the Farr residence.

The early phone system was a magneto system. Subscribers "rang up" the operator to make their calls; all lines were party lines, some with as many as 27 parties. In 1961, the old system was "cut over" to dial and everything changed. Customers could dial their own local calls, and party lines were reduced to eight parties at most. It was a major step

Eunice Farr became one of the country's few female public utility managers after her husband's death in 1940. She guided the firm until 1961.

The telephone office and switchboard were in this building until 1942, when a fire destroyed the structure.

for a company with 325 subscribers.

Other innovations followed. By 1964 the Valley's growing ski areas had completely filled the capacity of the phone system, and additional outside plant and a central office facility were needed. The Vermont Public Service Board approved a conversion to a one, two, and four-party system and the company converted, installing 72 additional miles of cable and rural distribution wire. To handle the 1,000 customers then on-line, Waitsfield-Fayston Telephone built its "first home" north of Waitsfield Village, during the summer of 1966.

Direct-distance dial (DDD) came in 1967—a change welcomed by the telephone company and its customers alike. In 1968 the company installed its first IBM computer, eliminating the handwritten bills and old-fashioned addressograph plates. With that computer, and the five it has had since then, Waitsfield-

Fayston Telephone developed electronic data processing to handle all aspects of the business-line assignments, automatically printed work orders, toll-call rating, general accounting and inventory record-keeping for all telephone company equipment. The firm became a pioneer, with new computer software to serve its needs.

Guiding the modernization process has been Dana Haskin, who became president of Waitsfield-Fayston Telephone in 1958, and Eleanor Haskin, its treasurer, the daughter of Alton and Eunice Farr. "Everything we do is computerized," said Dana Haskin in the summer of 1984. "We do things with computers that no other telephone company does in the country."

The Haskins matched the telephone company's growth to the growth of the Valley population, constructing new office facilities in 1968 and adding 90 miles of new lines. The same year, with financing from the Rural Electrification Administration, Waitsfield-Fayston Telephone became the first in Vermont to convert completely to a one-party system.

The growth of the area continued steadily, and the telephone company expanded and remodeled its facilities in 1971 and 1975. Digital computer switching replaced the standard dial system in February 1981, and in the Fall of 1982 the firm's Waitsfield Cable division began offering customers the option of cable television, including coaxial, two-way data transmission essential to computer banking and similar services. The transformation of Waitsfield-Fayston Telephone into a total telecommunications company was well under way.

The forced AT&T divestiture of telephone equipment subsidiaries in January 1984 also affected Waitsfield-Fayston. The company could no longer sell and install telephones. Instead, new customers had to buy their phones from Selectronics, the firm's retail store in the center of Waitsfield, or from other telephone

equipment suppliers.

In the years between 1976 and 1994, Waitsfield-Fayston Telephone Company (WFT), dba Waitsfield Telecom (WT) was deeply involved in industry changes, many of which began in 1979. Congress was beginning to deal with competition in the long distance market brought about by Hush-a-Phone and MCI circuits between Dallas and Chicago. Waitsfield Telecom's leadership believed that if they took a significant role in developing an industry strategy for the future, their own company would survive.

In 1990, Eleanor Haskin (Waitsfield Telecom) and Paul Violette (Contoocook Valley Telephone) considered trying to buy the Contel properties in their respective states. Shirley Manning (Lincolnville Telephone Co.) joined them. It wasn't until September 1992 that the dream started to become a reality. As a result of GTE announcing divestment of their New England properties, Eleanor, Paul and Shirley soon attracted other potential buyers and became the New England Independent Group (NEIG).

After a great deal of work and several rounds of bidding, GTE narrowed its selection to two prospective buyers. In addition to price, GTE was looking for the best fit—the bidder who could best operate the exchanges. Because GTE wanted only one bidder per state to purchase the stock, each of the three NEIG states formed an acquisition company. Vermont was directed by the team at Waitsfield Telecom. A definitive agreement was reached between NEIG and GTE on November 12, 1993 in Boston, MA.

The time between signing the agreement in November and the final closing date was a hectic one. All three state leaders agree that the prevailing spirit of teamwork was key. It was eight months of hard work—weekends didn't exist and conference calls occurred almost daily.

The Independents had to learn a great deal about GTE's systems and data. The plan was for a complete cut over, with GTE not providing transitional services after the closing date, except for some signaling system 7 (SS7) service and a few other miscellaneous services. Thus, the Independents had just eight months to not only get the legal documents in order, but to get the operational systems, such as billing, in place and ready to go. All data moved to the new companies on August 1, 1994.

While the tasks seemed overwhelming at times, the transition went quite smoothly due to the Group's extensive planning and preparation. The NEIG hired Larry Sterrs of Berry, Dunn, McNeil & Parker as the transition manager, who was the lead person in working with GTE. Individual state transition teams were formed, as well.

Key to the successful transition was the NEIG's communication with GTE's customers and employees. Each company distributed a variety of information explaining the transition, including bill inserts, advertisements, brochures and news releases. They also met with GTE's customers and employees, all 177 of whom were employed at the various new companies.

The acquisition meant significant changes. The Waitsfield-Fayston Telephone Company (WFT) became a sister company to the newly formed Champlain Valley Telecom (CVT), therefore quadrupling in size. The Company increased its number of employees, adding the former GTE employees, as well as hiring additional new staff.

The increased number of access lines enhanced WCVT's ability to deploy new technology such as SS7. Incidentally, the switching facilities acquired, while from different manufacturers than those used by some of the NEIG, in most cases were state-of-the-art, with the latest generics. The new CVT facilities were connected by fiber optic

Ramona Shaw at the company's switchboard prior to the conversion to a dial system in 1961.

cable, a SONET-based ring.

The credit for success of the venture goes to the employees of the companies forming the NEIG. These employees put in long hours in preparation for the transition, including the work of the GTE employees. In addition, the consultants and attorneys played an extremely important role because they worked so closely throughout the transaction.

"It feels good to be on the other end. It has been a tremendous learning experience—a once-in-a-lifetime opportunity. Telephone properties don't come up for sale that often, especially property so near your own," offers Vice President of Operations for Waitsfield and Champlain Valley Telecom (WCVT), Eleanor Haskin.

The growth of WCVT and the

required upgrades to plant and switching kept pressure on all employees to get the job done. In January 2000, the access line count was close to 21,000. In 1996, WCVT began a complete conversion to a Siemens EWSD digital switching platform to provide the latest services to its customers, which will be completed in June 2000.

The company is now in its second generation, and moving into its third generation. Because of the growth in technology, the future will bring many surprises and challenges. Waitsfield and Champlain Valley Telecom's company leadership is excited about the possibilities the future will bring.

A TIMELINE OF VERMONT'S HISTORY

1609: Samuel de Champlain is the first European to explore the lake which he later names after himself.

1666: Fort Ste. Anne built by the French on Isle La Motte.

1690: English build fort at Chimney Point on Lake Champlain.

1689-1763: A series of wars between France and England and their Indian allies was partly contested in present day Vermont.

1704: English prisoners of French and Indians taken in raid on Deerfield, Massachussetts, traverse Vermont on retreat to Quebec.

1710-1730: Greylock, an Abenaki chief, wars against the English.

1724: English build Fort Dummer on the Connecticut River.

1749: Governor Benning Wentworth of New Hampshire charters Bennington, the first township created in the New Hampshire Grants. This leads to conflicts over grants chartered by New York.

1763: End of French and Indian War brings settlers into the New Hampshire Grants.

1764: British crown upholds New York's claims on Vermont over New Hampshire's. Green Mountain Boys organize to resist New York claims.

1775: Fort Ticonderoga captured by Green Mountain Boys under Ethan Allen.

1776: Benedict Arnold loses naval battle on Lake Champlain, but stalls British advance southward.

1777: Westminster convention declares Vermont an independent state.

1778: One-eyed Tom Chittenden elected Vermont's first governor.

1783: End of Revolutionary War brings a surge of new settlers into Vermont.

1791: Vermont becomes the 14th state. The University of Vermont chartered.

1800: Middlebury College chartered. Population of state stands at 154,475.

Jedidiah Hyde log cabin, built in 1783, Grand Isle, Vermont. Courtesy, Vince Feeney

Farm life in 19th century Vermont. Courtesy, Historic Sites photo file, Special Collections, Bailey-Howe Library, University of Vermont

1802: First canal built in the United States completed at Bellows Falls.

1805: Montpelier chosen as state capital.

1812-15: War of 1812 controversial in Vermont. Much smuggling involving Canada.

1819: Norwich University chartered.

287

The Old Stone House in Brownington, built in 1823, and now the home of the Orleans County Historical Society. Courtesy, Historic Sites photo file, Special Collections, Bailey-Howe Library, University of Vermont

1823: Champlain Canal, connecting Lake Champlain to the Hudson River, opened, making Vermont less reliant on Canadian trade. Burlington becomes an important lake port.

1830: Serious flooding. All bridges on the Winooski River below Montpelier swept away. Mormonism founded by Joseph Smith of Sharon.

1836: State Senate established, replacing the old Council of Censors.

1848: First railroad line in Vermont opened, ushering in a decade-long boom in railroad construction.

1850: Population of state stands at 314,120.

1852: Adoption of the "Maine Law," prohibiting the manufacture and sale of liquor as a beverage.

1859: American educator and philospher John Dewey born in Burlington.

1861-65: Vermont enthusiastically supports the Union cause in the Civil War, with proportionately more men serving in uniform than any other northern state.

1864: A Confederate force operating out of Canada raids St. Albans.

1866: Irish-American members of the Fenian movement unsuccessfully attempt an invasion of Canada. A second attempt in 1870 also fails.

1881: Chester A. Arthur, a Fairfield native, becomes president.

1885: First electric lights in Vermont.

1898: Admiral George Dewey, a Montpelier native, defeats Spanish fleet in Manila Bay.

1900: Population of state at 342,633, almost unchanged since 1850.

1902: Local option law passed by legislature giving local governments the power to decide whether liquor could be sold in their towns.

1917-18: 16,013 Vermont men serve in World War I.

1918-19: The great Influenza Epidemic takes the lives of countless Vermonters.

1920: Robert Frost takes up residence in South Shaftsbury, beginning a life-long connection with Vermont.

1923: Calvin Coolidge, native of Plymouth, becomes president.

1927: Widespread flooding causes millions in damage. The Winooski

Plymouth, Vermont, as it was when its most famous native son, Calvin Coolidge, was president of the United States. Courtesy, Historic Sites photo file, Special Collections, Bailey-Howe Library, University of Vermont

River Valley particularly hard hit.

1936: Green Mountain Parkway proposal rejected by referendum.

1937: George Aiken becomes governor.

1938: Tropical hurricane causes extensive damage in Vermont.

1941-45: World War II saw the service of 49,942 Vermont men.

1946: Senator Warren Austin named first U.S. ambassador to the United Nations.

1950: Population of state stands at 377,747.

1953: Consuelo Northrop Bailey elected first woman speaker of Vermont House of Representatives.

A boy and his dog walk through the snow to the Ripton Country Store. Ripton, where Robert Frost summered between 1939 and 1962, had a population of 568 in 1890 that dwindled to 131 by 1960. In 2000, the population of Ripton was 628. Photo by Carolyn Bates

Thaddeus Fairbanks, St. Johnsbury inventor of the platform scale. Courtesy, Historic Sites photo file, Special Collections, Bailey-Howe Library, University of Vermont

1954: Consuelo Northrop Bailey elected Lieutenant-Governor. First woman in the U.S. to hold this office.

1962: Philip H. Hoff of Burlington elected first Democratic governor of Vermont in 108 years.

1970: Legislature passes Act 250 establishing strict guidelines for real estate developers.

1974: Patrick Leahy elected Vermont's first Democratic U.S. Senator since the founding of the Republican Party.

1976: Alexander Solzhenitsyn takes up residency in Cavendish.

1977: Ben and Jerry's Ice Cream opens its doors in Burlington.

1981: Independent Bernard Sanders becomes mayor of Burlington in a surprise victory over incumbent Gordon Paquette.

1984: Madeleine Kunin elected

Vermont's first female governor.

1984: Vermont utilities sign contract with Hydro-Quebec.

1990: Richard Snelling elected governor, for a fifth but not consecutive term, making him the longest serving governor since 1820. State population reaches 562,758, showing unprecedented growth in previous forty years.

1991: Howard Dean becomes governor on death of Richard Snelling.

1997: Act 60 creates a controversial statewide property tax intended to equalize funding for public education.

1997: Putney resident, Jody Williams wins Nobel Peace Prize.

1998: Champlain Valley devastated by ice storm.

Utility crews from all over the U.S. came in to help restore power. It took two weeks to get the Champlain Valley back to a semblance of order after the January storm, but limbs and trees were still being removed that summer. Burlington, long famous for its green canopy, lost so many trees that residents and sympathetic neighbors alike donated money to plant hundreds of new trees. Courtesy, Fred Stetson

Bibliography

Allen, Ira. *Natural and Political History of the State of Vermont.* London: J.W. Myers, 1798.

Beck, Jane, ed. *Always in Season Folk Art and Traditional Culture in Vermont.* Montpelier: Vermont Council on the Arts, 1982.

Beers, F.W. *Illustrated Topographical and Historical Atlas of the State of Vermont.* New York: F.W. Beers & Co., 1876.

Benedict, George Grenville. *Vermont in the Civil War.* Burlington: Burlington *Free Press* Association, 1886-1888.

Benton, Reuben Clark. *The Vermont Settlers and the New York Land Speculators.* Minneapolis: Housekeeper Press, 1894.

Bird, Harrison. *Navies in the Mountain: The Battles on the Waters of Lake Champlain and Lake George, 1609-1814.* New York: Oxford University Press, 1962.

Brown, Lesley I. *Independent Vermont and Revolutionary America.* Poughkeepsie, NY: Vassar College, 1977.

Bryan, Frank. *Yankee Politics in Rural Vermont.* Hanover, NH: University Press of New England, 1974.

Champlain, Samuel de. *Voyages in New France.* Translated by Charles P. Otis. Boston: Prince Society, 1878.

Chipman, Daniel. *The Life of Seth Warner, with an Account of the Controversy between New York and Vermont from 1763 to 1775.* Burlington: Chauncey Goodrich, 1858.

Collier, Christopher. *Connecticut in the Continental Congress.* Chester, CN: Pequot Press, 1973.

Coolidge, Guy O. "The French Occupation of the Champlain Valley, 1609-1759." *Vermont History,* vol. 6 (1938): 143-311.

Crockett, Walter Hill. *Vermont, the Green Mountain State.* New York: Century History Co., 1921-23.

Everest, Allan S. *The War of 1812 in the Champlain Valley.* Syracuse: Syracuse University Press, 1981.

Fuller, Edmund. *Vermont: A History of the Green Mountain State.* Montpelier: State Board of Education, 1952.

Graffagnino, Kevin. *The Shaping of Vermont: From the Wilderness to the Centennial, 1749-1877.* Bennington: Bennington Museum, 1983.

Hall, Hiland. *The History of Vermont, from its Discovery to its Admission into the Union in 1791.* Albany, NY: Munsell, 1868.

Hamilton, Edward. *The French and Indian Wars.* New York: Doubleday, 1962.

Hard, Walter. *The Connecticut.* New York: Rinehart and Co., 1947.

Haskins, Nathan. *A History of the State of Vermont from its Discovery and Settlement to the Close of the year MDCCCXXX.* Vergennes, VT: J.

The University of Vermont's Ira Allen Chapel, designed in Georgian Revival style by the influential New York architectural firm of McKim, Mead, and White, was constructed in 1926. Its steeple rises high above the green that was donated by Ira Allen in the late eighteenth century. Photo by John F. Smith. Courtesy, IC Photo Service, University of Vermont

Shedd, 1831.

Haviland, William A. and Marjory W. Power. *The Original Vermonters: Native Inhabitants Past and Present*. Hanover, NH: University Press of New England, 1981.

Hemenway, Abby, ed. *The Vermont Historical Gazetteer*. 4 vols. Burlington: A.M. Hemenway, 1867-1891.

Hill, Ralph Nading. *Contrary Country. A Chronicle of Vermont*. New York: Rinehart, 1950.

_____ . *Yankee Kingdom: Vermont and New Hampshire*. New York: Harper, 1960.

Himmelhoch, Myra. *The Allens in Early Vermont*. Barre: Star Printing, 1967.

Jackson, John Brinkerhoff. *American Space: The Centennial Years, 1865-1876*. New York: Norton, 1972.

Judd, Richard. *Vermont in the New Deal: Impact and Aftermath*. New York: Garland Publishing, 1979.

Lamb, Wallace. *The Lake Champlain and Lake George Valleys*. New York: The American Historical Co., 1940.

Lavoie, Yolande. *L'émigration des Quebecois aux Etats-Unis de 1840 à 1930*. Quebec: Editeur Officiel, 1979.

Ludlum, David. *Social Ferment in Vermont, 1791-1850*. Montpelier: Vermont Historical Society, 1948.

Morrissey, Charles T. *Vermont: A Bicentennial History*. New York: Norton, 1981.

Muller, H.N. and S.B. Hand, eds. *In a State of Nature: Readings in Vermont History*. Montpelier: Vermont Historical Society, 1982.

Newton, Earle. *The Vermont Story: A History of the People of the Green Mountain State 1749-1949*. Montpelier: Vermont Historical Society, 1949.

Nuquist, Andrew E. *Town Government in Vermont*. Burlington: University of Vermont, 1964.

Records of the Governor and Council of the State of Vermont. Edited by E.P. Walton. Montpelier: J. and M. Poland Steam Press, 1873-1880.

Robinson, Rowland. *Vermont: A Study of Independence*. Boston: Houghton Mifflin, 1892.

Rossiter, William S. *Vermont. An Historical and Statistical Study of the Progress of the State*. Boston, 1911.

Slade, William, comp. *Vermont State Papers . . . a collection of records and documents, connected with the assumption and establishment of government by the people of Vermont . . . .* Middlebury: J.W. Copeland, 1823.

Smith, Bradford. *Roger's Rangers and the French and Indian War*. New York: Random House, 1956.

State Papers of Vermont. Reports of Committees to the General Assembly of the State of Vermont . . . 1778-1801. ed. by Walter H. Crockett. Bellows Falls, VT: Wyndham Press, 1932.

Thompson, Zadock. *History of Vermont: Natural, Civil, and Statistical in three parts with a new map of the state. . . .* Burlington: Chauncey Goodrich, 1842.

Van de Water, Frederic. *The Reluctant Republic: Vermont, 1774-1791*. New York: John Day, 1941.

_____ . *The Upper Connecticut: Narratives of Its Settlement and Its Part in the Revolution*. 2 vols. Montpelier: Vermont Historical Society, 1943.

_____ . *Lake Champlain and Lake George*. Indianapolis: Bobbs, Merrill, 1946.

Wilbur, James B. *Ira Allen: Founder of Vermont, 1751-1814*. Boston and New York: Houghton Mifflin, 1928.

Wilgus, William. *The Role of Transportation in the Development of Vermont*. Montpelier: Vermont Historical Society, 1945.

Williams, Samuel. *The Natural and Civil History of Vermont*. Walpole, NH: Isaiah Thomas and David Carlisle, 1794.

Wilson, Harold Fisher. *The Hill County of Northern New England, Its Social and Economic History, 1790-1930*. New York: Columbia University Press, 1936.

Index

DATE DUE

MAR 0 8 2002			
APR 3 2002			
GAYLORD			PRINTED IN U.S.A.